THE BOOK OF
BLUNDELL'S

THE BOOK OF
BLUNDELL'S

CHARLES NOON

HALSGROVE

First published in Great Britain in 2002

British Library Cataloguing-in-Publication Data
A CIP record for this title is available from the British Library

ISBN 1 84114 181 X

HALSGROVE

Halsgrove House
Lower Moor Way
Tiverton, Devon EX16 6SS
Tel: 01884 243242
Fax: 01884 243325
email: sales@halsgrove.com
website: www.halsgrove.com

Printed and bound by
Bookcraft Ltd, Midsomer Norton

CONTENTS

FROM THE HEADMASTER

It gives me great pleasure to write the foreword to Charles Noon's *Book of Blundell's*, a project he has undertaken in the last two years, following his very successful biography of the nineteenth century Old Blundellian, Jack Russell.

Charles has put together a strong outline narrative, supported by his own particular eye for detailed anecdote and it is enlivened by his quirky comments. Furthermore this story of Blundell's through four centuries is splendidly supported by enriching illustrations.

It is a fitting conclusion to Charles Noon's thirty-year career as a Master at Blundell's, that, having written this book, he moves into retirement. For the last eleven years, as Head of the History department, his colourful lessons have brightened up many a Blundellian's day. His love of Blundell's and the surrounding district is quite clear to everyone who knows him, and I am pleased that he will remain connected to the School as its Archivist.

This book is an excellent immediate prelude to the great celebratory year of 2004.

Colin White

PREFACE

The obvious genesis for this book is the 400th anniversary of the founding of Blundell's School, which tradition ascribes to 1604. That date probably marks the opening of 'Old Blundell's' at Lowman Green in Tiverton and is when the old buildings were ready to accommodate a school. However there is enough evidence to suggest that teaching, financed by Peter Blundell's will, had been going on in other premises in Tiverton since 1602, or even 1601.

Such a landmark is a time to take stock. Peter Blundell's money set up and endowed what was the largest school in the West Country to safeguard the Protestant faith by training scholars in grammar, so that they could go to the universities and become 'good and godly Preachers of the Gospell'. This could not remain for ever the School's sole purpose and in the nineteenth century there was a widening of aim, which can be seen in the various mottoes chosen to grace the School crests: 'In patriam populumque fluxit' and 'Pro Patria Populoque.' It has in all good times been a part of the School that education had a wider purpose than the equipping of individual pupils with the skills necessary for earning a living. When the School became an engine for class and sectional self-interest, as in the period 1775–1840, it ran into serious trouble. If the School continues to serve the wider community it will deserve to survive another 400 years. If not, not.

Now some apologies and thank-yous. I must apologise for some of the obvious bias in this book. Only after finishing it did I realise how 'staff-focused' it is. An Old Boy would probably have written with a different focus, as would a parent or an outsider. Also it is curiously difficult to write the story of an institution without slipping into a reign-by-reign approach and almost all the chapters are based on the regnal dates of Headmasters. This approach makes it difficult to recount the story of teachers like, for example, Jazz Hall who endured or enjoyed life under six Headmasters. In a book limited in pages and number of illustrations it is impossible to do justice to all. Some things have to be omitted and many glossed over. In that the games' history of the School has been well written up by Ted Crowe in his account of Blundell's Rugby and by Chris Reichwald in his *Blundellian* articles, I have tended to concentrate on areas that have not previously received coverage. On the other hand I have concentrated on the conflict with the Town between 1830 and 1850, an aspect ably covered by Brian Jenkins in his book *The Removal of Blundell's*, because my point of view was very different. It was always very difficult to know where to draw the line between what was achieved by boys at school and by boys after they had left. If something were already well known, through photographs in the pavilion or elsewhere, it often seemed less necessary to include it within these covers.

Thanks are due to those who have managed to preserve the material, the School Archive, from which this book has been written. I am indeed grateful to that host of individuals who cherished their school-days and who have kept photos and diaries which have come down to us, and hope that more will be moved to send their records to the School Archivist for safe keeping. E.G. Peirce first saw the need to organise and preserve the documents of the School's past. J.B. Jenkins continued the work and in the last two years the task of cataloguing all the photos and documents has been completed. The historian is always standing on the shoulders of his predecessors. I am grateful to Dr Jones of Balliol, a School Governor, for his enthusiastic support in all matters connected with the preservation of our past.

I am especially grateful to my wife and to Chris Price for reading and checking the first drafts. And to all those kind souls who responded so generously to my requests for photos. I can only hope that I have made proper acknowledgement in the captions. I have not always been able to use all that you have sent me. I also record my thanks to Steven Pugsley of Halsgrove, whose idea this book was, and to the staff at Halsgrove who helped produce this book. And finally to the Blundell's IT Department of Martin Dyer and Nick Markell for their help and tolerance of my importunities.

One last word: if you have any photographs, please name everybody in them. Photographs without names are a frustrating nuisance!

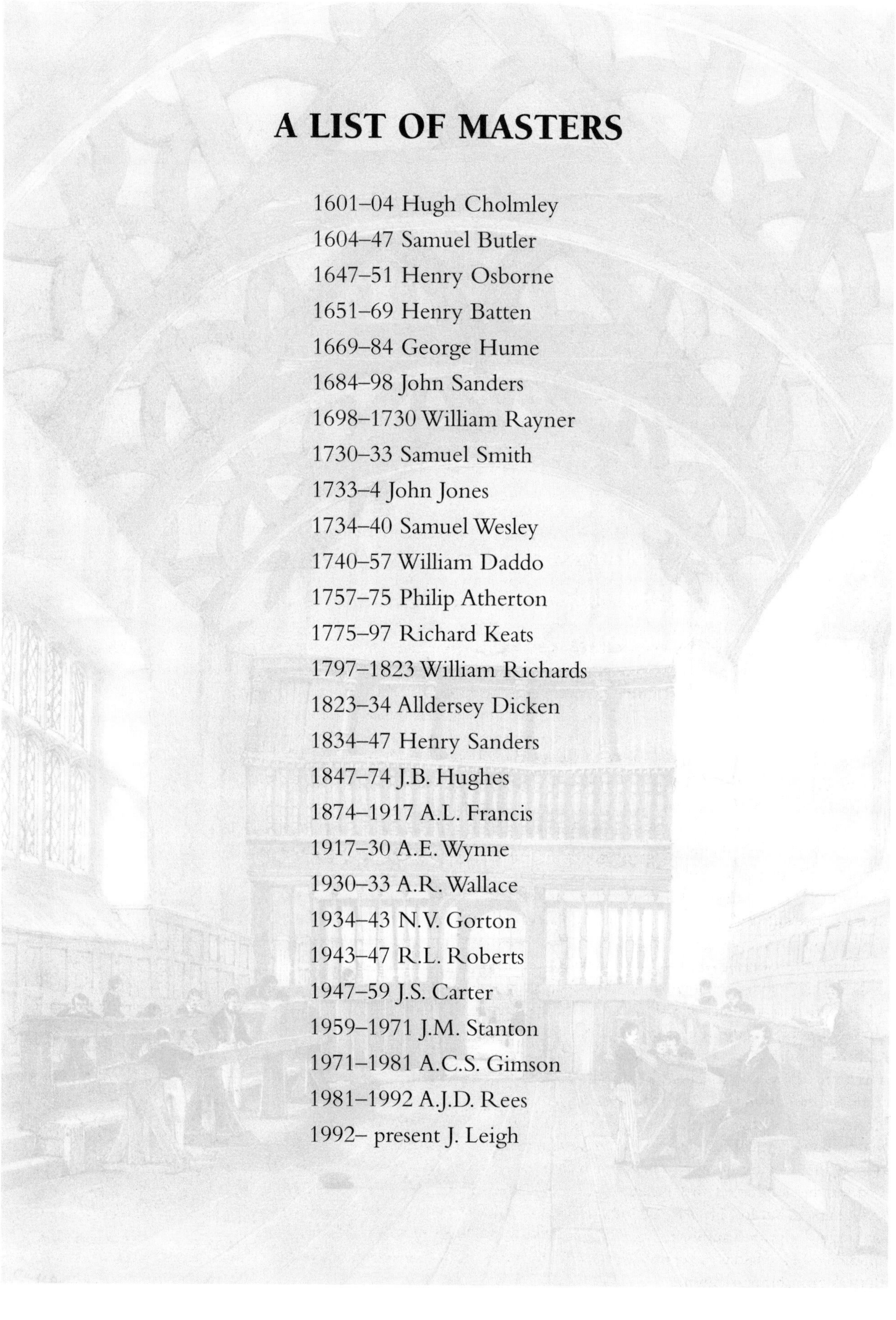

A LIST OF MASTERS

1601–04 Hugh Cholmley

1604–47 Samuel Butler

1647–51 Henry Osborne

1651–69 Henry Batten

1669–84 George Hume

1684–98 John Sanders

1698–1730 William Rayner

1730–33 Samuel Smith

1733–4 John Jones

1734–40 Samuel Wesley

1740–57 William Daddo

1757–75 Philip Atherton

1775–97 Richard Keats

1797–1823 William Richards

1823–34 Alldersey Dicken

1834–47 Henry Sanders

1847–74 J.B. Hughes

1874–1917 A.L. Francis

1917–30 A.E. Wynne

1930–33 A.R. Wallace

1934–43 N.V. Gorton

1943–47 R.L. Roberts

1947–59 J.S. Carter

1959–1971 J.M. Stanton

1971–1981 A.C.S. Gimson

1981–1992 A.J.D. Rees

1992– present J. Leigh

THE FOUNDING FATHERS

Peter Blundell is still a man of mystery, about whom little is established fact. He definitely died in the spring of 1601 as his will was proved in April that year. He was definitely a very wealthy man, as his estate was worth between £30,000 and £50,000 (values of the day, and deliberately wide to avoid quibbling), and because his death occurred in a time of inflation so figures must be multiplied by at least a thousand. (The Headmaster of his new school would be offered the very generous salary of £50 p.a. and who knows of a secondary school Head who now works for £50,000!) He probably earned much of his wealth from the profits of cloth, but such vast wealth may also have come from government finance and Blundell may have been one of the hard-faced men who did well out of the war with Spain. The plaque that used to stand above the gate of Old Blundell's confidently asserts that he died aged eighty-one, so he should have been born in 1519 or 1520. But the earliest parish records anywhere date from the late 1530s and, as anyone who has worked from them knows, the old are not accurate about their age. Strangely, all accounts agree that he was definitely unmarried in an age when marriage was, as it still is, not a statement of sexual preference, but the cheapest and most effective way of getting a housekeeper. His will, with its numerous bequests to his extended family of Blundells, Chilcotts and Prowses, suggests strong family attachments.

Peter Blundell, founder and man of mystery.

A further puzzle is that such a wealthy man, with friendships reaching to the highest level of the Tudor state, is so unknown. He nominated his friend Sir John Popham as his executor. Sir John was a Wellington man, but also Chief Justice of England, who in a long career ending in 1607, took a key and ferocious part in many of the great legal episodes of his day. He was a prosecutor of Mary Queen of Scots and he condemned Guy Fawkes. It is clear that, in spite of other calls on his energies, Popham approached his duties as executor with great vigour and I suggest that he did so because of a Puritanism that he had shared with Blundell. A Spanish ambassador once called Popham 'a terrible Puritan'. In his will Blundell used the phrase 'for the increase of good and godly preachers of the gospell' as the explanation why Popham should establish scholarships at Oxford and Cambridge for pupils of his School. That phrase is a clear indication of Puritanism, with its emphasis on 'preaching' rather than on the sacraments, and of the interest that Blundell and Popham had in making the West Country safe against the assaults from without of Spanish Catholicism and the wiles of the fifth column of Catholics from within England, so soon to be given terrifying shape in the Guy Fawkes' plot of 1605.

This anti-Catholic zeal perhaps explains another puzzle: the sheer size and magnificence of the endowment. Blundell asked for a school of 150 grammar scholars, that is students of Latin and Greek, capable, if they had the ability or so chose, of going to the universities and becoming ordained. (In 1609 his nephew Chilcott founded an 'English' school for those with more limited academic ambitions: the Chilcott School in St Peter Street.) Let there be no doubt about the scale of Peter Blundell's Free Grammar School in Tiverton. In its time it was the largest school in the West and must, from the start, have been intended to be the regional powerhouse for the true and Protestant religion. Strengthening this suggestion is the previous history of Samuel Butler, a graduate of University College, Oxford, the 'traditional' first Headmaster. He had started his career as a Barnstaple schoolmaster, but lost his place in 1603 or 1604 because of an enquiry as to whether he taught by proper authority, i.e. whether he had episcopal approval. When they appointed him Master, the entirely secular Feoffees of Blundell's were not put off by Butler's probable Puritanism.

Sir John Popham: a man not to be trifled with.

It has already been stated that Popham moved fast. We cannot follow the building of the School or tell when the buildings by the Lowman opened for business. The Great Account Book starts in 1610, but shows an institution already in being; only tradition declares that the School began in 1604 when Samuel Butler became the first Master. But tradition may well be wrong. Popham is known to have approached the Master of Cambridge's most Puritan college, Emmanuel, in 1601 for advice about whom to appoint to run the School. The Master, Dr Chaderton, recommended an Emmanuel man, Dr Hall. Hall accepted Popham's offer, but almost immediately decided to decline it, having been offered a richer preferment, the Rectory of Halsted, from Lady Drury. He then had the difficult task of going to Popham to withdraw his acceptance of Blundell's School and, to sweeten the scary Chief Justice, Hall in turn recommended his 'old friend and chamber-fellow, Mr Cholmley', whom Popham then appointed. Hall's memoirs end the episode with the words 'so, as we two (himself and Cholmley), who came together at the University, now must leave it at once'. So where would Cholmley be going except Tiverton? We know that he did indeed go because in February 1604 he was appointed Rector of Clare Portion by James I, an appointment, which, by the terms of Blundell's will, he could not take up without resigning the mastership of the School. It is very unlikely that Cholmley would have been given Clare unless he already had a Tiverton connection. He was also given the wardship of Tiverton's then most important landowner, Sir John Trelawney. Cholmley had been educated at Ashby-de-la-Zouche and does not seem to have had any other Tiverton connection other than that he, rather than Butler, was the first Headmaster.

This belief that the School started before Butler's appointment as Master in 1604 is strengthened by a piece of research by Stanley Mahood, who found a letter written by Hume in 1673 in the Wase papers at Oxford. Mahood quotes Hume as follows:

Mr Cholmley, some time canon of your Church, was the first schoolmaster, but I never heard he taught in the school. Yet he taught somewhere else and received the stipend for some time.

Moreover, Cholmley maintained a close link with the School as the evidence from the Great Account Book shows. In the early days the Feoffees paid for an annual sermon on St Peter's Day and Cholmley preached in 1618, 1620, 1621, and 1622. It

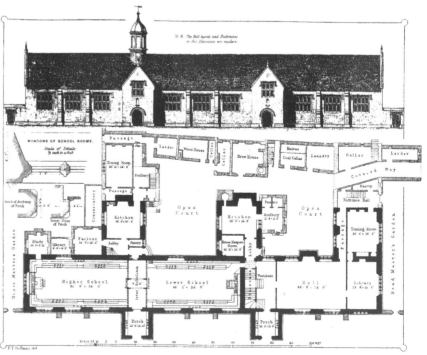

A plan of Old Blundell's. The later additions have a darker outline. The buttresses date from 1840.

Blundell's School, Tiverton, Devon.
(Ground Plan and Front Elevation.)

seems the conclusion must be reached that Cholmley was Master of Blundell's School from 1601–04 and that he ran a school in Tiverton, probably holding classes in St Peter's Church or some other building and perhaps by 1603 in the school buildings. The Emmanuel College archives assert that Cholmley was Headmaster at Tiverton from 1601 to 1604. At best all we can do is pretend that 2004 is the 400th Anniversary – it could be the 403rd.

Peter Blundell specified with minute exactness how he wanted his new school to be built. He left it to Popham to find the 'fytt and convenient platt and piece of ground' but in the building of the 'faier School House' he left little to the Chief Justice's discretion. Specifically reserved for teaching would be a building 'one hundredd foote in length and fower and twenty foot in breadth.' The floor of the school was 'to be well plancked with plancks of oke and to be devided on or neere the middest with some fitt partition of fower foot in height or thereabouts and to be strongly wainscotted round abowte, to extend abowte five or six foote above the settles and formes.' All the windows were to be 'well and strongly glassed and barred with iron bars'. So accurately was the commission carried out that Dunsford, reporting in 1790, stated that the Upper School was 51 feet long and the Lower School 48 feet long and each 24 feet wide! There was also to be a:

… hawle, buttery and kitchin' with 'fitt and convenient roomes over the said hawle, buttery and kitchin and in the hawle and chamber over the same one or other chimney, and in the kitchin one faier great chimney with an oven and a chamber over the kitchin with a chimney therein.

Which of course is what you see when you enter the Old School. To the left and centre is the big schoolroom, divided in two halves, and to the right the domestic offices and the Master's House. Popham was also instructed that the school house should have a 'convenient garden and wood yard' and that, overhanging the Lowman there would be a necessary house, where for the next 275 years the bowels of the school community would communicate directly with the Lowman. (It is now a garage.) Blundell also stipulated that the whole was:

… to be well walled and enclosed with a strong wall, the going in and forthe to be at one only place with a fair strong gate with a little doore as is usual. And that the whole may be substantially done my will is that my executors shall bestowe therein twenty fower hundred poundes within the least.

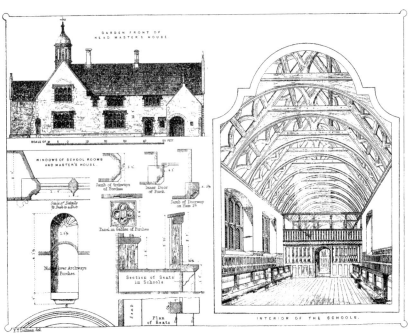

The School Rooms.

An eighteenth-century map to show Blundell's and Tiverton.

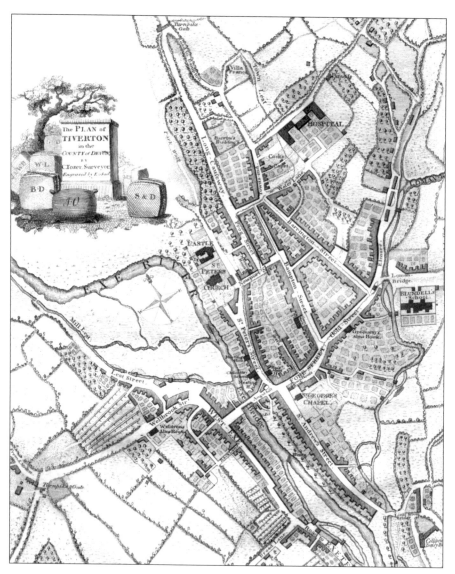

And it was substantially done and has stood the ravages of time. Apart from retiling and the sort of repairs that any building inhabited by the human boy needs, the only major repair has been to strengthen the walls with buttresses in the early-nineteenth century. At about the same time, when numbers crept over 200 for a space, some rather poor buildings were tacked on to the rear of the School to accommodate the extra boarders.

The only other surviving addition is the Porter's Lodge to house the controller of the 'going in and forthe'. The Feoffees or Governors decided to build the Lodge in 1695 and the first Porter moved in in 1698, as the Great Account Book records in January 1699 that they 'paid the Porter half a year's salary due last Christmas… £1'. Somewhere around the Green probably lie the foundations of another building, which has been lost. Dunsford records that in 1626 the plague was so violent in Exeter that the Assizes were held in Tiverton at Blundell's. At these Assizes two criminals were sentenced to death, a Dutchman for robbery, and a man called Comings from Chevithorne for sheep stealing, and were hanged at Whitedown (Whiddon) on the Cullompton road. In 1649 Dunsford, culling earlier sources, also reports that the Assizes were held in the School and two judges sat: Mr Justice Rigby sat in the Upper School and Lord Chief Justice Wild sat in the 'Fives-place, in the school-house green'. Presumably the 'Fives-place' had a roof and at least two walls so it may have been in one of the angles of the green. It awaits discovery.

The parts of Blundell's will that later excited controversy were those that focused on what would go on in the buildings and who and what would be taught. On the surface Blundell was emphatic and clear. There should 'not be taught more than above the number of one hundred and fiftie scholers at one tyme', to be children:

> ...born, or for the most part brought upp in the towne and parrish of Tyverton; and if the same number be not filled upp, my will is that the wante shall be supplied with the children of forreyners; and these forreyners only to be admitted with the assent of such tenne householders of the towne of Tyverton as for the tyme beinge shall be most in the subsidie bookes of our sovereigne Lady the Queenes Majesty and of her successors for ever. And my meaning and desire is that they will make choice of the children of forreyners such are of honest reputation and feare God, without regarding the riche above or more than the poore; and that there shall bee noe scholar bee or continue in the said schoole, as a scholer, but boyes, and none above the age of eighteen yeares or under the age of six yeares, and none but a grammar scholler.

Balliol College 1566, then a poor college in need of endowment.

So, boys aged six to eighteen. Yet even that would one day cause a difficulty. Did it mean that a scholar had to leave on his eighteenth birthday or before his nineteenth? 'None but a grammar scholer' meant that they must be taught 'grammar', i.e. Latin and Greek, but did that mean they could be taught other things besides 'grammar'? And what might happen when 'subsidies', the standard tax of Tudor England became things of the past and there were no more 'subsidie bookes'? Presumably too the 'forreyners' would have to be boarders, and as such a source of profit to the Masters, who might be tempted to angle the school towards those sources of profit.

Perhaps Blundell had this possibility in mind when he added the stern injunction that the Schoolmaster should have 'yearlie for ever fiftie poundes' with the use of the rooms and buildings and the Usher would have 'twenty marks', i.e. £13.6s.8d. a year and 'a chamber'. He continued:

> My hope and desier and will is, that they hould themselves satisfied and contente with that recompense for their travell, without seeking and exacting any more either of parents or children ... for my meaning is, yt shall be for ever a free scholl and not a schole of exaction.

In a way nothing could be plainer and might have been if the world had not changed. The first change was that between 1600 and 1750 Tiverton's population fell by between a third and a half so that by the latter date we find the school with under a hundred pupils and those mostly boarding 'forreyners'. Then with the changes of the Industrial Revolution education would mean more than 'grammar'.

Eventually the problem for Peter Blundell's Free Grammar School at Tiverton was that he endowed it so well. It was such a juicy bone that it was very well worth fighting over. To support the school well enough to maintain the buildings and pay for the Master's and Usher's stipends, it was endowed with lands in South Prawle and Tiverton that for 300 years provided the school with a more than ample sustenance and, in most years, a surplus, so that the main problem of the body of twenty-five self-perpetuating 'Feoffees', that Blundell set up to run the school, was 'what shall we do with the money?' Besides choosing the Master and Usher and supervising the lands and accounts the Feoffees had to oversee the relationships between his school and the universities. His will continued: 'for the increase of good and godly preachers of the gospell' his executors should spend £2000 in the founding and establishing of scholarships in the Universities of Oxford and Cambridge. They should buy lands, the profits of which should be employed in the maintenance of these scholars forever. These scholars should:

Sidney Sussex. A newer College than Balliol but equally needy.

> ...be elected and chosen by the said Feoffees, with the advise of the scholemaster there for the tyme being, out of the saide grammar schoole of Tyverton and not elsewhere, and that of the aptest and most towarde in learninge and such as are least able to maintain themselves.

By 1610 relationships had been established between the School and Sidney Sussex in Cambridge and Balliol in Oxford, Popham's old college, that were to last until the wide reforms of the post-war period. These relationships were formalised in massive parchment indentures. Things settled into two scholars being appointed to each college and two fellows being on the foundation of each college, the fellows to be

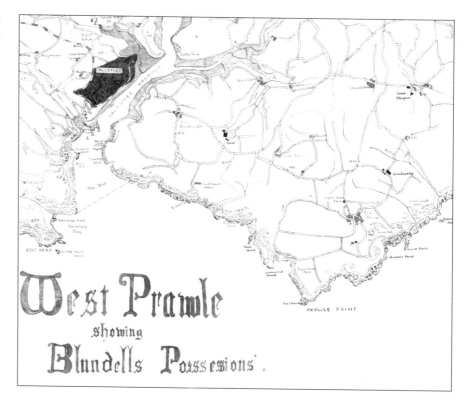

Prawle Point in South Devon. Most of the peninsula was owned by the Feoffees.

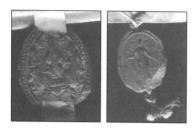

Peter Blundell's signature.

Seals from the foot of Peter Blundell's will.

chosen from the scholars, an arrangement that continued until the last century, almost always amicably in the case of Sidney, but with some hiccoughs with Balliol.

Blundell's great endowment was increased over the years by John Ham, Benjamin Gilberd, John Newte and Richard Down, names that roll towards us every year from the Thanksgiving Prayer. In 1678 John Ham left monies to the maintenance of a Fellow and Scholar at Sidney or Balliol to be chosen from the School, stipulating that the first beneficiary should be his son. In 1783 Gilberd left money to provide £60 income a year to be used by the Feoffees, which was used to provide two extra scholarships. In 1806 Down bequeathed an endowment of a scholarship, to any scholar who had achieved admission to any college, but the award was to be made by the Mayor of Tiverton, the Rector of Tidcombe and the Master of the School. Newte's gift, made in 1715, bypassed the Tiverton Corporation and the Feoffees by the testator stating that the award should be to a Blundell's pupil, but made by the three Rectors of Tiverton, the funds to be in the keeping of Balliol College. By the early-nineteenth century these endowments had increased the attractions of Blundell's and encouraged 'forreyners' to send their sons to the School.

But much of this lay in the future. The Great Account Book begins in 1610 and between then and 1616 the School had received seven years of income totalling £780.16s.3d. and had spent in the same seven years £767.6s.6d. In these years income had varied between £95 and £117, expenditure between £92 and £111. Peter Blundell's great school was well and soundly launched on its great 400-year voyage, steered by the 20 or more Feoffees named in the will, whose numbers were kept up by regular elections and co-options. Blundell was most specific about the choosing of new Feoffees: they were to be the heirs of deceased Feoffees. If no heirs were available 'then others near inhabiting of honest report and reputation should be chosen'. Over the first two and a half centuries they met almost annually. In spite of low standards of public morality, there was no peculation and there was a firm grasp of continuity with the past. Well into the nineteenth century, minutes refer to the founder as 'the late Mr Blundell', and in 1840 15 of the Feoffees were heirs of deceased Feoffees, two were heirs of living ones and at least five were connected with families named in the original will of the founder.

2

GODLY PREACHERS TO HIGH TORIES

Samuel Butler was Master from 1604–48, a span only matched by A.L. Francis. Information about early Blundell's is scarce and comes obliquely from biographies and other records. The archives of Gonville and Caius College show three of Butler's pupils. Richard Eveleigh of Clyst Hydon was born in Armada year and entered Caius in July 1606, but did not state how long he had studied in Tiverton School. John Bowbeare of Bampton, born in 1593, entered Caius in 1610 and stated that he had spent five years at Tiverton School under Mr Butler. It is clear, therefore, that the School was doing its business for sure from 1605. It is also possible that Eveleigh studied under Cholmley as well as Butler – he would only have been thirteen years old in 1601.

The third Caius entrant was Thomas Stukely of Affeton, whose mother was aunt of George Monk, the Cromwellian General, who later would restore the monarchy in 1660 and become first Duke of Albemarle. Stukely was at Blundell's from 1616–1619. Other 'important' political names are John, Richard and Edward Eliot who were Butler's pupils between 1620 and the early 1630s. Their father was Sir John Eliot, one of the greatest heroes of the Whig school of history. Sir John, the ancestor of the Earls of St Germans, was Vice Admiral of Devon in the 1620s, at the time of some grossly mismanaged expeditions against France and Spain. The experience of coping with undisciplined and unpaid English troops, 8000 of whom were billeted by the Government on his Devon neighbours in 1625, turned him into a bitter opponent of the incompetent Charles I and his favourite, the Duke of Buckingham. G.M. Trevelyan described the climax of Eliot's Parliamentary career in 1628 and 1629, when he was one of the leaders of the cause against royal tyranny, as follows:

In the stately, simple, poetical English of the time, Wentworth, Seymour and Seldon, Phelips, Eliot and Pym pleaded the cause of posterity, while Hampden, Cromwell and hundreds more listened with a passion that sometimes broke forth in tears.

He took a lead in carrying the Petition of Right against Martial Law, Billeting, Arbitrary Taxation and Arbitrary Imprisonment. In the next year, 1629, the conflict widened to include religious issues (Charles was suspected of favouring Catholicism), and taxation (Charles was illegally collecting tonnage and poundage). Eliot introduced into the Commons the 'Three Resolutions', condemning innovations in religion which extended Popery, the collection of un-Parliamentary taxes, and the paying of such taxes.

Such were the Three Resolutions of the last and greatest day of Eliot's Parliamentary career, passed by the shouts of the angry members, thronging and swaying round the chair into which they had forced back the frightened Speaker, whilst the blows of the King's officers resounded on the fastened door. When they had so voted, they flung all open and poured out flushed into the cold air of heaven, freemen still and already almost rebels.

Eliot was arrested and thrown into the Tower, where he died in 1632. His eldest son, also John, petitioned for his body to be returned for burial at Port Eliot in Cornwall. The King refused. John Hampden, of Ship Money fame, became the guardian of the orphaned sons of his friend, and, as the youngest Edward was at the School when his father died, it is possible that Hampden visited him there.

Evidence from a further pupil of Butler's adds to the picture. George Bull was born near Wells in 1634 and attended Peter Blundell's School, before moving on to Oxford in 1648, aged fourteen. Writing in 1713, his biographer described the School as:

… not more considerable for its liberal endowment than for its stately and noble structure. The scholars generally exceed than fall short of the prescribed complement. It not only

flourisheth at present, but hath made the most considerable figure of any in that part of the nation ever since its first foundation.'

Bull's biographer was almost certainly right about the numbers. All the seven pupils mentioned, the three students of Caius, the three Eliots and Bull, came from far enough away to have been, of necessity, boarders. Moreover, if at this early date Butler was attracting pupils from as far away as Wells and Port Eliot, the School must have been flourishing.

The Balliol and Sidney Sussex scholarships took some time to get established. Popham nominated two scholars to Balliol in 1602, but the first pupil from the School only went up in 1615 and the College rejected the second in 1617; there are only four Balliol Scholars recorded before 1630. Relations were better with Sidney. Popham had appointed four scholars by 1603; the first pupil from the School went up in 1610 and 36 more followed during the century.

In these early years, as the presence of Stukely and the Eliot brothers shows, the School remained true to Blundell's and Popham's Protestant vision. Almost from the beginning it seems that the founder's name-day was kept with the special observance of a dinner and a sermon. In 1610, the earliest year for which we have a detailed record of expenditure, there seems to have been no St Peter's Day ceremony, but in 1611 Mr Butler was paid £3.10s. for the expenses of the day and in 1612 he was paid £5. In 1613 the bill was divided between £3.10s. for the feast and ten shillings for a sermon by Mr How. There was a St Peter's Day sermon every year until 1622 when the accounts cease, only to restart in 1633 when James Hartnoll preached for the usual ten-shilling fee. Almost certainly, the custom of 'Preacher and Feast' was observed in the 'missing' years. Interestingly the putative 'first' Master, Hugh Cholmley, preached four times – in 1618, 1620, 1621 and 1622, and only one other preached twice. In the 1630s Archbishop Laud tried to stop all preaching except by the parish priest and he tried to pursue a vigorous policy of infiltrating royalist nominees into the churches of known Puritan areas. When Hartnoll died in 1634 the Crown overrode local rights of presentation and installed Peirce, a Laudian, who held Priors and Clare portions of St Peter's Church, and who may well have denied the church to the Feoffees' preacher. For whatever reason there is no further mention of St Peter's Day sermons after 1637. No clergyman, who afterwards supported the King in the Civil War, was invited to preach.

The Feasts, however, continued until 1640. In 1611 the dinner might have cost £3.10s. but after 1616 it rarely cost less than £5. Sometimes, as in 1617, wine was mentioned. In 1634, when the accounts reopened they spent £12.2s.6d., almost the same amount as the Master's salary for three months. It is difficult to know what to make of these 'feasting' figures, which in some years mount to almost ten per cent of the income of the foundation, as we do not know how many sat down, for it is possible that in some years the senior pupils joined in.

What is clear is that any study of the accounts indicates that the endowment was adequate. Peter Blundell had been quite clear on the point that his executors should buy more land if the endowment were inadequate for a Free School. In his will he also made another point most forcefully:

> *My true meaning resteth in the Trust, Providence, Circumspection and Care of the said Feoffees, which I hope they shall accomplish and perform accordingly, even as they will answer the same before the Majesty of Almighty God and the dreadful day of Judgment when the secrets of all hearts shall be disclosed.*

In almost every year in the pre-Civil War period there was a comfortable surplus, so there was no need to stint repairs of the fabric or the replenishment of the inner man.

A few other details come from this early period. In 1625 the plague was in Exeter and the Assizes were held in Tiverton in the School and it was reported that a Judge sat in the Fives court. The only other possible confirmation of the existence of Fives playing is an entry for the 1690s of a sum for repairs of the 'Ball Place'. In 1611, 18s. was spent on stools and in 1615 the privies were repaired. In 1621 a stone footbridge was built over the Lowman so they could come dry-shod to school. In 1622 extra clasps were added to the long black box, probably to what is now called 'P.B.'s Tuck Box'.

Peter Blundell's Tuck Box.

Tiverton and the School had an exciting Civil War. Where their activities can be traced the Feoffees, like most of urban Devon, were for Parliament. One of the Feoffees, Mr Were, secured Tiverton for Parliament only to lose it to a Royalist force in 1643. In 1645 Fairfax's Parliamentary Army came over the hill from Cullompton to besiege the Royalists in the castle. Fittingly, he made the School his headquarters, during what must have been an interesting Autumn Term. A minority of Blundellians, notably the Sainthills of Bradninch and the Newtes of Tiverton, supported the King.

In February 1647 old style, 1648 new style, just after the fighting in the West Country had ended, one of the School's great servants, John Ham, was appointed Treasurer, a post he held until his death in 1678. Like all previous Treasurers he was a member of the Blundell clan. The first Treasurer, John Blundell, had been the founder's nephew, the second a great-nephew. The third, William Slee's brother, had married a descendant of the founder's sister and John Ham was the offspring of a Slee-Blundell marriage. It would be 1734 before the Feoffees appointed a Treasurer who was obviously outside the Blundell family. Ham kept the Great Account Book with a new rigour and fullness and he chased arrears of rent with terrier tenacity. By the time he died the running surplus had reached over £500 even though £600 had been donated to Balliol in 1676 to fund more scholarships. In his period average income was about £350 and expenditure below £300. Ham's surplus also allowed the building of the 'New House' to the rear of the old buildings. When he died he left sufficient funds to the School to found Ham's exhibitions, although confusions over the administration of his will and reluctance by his executors to hand over the monies delayed the first nomination until 1740.

Another of Ham's successors, Donald Caskie, Bursar 1974–94.

Ham also kept all his receipts, and by some curious marvel, when so much else has been destroyed, they have survived. He was scrupulous; for instance, the bill for the clock repairs for 25 December, 1672 (obviously not a holiday then). George Hume the Headmaster paid the clockman, John Collins, and then got Ham to repay him and all was recorded, signed and countersigned. It is a feature of some of these bills and receipts that Ham often rounded them down.

More interesting are the Feast bills. The bill for 6 April, 1664 is useful as it shows two types of diner with 'ordinarys', i.e. menus that are different. My guess is that the 28 'ordinarys' are the Feoffees, Master and Usher and the 18 lesser 'ordinarys' are the older boys. The drink seems a 'useful' amount for 28 adults and 18 boys – 28 bottles of sack (probably 40 pints), 25 quarts of cider (50 pints), 4 quarts of claret and 20 gallons of beer. Surely the hire of 13 horses can only be to help some diners homewards. A bill of 1666 divided the diners into three groups – 'ordinarys' at the gentlemen's table at 2s. each, 'Mr Spurway and the two

A bill of 1672 for winding or mending the clock.

A Feoffees' Feast of 1664. James Clarke was a Tiverton publican.

A Feast of 1678 showing the bill of fare.

The School, the earliest accurate engraving showing the twin roofs of the Porter's Lodge. The door in the right corner leads to the privies or 'House of Ease'.

servants' at 1s.6d. each and the 'second table' at 1s. each. The bill for January 1678 shows the raw materials for the Feast: two pieces of beef, butter, eggs, apples and pears, poultry, woodcocks and partridges, bacon with the poultry, for oranges and lemons [?], for [???] and sausages, a loin of veal, a shoulder of mutton, 5 pounds of suet, 5 pounds of sugar, fruit and spice, tobacco and pipes, for persons that attended, for fire in the kitchen, hall and parlour, for flour, for bread, for [???], for the final [???], for 14 bottles of sack and four of claret, for beer and cider.

Ham also made the Masters and Ushers sign for their salaries. Samuel Butler had died or retired before Ham got into his stride and we only have specimens of his hand as witness to legal documents. His successor, Henry Osborne, lasted only from 1647 to 1651 and made little mark, but Henry Battyn, 1651–69, signed a number of Ham's documents. His is rather a prissy signature, unlike the flourish of George Hume who was Master from 1669–84. Curiously, the Feoffees went out of their way to get Hume by offering him £50 to come. He was obviously a well-known teacher and already advanced in years because they then had to pay him £150 to retire. The Feoffees' minutes, known as the 'Book of Orders', blandly stated that Hume:

> … surrendered his place in respect of his old age rendering him unfit to continue the employment and the Feoffees in compassion to his age and family do order that the Treasurer do pay Mr Hume the sum of £150 and that this act be not drawn hereafter into any future precedent.

However, it is clear that in the years of his vigour Hume did the School proud as in 1671 he was paid £3 to 'plank' the stables to store apples 'as his house is so full of boarders', and it was in this context that the 'New House' was built at the back of the School. After they had got rid of Hume, the Feoffees made a 'safe' appointment by choosing an 'old boy', John Sanders, a 1670 Blundell's Scholar and Fellow of Sidney Sussex, who was Master from 1684 until his death in 1698. The addition of his years was the building of the Porter's Lodge and the appointment of the first Porter, agreed at the meeting of the Feoffees on 29 June, 1695 when they:

> … ordered that three of our number doe forthwith direct and agree for ye building of a Porter Lodge at ye Schoole greene gate, ye cost to be paid by our Treasurer by ye order of any two of them and such person to be appoynted porter there as they shall think fitt.

When the Lodge was completed in 1699, Edward Gorman was appointed Porter with the salary of £2 a year and a new gown every three years. However, like the Master and Usher, he did not rely on his salary alone. When things were tidied up in the nineteenth century, the 'sweeping tax' paid to the Porter by all boys was commuted into a regular salary, so presumably Gorman and his successors received something similar.

A financial surplus, a full school, flourishing arrangements with the universities: it had all gone very well during the first hundred years.

3

'THE GREATEST GLORY OF THE TOWN'

This is how is how Thomas Cox, who wrote *Magna Britannia*, a description of Britain in 1720, described the School. It is tempting to see the eighteenth century as Devon's Golden Age of peace and prosperity after the religious strivings and civil wars of the seventeenth century, and before the railway sucked much of its vigour towards the metropolis, and the new power of coal and industry relegated those areas which were mainly agricultural, to the backwaters of national life. However, the Town's eighteenth-century economic history falls into three distinct phases, as so often, punctuated by fires. Until mid-century it enjoyed the last burst of its ancient weaving prosperity, selling cloth, mainly serges, to Holland and Germany. Then followed a long downturn as trade was interrupted by the seemingly unending French wars and local vigour dwindled. In the final years of the century, Tiverton, whose population had perhaps fallen from 9000 in the 1740s to 6500 in the 1780s (the first census taken in 1801 gave the population as 6505, well below the estimate of 8000 that was given by an official of James I in 1615), began its third phase of increasingly rapid recovery as a new generation of entrepreneurs, of whom the most successful was John Heathcoat, introduced new products. The population rose to over 11,000 in 1851, perhaps double that of the eighteenth-century trough.

William Daddo, Master, 1740–57. He was almost certainly a pupil of Rayner, Master from 1689–1730.

These fluctuations controlled the fortunes of the School. In the last flush of the old prosperity under Rayner, 1698–1730, and Daddo, 1740–57, it is recorded that the School was full, but from 1760 to 1800 that was probably not the case. After 1770 we can be quite sure that the School was between a third and a half empty, because in that year a very active Feoffee, Benjamin Incledon, presented the Master with a register. From this time we know the name, age, parentage, place of origin and duration of time at the school of every pupil. After the Great Account Book starting in 1610, and the Feoffees' Book of Orders starting in 1663, it is the third great pillar of our understanding of the School. Probably its first decade marks the numerical nadir of the Old School: in the 1770s numbers according to the then Headmasters, Atherton and Keats, ranged from a low of 90 in July 1776 to a high of 103 in February 1775. But research done by Rankelor, a Blundell's teacher of around 1900, shows a grimmer picture. He took June as his month of calculation and he showed numbers steadily falling from 90 in 1777 to a bottom of 55 in 1782 and then rising very slowly to 109 in 1793, the numbers conforming very accurately to the prosperity of the Town. Numbers of pupils would rise to over 200 in the early-nineteenth century.

If the economic fortunes of Tiverton changed in the eighteenth century, so did its politics. Blundell founded his school to be a powerhouse of the 'true religion', i.e. a purified Protestantism. The Town, the wider Devon community and the School took a clear stand in the Civil War against a perceived royal tyranny tainted by Catholicism, but a minority of Blundellians, forerunners of a later norm, were for the King and his Church. The most famous of these Royalists were Peter Sainthill of Bradninch and Richard Newte of Tidcombe. Peter Sainthill had been born in 1593 and past writers have always assumed he was a Blundell's Scholar. By 1640 he held a number of Westcountry offices and was elected to represent Tiverton in the Parliaments that led to civil war. In 1644 tradition has it that the King stayed a night at Sainthill's home. He died in exile at Leghorn in 1648, but his son, Samuel, became a Feoffee in 1679. Richard Newte was the son of Henry Newte, the first Town Clerk according to the Charter of Incorporation of 1615. This Henry Newte obtained the advowson of two of the three 'portions' of St Peter's Church and in 1641 appointed Richard to Clare and Tidcombe. An inscription in St Peter's records his status as an 'Old Blundellian'. In the annals of the sufferings of the Royalist clergy he has a prominent place as someone stigmatised by the Parliamentarians as a Grand Malignant. His Tidcombe Rectory was plundered and his pregnant wife threatened with loaded pistols (a regular war atrocity story of the time, rather akin to the Hun catching babies on their bayonets in Belgium in 1914). During the Protectorate he had to live hand to mouth, but returned in 1660 and became Chaplain in Ordinary to the King in 1666. He contributed to an arrangement with Balliol and in 1671 his son John, also educated at Blundell's, became a Balliol fellow. He succeeded his father as Rector of Tidcombe in 1676 and his attitudes are clear from Dunsford:

> *He had imbibed the principles of passive obedience and non-resistance, with which he was reproached after the Revolution in 1688* [i.e. he supported James II and the Jacobites rather than William of Orange and the Hanoverians]. *Mr Newte was much attached to the interest of the Church of England, and assiduous in promoting the principles of it in the minds of the rising generations by his preaching and many benefactions.*

John Newte, Balliol Scholar of 1671, scion of a famous Tiverton and Blundell's family and a pupil of Batten and Hume.

Richard was succeeded by his son and grandson, both Samuels, and grandson Samuel by great-grandson John, who died in 1792. Out of the seventeenth century, and a school founded to encourage Puritanism, had grown the Newtes, High Churchmen, Establishment men, who by the end of the eighteenth century would be seen as Tories of the 'old school'.

It seems clear that the Newtes increasingly typified the way the School was going. Samuel Sainthill became a Feoffee in 1679 and the most famous Blundellian academic of the later-seventeenth century, George Bull, eventually in 1705 Bishop of St David's, was an epitome of High Anglicanism. His three great books, *Harmonia Apostolica*, *Defensio Fidei Nicaenae* and *Judicium Ecclesiae Catholicae* illustrate by their titles how far the Puritanism of early years had strayed. There was a last burst of the old religious quarrels in Queen Anne's reign. In Tiverton this can be seen in the hot election of 1710. For the Whigs and Religious Toleration stood Thomas Bere of Huntsham, whose son was elected a Feoffee in 1713, in partnership with R. Mervin, Esq.; for the Tories and the exclusive rights of the Church of England and the possibility of a Stuart restoration stood Sir Edward Northleigh, the Attorney General, and John Worth, a Feoffee elected in 1695. Only the Corporation of Mayor and twenty-four Burgesses had the right to vote. In his memoir John Blundell, writing in 1707, gives the result as Tories 13, Whigs 12, and he names the only Feoffees on the Corporation, Peter Atkins, Arthur Culme and Henry Blagdon as voting with the Tories.

George Bull, 1634–1709, a pupil of Butler and the epitome of the Highest Anglicanism, also Bishop of Bristol.

This shift from Dissenter and Puritan to High Church Anglican can also be seen in the Wesley family. Samuel Wesley, Master after 1733, had a father who moved from dissent back into the Anglican Church and his mother's father had also been a dissenting minister. As a boy Samuel Wesley was a Chapel Royal chorister at Westminster and at Oxford he was deeply influenced by the Dean of Christ Church, Dr Atterbury, the most notorious Tory Jacobite of his age. When Bishop of Rochester in 1722, Atterbury was fanatic enough to support a rebellion to put the 'Old Pretender' on the throne as James III, for which he was exiled in 1723. It says much for Wesley's honesty that he remained loyal to Atterbury. That a man of such notorious Toryism could be appointed Master in 1733 can only be evidence of the equal Toryism of the Feoffees. Confirmation of this shift is the election of Sir William Wyndham as a Feoffee in 1735, when he was a leader of the Tories in Parliament against Walpole.

The growth and flourishing of certain customs within the School also indicate the swing behind Toryism in Church and State. In 1645 Fairfax had been welcomed as a deliverer from the tyrannies of the Royalist garrison in the castle, and Master Butler, Usher Amory Butler, scholars and most Feoffees were probably glad for him to use the School as a headquarters. After 1660 the School wholeheartedly took part in the coarse annual mockery of Oliver Cromwell and the annual commemorative rejoicing that marked the anniversary of Charles II's landing at Dover on 29 May, 1660.

This celebration may not have been as elaborate in the early-eighteenth century as it later became. The custom was for the scholars to sally forth into the surrounding countryside and hack down great quantities of greenery, especially oak.

Samuel Wesley, curmudgeonly elder brother of John Wesley, Master from 1734–40.

They would use this to decorate the Upper School so that it represented nothing more than a forest glade, the boys perching dryad-like amidst the bowers. A great bough was hoisted above the Master's desk, and at eleven o'clock the Great Man would take his seat. The entertainment was provided by 'spouting', that is every pupil had to declaim 20 or more lines of verse. The accounts that have come down mention that the most popular poem was 'the Death of Sir John Moore at Corunna' and those accounts must belong to the next century. Another story has a blushing imp declaiming 'Go lovely rose' and forgetting the rest, so that might have been earlier. In later years the 'spouting' was followed by sports and in even later years a cricket match followed the sports.

Not all Blundellians were Tories. One of Rayner's pupils was William Hayter, born in Chagford in 1702. He was distinguished enough at Blundell's to be awarded a special Exhibition, which allowed him to graduate from Exeter College in 1724. Rapidly he became Chaplain to the Archbishop of York and in 1730 he became Archdeacon of York. Horace Walpole claimed that this rapid promotion by the Archbishop, Dr Blackburne, was because Hayter was Blackburne's son, conceived when Blackburne was a Canon of Exeter Cathedral and Sub-Dean. The *Dictionary of National Biography* coyly states, 'Rumours injurious to his reputation were circulated and in 1702 they forced him to resign his sub-deanery'. And 1702 was indeed the year that the Rector of Chagford's wife added to her family. Blackburne married a rich and well-connected wife and became Bishop of Exeter, but his first foray into the outside world was to go buccaneering on the Spanish Main. It is said that when one of his buccaneering chums came back to England to retire and asked what had become of his old matey, he was flabbergasted to hear he had become Archbishop of York. Horace Walpole, commenting on his Primacy, sniped that nothing remained of his previous career of piracy – except his seraglio.

William Hayter was at Blundell's in the 1710s. Perhaps the only Blundellian to have been the bastard of an Archbishop, he was Bishop of London and tutor to George III.

By permission of the Church Commissioners

Blackburne's influence helped Hayter to the See of Norwich in 1750. Walpole described Hayter as 'sensible and well-bred', and the Pelhams had him appointed as tutor to Prince George and his brothers. The court was a hotbed of politicking and the boys' mother, the widowed Princess of Wales, who was no more sensible than usual, disapproved of Hayter's severity. One suspects that Hayter's timetable for the princelings was based on his Blundell's experience. Rise at seven, translate Caesar till breakfast at eight-thirty. From nine to ten History and Geography and at ten their pre-breakfast work on Caesar would be corrected and more Caesar prepared. From eleven to twelve a variety of writing, arithmetic and dancing and French. From twelve to three, riding and exercise until dining at three. After dinner their mother and a German Master would visit. From seven to nine improving books would be read and improving conversation on such matters as the constitution would be conducted. Sermons and Catechism on Sundays. When he caught the young George reading a book that justified the absolutism of James II he called for the dismissal of elements of the Princes' household whom he considered to be Tories. However, he was himself dismissed through the agency of the Princess of Wales. The 'what-might-have-happened-if school of history' may suppose that, if Hayter had weaned the Prince off his dangerous 'George be King' notions the American colonies might have been saved. He incurred unpopularity from his clergy by his willingness to accept Dissenters as human beings and by his support for a measure to give the Jews full civic rights. In 1762 he died of gout and dropsy.

Another of Rayner's pupils who reached the episcopal bench was John Conybeare of Pinhoe, who left Blundell's for Exeter College in 1710, where he became Rector in 1730. He was a strenuous opponent of Deism and in sermon after sermon, tome after tome, defended Revealed Religion from the insidious attacks of the Deists. As further reward for these exertions he was appointed Dean of Christ Church, and eventually Bishop of Bristol. Like Hayter he was also afflicted with gout and died in 1757. He must have been an above average preacher as a posthumous edition of his sermons had 4600 subscribers. However Whig Hayter and Whig Conybeare in their day were as unusual Blundellians as Tory Sainthill had been in his.

John Conybeare left Blundell's in 1710. He became Rector of Exeter College and a sound Whig bishop. Like Hayter he suffered from gout.

By permission of the Rector and Fellows

If mirroring the economic fortunes of the town of Tiverton, and becoming more Tory were two developments, a third was an increasing divorce between the School and the Town. As the years went by the Town Corporation became part of the great machinery of patronage and the Burgesses sold their votes to men like Sir Walter Yonge, the friend of Walpole, who, Dunsford stated, 'had great influence over the Corporation for many years and generally directed their choice of members of Parliament.' His influence was followed by the control of the Ryder family. Between 1735 and 1832 one of the MPs was always a Ryder, and after 1768 the other usually a Duntze. In the declining economic environment of the later-eighteenth century members of the Corporation clung on to their place to get the rewards that the Borough's patrons could provide. Increasingly, the Feoffees chose non-Tivertonians to fill up their numbers; for example, of the 37 Feoffees elected between 1728 and 1751, only one lived in the Town, although four lived in mansions within the parish of Tiverton, leaving 32 from outside. And this would eventually cause problems.

It is a mark of eighteenth-century Blundell's that more and more light creeps into the scene, until by the time of Master Richards, 1797–1823, we feel we know the School. Of Rayner's mastership, Dunsford, writing in 1790, reported:

He is said to have been well skilled in classic learning, an excellent Master, and remarkable for strict discipline. The School flourished so much in his time that an assistant became necessary to him in the higher school. Many respectable scholars were bred under his tuition.

Martin Dunsford, a pupil of Rayner who wrote a history of Tiverton from the reforming point of view.

A mid-eighteenth century very minor poet, Kiddell, paints portraits of the Masters he knew, beginning with Rayner. After an encomium to the School itself he comes to Rayner:

I see, I see, through a long length of days,
Some of the Masters who shall swell thy [the School's] praise.
Skill'd in all tongues, see Rayner [1698–1730] tread the stage,
Severe his virtue, awful in his rage;
While others follow all the musty rules
Of barb'rous monks, or slow phlegmatic fools,
From ev'ry weed, lo! Rayner clears the ground,
And in his grammar all the man is found.

'Smith next, [1730–33] who, with inimitable art,
Tempers the Master with the parent's part;
Lures the young mind his precepts to regard,
And makes e'en learning be its own reward.

Jones [1733–34] ever gentle, moulds the soul with ease,
Born to instruct, and only lives to please.

Wesley [1733–39] alone, curst with excessive pride,
Wesley alone shall want me as a guide;
To him I leave dry puns in scales to poise,
And wield a birch, the terror of all boys.
But see, his successor [Daddo 1740–57], my fav'rite son,
Completes the work that Jones had just begun;
Of manners mild, he scorns the fasces aid,
Great in his genius, in his temper staid;
Partial to none, yet lov'd alike by all,
His works shall praise him, thousands weep his fall.

These lines are a bit harsh on Wesley. He was probably a soured man and was too metropolitan in his tastes for Tiverton; in one letter to brother Charles in America he wrote, 'I am in a desert here as well as you, having no conversable being but my wife, till my mother came last week.' But he was a man with a national literary reputation and he responded to Kiddell in easier metre:

I've alarmed the country round
By raising board to twenty pound,
Huge provocation, I confess,
So great it never can be less.
Poor Sanders [1684–98] drudged incessant here,
The longer part of twenty year
What riches did his kindred find?
He left his victor plate behind.
Full thirty years has Rayner stay'd,
Rayner, oft praised, but never paid!
His boarders, though so gainful thought,
Cost hundreds more than ere they bought.

Useful to know that in mid-century boarding fees were £20. A hundred years later they would be £50. Wesley also paid homage to the founder and cannot have been unmoved by his charge:

Exempt from sordid and ambitious views,
Blest with the art to gain, and heart to use,
Not satisfied with life's poor span alone,
Blundell through ages sends his blessing down.
Since worth to raise and learning to support,
A patriarch's lifetime had appeared too short;
While letters gain esteem in Wisdom's eyes,
Till Justice is extinct, and Mercy dies,
His alms perpetual, not by Time confined,
Last with the world, and end but with mankind.

Wesley should also be compulsory reading for all teachers meeting parents, and all parents listening to teachers. His poem, which includes the lines, describing the teacher who:

With meekness and attention hears
Sisters and aunts and grandmothers…

… is too naughty for lengthy quotation. He died at fifty, in harness, in November 1739. It is curious that four Masters died in the Master's House in the 1730s – Rayner, Smith, Jones and Wesley. After Wesley all the Masters resigned and enjoyed years of retirement, and in the seventeenth century, of five Masters only one died in office.

Between Rayner and Daddo it seems the School flourished and its fortunes can be seen through the lives of its more famous clergy. John Conybeare, 1692–1755, and Hayter, 1702–62, both Rayner's pupils, have already been mentioned. That Rayner's Blundell's could produce two famous Bishops and the reprobate Bampfylde Moore Carew, known as King of the Gypsies, is some sort of witness to a broad education! Richard Beadon and Thomas Davey were both pupils of Daddo and their lives at Blundell's probably overlapped in the 1740s. Davey, the elder, of a family prominent in Tiverton since the sixteenth century, was the son of the Feoffees' Treasurer, and was awarded a Balliol scholarship and a Newte exhibition, useful preparation for a life of clerical plurality. He collected four parishes and became Master of Balliol in 1784 until his death in 1798. He would have slipped away to anonymity if Southey had not immortalised him with some undergraduate doggerel:

Thomas Davey. A Balliol Scholar who became Master.

By permission of Dr Jones

I go, God save me,
To Doctor Davey
And when he came,
My own sweet name
In modest manner said.
Dear Tom, his Wig
Is not so big
As many Doctors more,

And so I may
Presume to say
His wisdom is the more.
He then a book
Very shabby to look
Gave me, wasn't that kind?
For which nice gift
Indeed I left
But one pound four behind.

Richard Beadon, another of Daddo's pupils, who became successively Bishop of Gloucester and Bath and Wells.

Richard Beadon was born in 1737 and went to St John's, Cambridge, where the Tripos system of examinations had been introduced. He was a Wrangler and won prizes for his Latin prose. He became Vice-Chancellor, Archdeacon of Lincoln, Master of Jesus, where he, like Hayter, came into contact with the royal family in the form of William Frederick, later Duke of Gloucester. Court favour brought him the Bishopric of Gloucester in 1789, whence he was translated to Bath and Wells in 1802, dying at the advanced age of 85 in 1822. He was arguably the laziest bishop in England.

Sound scholarship, good manners, rich living – how comfortably roll by these lives of the Hanoverian Blundellians!

Kiddell's lines apart we know more and more. The essential elements of school life are quarrels between staff and Master, some elements of life as lived by the scholars and knowledge of the continuing community, the 'Old Boys'. And these we begin to have. The most dramatic evidence of 'boy life' comes from the Feoffees' Orders of 1730: 'Ordered that all Cockfighting at the Schoolhouse on Shrove Tuesdays be abolished for the future.' Apparently, cock-fighting was quite normal in schools, so much so that when St Paul's was founded in 1518 it was expressly forbidden in the statutes. Connected with Shrove Tuesday cock-fighting was payment to the Master of a 'Cockpenny', the payment of which survived at Sedbergh until the 1860s at a rate of £1 to the Master and ten shillings to the Usher. One wonders whether such a prohibition was effective; certainly it had to be repeated in 1740 and the practice probably did not stop then. The Lowman site was prone to flooding and in the period of Rayner through to Daddo, there is evidence of the fun that boys could have from a real flood. The Green was well flooded in 1695 and 1753, and it was apparently accepted usage that the boys could get into the school brewery and use the tubs as punts and pole around the Green, having a holiday. The Feoffees were sharp about holidays. In 1699 they had ordered that:

> … *the Scholemaster shall not be allowed to grant above one play day in a week but by ye request of one of the Gents that are Feoffees and that in such weeks only wherein there is no Holy Day.*

Without the pressure of public exams presumably the temptation was overwhelming for the Master and Usher to go to the races or the equivalent of the Headmasters' Conference, as the prohibition had to be repeated in identical terms by the Feoffees in April 1734.

Perhaps because of the arrival of Wesley, 'curst with excessive pride,' the Feoffees had to adjudicate between the Master and the Usher, the former Blundell's Balliol Scholar of 1718, William Somaster. They resolved that:

> … *the Usher and Assistant Master, at all times from henceforth be under the direction of the Headmaster, and the said Headmaster is to have the inspection of the lower as well as the upper school and that the clerk do leave a copy of this order with the said Headmaster, Usher and Assistant Master.*

Ouch. One knows roughly what the pupils did 'in school'; they learnt Latin and Greek, what used to be called 'grammar'. Evidence from a notebook written by boys aged ten to thirteen in the 1780s shows that they were acquainted with Shakespeare, Smollett, English history and classical mythology and that their English vocabulary was much wider than that of an average 9A pupil of today. They also probably did arithmetic, tackling complicated sums without logarithms or calculators.

The interest of a school is also what happens outside the classroom and early-eighteenth-century Blundellians seem to have been of a roving disposition. In 1756 the Feoffees:

> … *recommended to Mr Daddo and Mr Atherton and the Masters for the time being that they suffer none of the scholars to go without the gate of the school without the express consent of them or one of them.*

For many years before this injunction, and for many years afterwards, Blundellians invaded the neighbouring countryside. Sometimes it was to collect greenery to decorate the School on 29 May in celebration of the Restoration. At other times it would have been to exercise their dogs and even to form packs for hunting. One such at this early period was Bampfylde Moore Carew, the son of the Rector of Bickleigh, who joined Rayner's school in 1705. Not content with normal truancy, he ran away to join the gypsies and eventually became their leader or 'King'. After numerous adventures, which brought him national notoriety, he died in 1758. His last days at school are described by Snell as follows:

Bampfylde Moore Carew, King of the Gypsies, a less orthodox Old Boy.

> *At this time the boys at Tiverton school had a fine pack of hounds, and, among the subscribers were John Martin, Thomas Coleman and John Escott, all young men of good family, Coleman being the son of the Squire of Gornhay. It happened one day that a neighbouring farmer, who was a great sportsman and a whipper in to the enterprising Blundellians, waited upon them with the information that there was a fine deer, with a collar round its neck. The scholars set off in a body with Martin, Escott, Coleman and Carew at their head to hunt the animal. The time of this event was just before harvest, when there was much corn standing in the fields, and, as the chase was hot and lasted several hours, considerable damage was done to the crops. The 'field' however succeeded in killing the deer, which, from the inscription on its collar, was found to belong to Colonel Nutcombe of Clayhanger. Meanwhile the farmers and landowners, for whose interests the youthful Nimrods had shown such a princely disregard, wended their way to Mr Rayner and demanded vengeance. An inquiry was instituted and the culprits, foreseeing the result, deemed it expedient to be 'aeger' [sick].*

It was on this day of 'aeger' that Carew fell in with the gypsies at Brickhouse and joined them. Roving the countryside in bands of juvenile Nimrods persisted. At the beginning of the next century, in 1809, 'Jack' Russell joined the School determined to achieve a scholarship to obtain the necessary qualifications to follow his father into the Church of England. He only just escaped expulsion for keeping hounds and playing truant.

Within the gates they could cock-fight and perhaps play Fives in that court referred to as the site of the 1649 Assizes. There were available to them the usual amusements. The Town's bull-baiting area was nearby and no doubt the scholars took part. Curiosity is roused by another order of the Feoffees in February 1709:

> *That no persons whatsoever shall be permitt'd to use or exercise any play or diversion within the limits or bounds of the School without the permission and consent of Mr Rayner the Master, and that the Porter for the future shall keep such persons out.*

The previous Feoffees' meeting had been in July 1708, so whatever was being forbidden had presumably happened since then. Perhaps it might have been a Christmas play or perhaps 'play or diversion' meant what we would call sport and perhaps Kiddell gives us a clue. In an extended passage he writes an account of what must have been a game of primitive football:

> *Here oft the swains, when winter chills the blood,*
> *And feels the current of the murmuring flood,*
> *Amidst whose beds of ice, or show'rs of snow,*
> *Send forth the ball, a signal to the foe,*
> *The sturdy foe, all mark'd with many a scar,*
> *Attempts the prey, and so begins the war:*
> *Each kicks, and spurns, and proud of high renown,*
> *Conceals the smart, nor will his anguish own;*
> *But, bleeding, shouts, and furious hurls the ball,*
> *And, if he falls, he conquers in his fall!*
> *To him another hero soon succeeds,*
> *Alike his courage, and alike he bleeds:*
> *In vain with fury does his bosom flame,*
> *In vain he hopes to celebrate his name;*
> *His feet fly up, his body beats the ground:*
> *Hark the ice crackles, and the streets resound,*
> *How near the goal, and fir'd with strong disdain,*

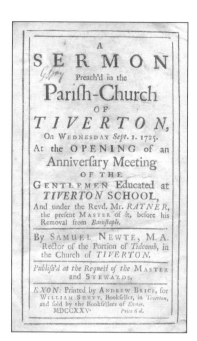

1725. *The earliest evidence of Old Boys' Day, but probably this occasion was not the first.*

These labour not to lose, and those to gain;
Hero with hero long for fame contends,
And long they suffer ere the battle ends:
This tho' with force, and that with art assails,
Yet force, or art, or courage nought avails:
And now they sport, and now again engage,
And ev'ry turn redoubles all their rage;
'Till as their rage renews, their strength decays,
And impotent, they part, with equal praise.

But organised games as the twenty-first century knows them can only be found in the nineteenth century.

A sign that the School was in rude health is the appearance of regular Old Boys' Days. The first real evidence is a published sermon of Samuel Newte's, dated 1 September, 1725, 'preach'd in the Parish Church of Tiverton at the opening of the anniversary meeting of the gentlemen educated at Tiverton School.' It is published 'at the request of the Master and Stewards'. In the archives there is another sermon 'preached in St Peter's Church in Tiverton on 6 September, 1753, being the annual meeting of the gentlemen educated at Blundell's School.' The frontispiece lists eight stewards: George Fursdon, William Troyte, John Callard, George Cooke, Hugh Ackland, Edward Collins, Henry Osmond and Nutcombe Quick and claims that 'this discourse was published at their request.' The similarities are too striking for any other conclusions than, firstly the meeting of 1725 was not the first, and secondly that there was a series of meetings between 1725 and 1753. There is clear evidence of a meeting in 1751 as John Wesley was in town and he recorded details in his journal, Thursday 29 August:

There was a sermon preached at the Old Church [i.e. St Peter's not St George's] before
the Trustees of the school. At half an hour past twelve the Morning Service began. But
such an unsufferable noise and confusion I never saw before in a place of worship: no, not
even in a Jewish Synagogue. The clergy set the example; laughing and talking during the
greater part of the prayers and sermon. A young gentlewoman, who was with us where we
dine, hastened away to prepare for the ball. But before she was half dressed, she was struck,

An invitation to the Old Boys' Feast of 1727.

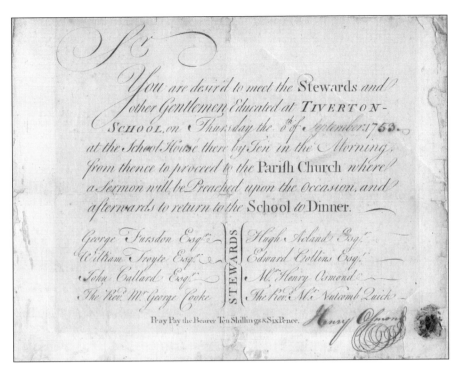

And of 1740.

Sr

You are desir'd to meet the Stewards *and other Gentlemen Educated at* TIVERTON-SCHOOL, *on Thursday the 6th of September 1753. at the School-House there by Ten in the Morning, from thence to proceed to the* Parish Church *where a Sermon will be Preached upon the Occasion, and afterwards to return to the* School *to* Dinner. ——

George Fursdon Esqr.   Hugh Acland Esqr.
William Troyte Esqr.   Edward Collins Esqr.
John Callard Esqr.   Mr. Henry Osmond
The Revd. Mr George Cooke   The Revd. Mr. Nutcomb Quick

STEWARDS

Pray Pay the Bearer Ten Shillings & Six Pence.

and came down in a flood of tears. Nevertheless she broke through, and in a few hours danced away her convictions.

Towards the close of the sermon in the evening a rabble of gentlemen's servants gathered together and endeavoured to make a disturbance. The next morning a 'mob of footmen', presumably the Old Boys' servants, made a more vigorous riot. When again there is evidence of Old Boys' meetings in 1788 all accounts say that they were restarted after a discontinuance of about thirty years. A possible explanation is the Lisbon earthquake. The religion of the period laid great stress on the reasonableness of belief, the rationality of the universe and God's controlling hand. But on 1 November 1755 earthquakes, tidal waves and fires devastated Lisbon, many thousands being killed in the collapsing churches. In December George II issued a special Proclamation observing, 'The manifold sins and wickedness of these Kingdoms have most justly deserved heavy and severe punishments from the hand of Heaven.' The King pointed to the dreadful example of Lisbon and ordered a national day of fasting on 6 February 1756. The idea caught a changing mood. John Wesley produced a searing pamphlet called 'serious Thoughts occasioned by the late earthquake at Lisbon', which ran into six editions. Horace Walpole wrote:

Between the French and the earthquake [The Seven Years' War had begun] *you have no notion how good we are grown; nobody makes a suit now but of sackcloth turned up with ashes.*

And of 1753.

In 1757 the Militia was forbidden to drill on Sundays. George III was an enthusiast for Christian propriety and discouraged Sunday card parties; domesticity and simple piety became fashionable and perhaps the Anniversary Meetings of Gentlemen Educated at Blundell's School was one of the casualties.

In a final attempt to grasp the shadows of this distant period, let us end with the words of Francis Fort, Rector of Huntsham, as he preached the 'Anniversary' sermon of 1753, before the eight Stewards 'and his much esteemed friends and beloved School Fellows'. Fort had been born in 1696 and had been awarded a Sidney Sussex scholarship in 1713, so had been a pupil under Rayner. He had become a Fellow of Sidney before being elected to a fellowship at Exeter College in 1721, and being the Preacher of 1753 took as his text Acts xxii.3, 'Yet brought up in this city, at the feet of Gamaliel'. He started off with a nice fancy that God in his wisdom had sent 'mean, obscure and ignorant apostles' to preach to the Jews, but sent the well-educated St Paul, who had been taught by Gamaliel, to the Greeks. We, who have suffered under successive Ministers of Education, Directors of Studies and the like, may enjoy his warning that:

> *… some indeed, like other vain and whimsical projectors, are ready to propose more cheap and speedy methods of instruction. But then these schemists are, for the most part, airy and deceitful, they finish scholars like buildings, in a very slight and irregular manner, and, too often without a proper foundation.*

He ended as follows:

> *We may be able to make some requital to our earthly benefactors… And surely none of our friends, not even our parents excepted, have a juster claim to these reasonable offerings of our hearts than those Gamaliels at whose feet we were brought up – those Masters to whose skill we owe the removal of our native ignorance; to whose kindness the correction of our youthful follies. One of these* [Rayner], *who for many years presided over this school with so much credit and success, and to whom many of us are indebted for our first good principles of religion, as well as learning, we can never think of, or speak of, without the warmest emotions, and heartfelt expressions of grateful respect. And it must be a satisfaction mixed with joy, to all those who wish well to the common place of their education, and to the memory of their good old Master, to see the seat of this wise and learned Gamaliel so well supplied by a scholar of his own forming, and one, who so happily imitates his skill, and so prudently copies his example.* [Daddo, a Cornishman born in 1712, who was obviously Rayner's pupil.]
>
> *All those then who are truly sensible of the great benefit of a liberal education, will take care to pay a proper regard to both these duties; first to glorify God, and then to be thankful to man…*
>
> *And to express both these duties in the most publick and solemn manner – to show our gratitude to God and man is the intent of our present annual religious assembly. And, if after this, to raise our spirits, to warm our hearts, and enlarge our affections, we indulge, a little more freely than usual, at a festival entertainment, we do no more than the wisest and best of men have done in all the ages and nations, and none but a few mistaken zealots, or morose bigots* [Wesley] *will presume to censure us for it.*

And off they went to dinner and a ball in the evening. It has never been a school for morose bigots.

ATHERTON AND KEATS

After the rapid 'turnover' and mortality of Headmasters in the 1730s when Rayner, Smith, Jones and Samuel Wesley had all died in the Master's House, it is a relief, unless you hate such men passionately, to return to the longevity usual to the mastership. From 1604 to 1730 there were six Masters, an average span of twenty-one years. From 1740–1823 there were four Masters – Daddo, Atherton, Keats and Richards – again averaging just under twenty-one years at Lowman Green, all having reigns of remarkably similar length: Daddo seventeen years, Atherton eighteen years, Keats twenty-two years and Richards twenty-six.

Philip Atherton was one of only two Ushers who stepped up into the shoes of the mastership. The Feoffees' Order appointing him Usher in 1746 on the death of Daddo refers to him as 'of Tiverton'. He was then aged twenty-eight and a graduate and Fellow of Balliol, Daddo's old college, so he may have been specially recruited with a promise of the reversion. Martin Dunsford, who had been his pupil in the Lower School from 1752–57, and a man who in later life flew the flag for the Radicals in Tiverton and thus was not likely to look at Blundell's through spectacles of any rosy hue, described him thus:

> He discharged the duty of Usher eleven years with so much reputation that, on Mr Daddo's resignation, he was elected Master of the School. He was eminent for classic learning, and under his care the reputation of the School was greatly raised. He possessed a good understanding, was of a mild temper and benevolent disposition, which secured him general respect. After a faithful service of twenty-nine years, in the useful and important employ of sowing the seeds of learning, and cultivating the principles of virtue in the minds of the numerous pupils committed to his care, Mr Atherton resigned the school in 1775; died the 19th of March, in the 59th year of his age; and was buried in the Chancel of St Peter's Church.

Philip Atherton, Usher 1746–57 and Master 1757–75, of mild temper and benevolent disposition.

Words from the heart from a former pupil. Atherton's burial in the Chancel is explained by his performance of duty in St Peter's. His memorial on a pillar by the lectern confirms that he was 'one of the ministers of this church' and records show he was doing duty after 1754, continuing until his retirement from the mastership in 1775. He was also Vicar of Nynehead in Somerset. Beavis Wood states that, in 1775, Atherton was also deputy Recorder of Tiverton. On his death in 1777 Beavis Wood referred to him as 'our late worthy friend'. So he jogged along in some comfort and with some status in the Town. There is also other evidence to show him as a 'figure' in a pocket borough dominated by the Ryders, whose man of business was Beavis Wood and whose local allies were Oliver Peard, until he blew his head off with a blunderbuss in 1765, and Sir John Duntze of Rockbeare. Atherton was on the board of the first Turnpike Trust and he was a trustee for the Worth and Hartnoll families. His family benefited from his being useful, as one of his sons-in-law became an Exciseman and the other a Customs Officer, valuable posts and part of the patronage that greased a pocket borough. When his wife Betty died a few years after him, she left £1600 in cash as well as lands worth an unspecified amount.

His most famous pupil was Dr Eveleigh, the son of the Rector of Winkleigh. He entered Blundell's in 1760 and went to Wadham with one of Ham's Exhibitions and was elected a Fellow of Oriel in 1772, becoming Provost in 1780 until his death in 1814. As was the comfortable custom he was also Canon of Rochester and held an Essex parish. Under him Oriel maintained and extended its position as the foremost academic and religious college in the University. Keble wrote of him:

> I had known him as long as I can remember anyone. He was, I verily believe, a man to bring down a blessing on any society of which he was a member.

Dr Eveleigh, Atherton's pupil and Provost of Oriel College, 1780–1814.

By permission of the Provost and Fellows

Perhaps he had learnt these traits from the 'mild temper and benevolent disposition' of Atherton.

Atherton was certainly loved by more than Dunsford. In the back of an old ledger is a poem, written in 1768 by Henry Hutton, the Balliol Scholar of that year, entitled, 'On his Leaving Blundell's School in the mastership of the Revd Mr Atherton.'

Rude and unskill'd in all the Rules of Art,
Void of all merit but a grateful Heart,
The Muse attempts in unharmonious Strains
To paint the blessings of Palladian Plains.
O Thou who taught that humble Muse to sing,
Whose precepts oft supplied the poet's wing,
Hear while again she tries to tune the Lay,
While yet encouraged by thy friendly Ray.
Those two his other half, forgive the muse,
Her failings pardon and her faults excuse,
Forc'd by sad fate she bids a long farewell
To those blest fields where Joy and favour dwell;
Forc'd by your kindness she would fain rehearse
Past scenes of pleasure in unpolish'd verse.
Close by the bank where gentle Lowman glides,
Ere swelling Ex receives its murmuring tides,
Behold the Dome, which Blundell deigned to raise!
Blest be his name and sacred be his praise!
Within these walls by heavenly virtue fir'd,
How many youths by wisdom's self inspir'd?
'Tis here she dwells, 'tis here the Goddess reigns,
The seat of Empire hers and these her plains;
Here Attic learning is again reviv'd
Such as in antient days great Athens view'd.
Here Roman worth still charms the youthful mind,
Still Titus rules, the darling of Mankind.
Again victorious Caesar seems to fight,
And Scipio's generous deeds again delight.
Here Rome's diviner bards in glory live,
Crown'd with that flame, which once themselves could give,
Still gentle Horace smiles, whose easy page,
Alone could please and ridicule the age,
Could laughter raise, yet wit with virtue blend,
And with the Satyrist unite the friend.
Here train'd to learning we with pleasure read
Of each great action, each distinguish'd deed,
Peruse majestic Homer, or admire
A Tully's eloquence or Virgil's fire.
Instructed then what bosom does entreat?
What heart but glows with simulative heat.
E'en I the meanest of the tuneful throng,
To whom no laureate in bays belong,
E'en I invoke the Muses, ignobly vain,
And, taught by you, to you devote the strain.
Thus Phoebus once, the Sybylli bosom fir'd
With future knowledge and her breast inspir'd;
She felt the power diffus'd in every part,
And all the God possessed her swelling heart.
Then her prophetic voice long silence broke
And, as Apollo taught, the Goddess spoke.
Content and Virtue shed their blessings here,

And innocence dispels each glowing care;
Here rosy health, with every blooming grace,
Cheers every heart and brightens every face.
Soon on each day the festive hour returns:
See how the youth with warm impatience burns,
See how the ball flies o'er the little plain,
Swift as Camilla when she scores the Main;
By turn they run, by turn again pursue,
A glorious conquest ever in their view,
They met, they fall, again the Heroes rise,
Scorn every danger, every toil despise,
Rush on impetuous until they win the Game,
And with triumphant shout their Joy proclaim!
Some to the bank of wandering Ex repair,
And with alluring art the Trout ensnare,
Skill'd on the gentle wave to throw the line,
While sure success awaits the shrewd design.
Oft through the walk Oh! Colliepriest I've stray'd,
When the low sun his milder beams display'd;
There glides the murmuring stream with awful sound,
There oft great Addison, immortal sage,
I read thy precepts, thy instructing page,
Admir'd thy work, thou Guardian of mankind,
Chaste as thy soul, as thy self refin'd;
Here have I seen what Pope, what Milton sung,
And mourn'd Narcissus' fate with virtuous young.
There, there were pleasures once allotted me
Once from each care, from every trouble free!
Farewell ye joys, ye pleasing scenes adieu!
The golden age scarce happier moments knew!
O still may wisdom shed her blessing here,
And make the name of Blundell ever dear!
Oh still may gratitude revere the man,
Whose universal love first drew the Plan.
From Blundell learn what virtue can bestow:
The noblest honours which are found below.
Let his benevolence inspire your breast,
Like him be good, and then like him be blest!
While states and Empires fall, for fall they must,
And monarchs lie forgotten in the dust,
Still Blundell lives, still blooms with growing fame,
And every day adds honour to his name!
His monument shall stand till Earth decays
And Ages yet unborn proclaim his praise.

Not only a nice, but a useful, poem. It contains clear evidence of what an eighteenth-century Blundellian was exposed to in the schoolroom: Roman and Greek history, the poetry of Horace, Homer and Virgil in the Classics. Yet they were well read too in English literature; Shakespeare may have been out of fashion, but Addison, Pope and Milton were sound fare for the soul. The recreational presence of football is confirmed and Kiddell reinforced. All Blundellians fished, swam, hunted and went for walks, and, if Hutton is to be believed, rejoiced in their heritage. It also illustrates the blessings of a coherent culture, where all educated readers would understand all the metaphors and allusions.

When much-loved Atherton resigned there was a delightful fuss. The Feoffees' Book of Orders gives little clue of the storm brewing, merely recording for their meeting of 17 May, 1777, unusually well attended with 20 Feoffees there, that:

The Revd Mr Keats, Master 1775–97, a likeness from the early years of his mastership.

The Revd Mr Keats of Charlton in Hants, Master of Arts be elected and chosen Master of the Grammar school in Tiverton in the room of the Revd Mr Philip Atherton and to have fifty pounds yearly paid him with all the advantages and profits belonging to the said Schoolmaster to commence midsummer day next.

In a letter to his patron, Nathaniel Ryder, written on 22 May, Beavis Wood wrote:

It was generally expected that Mr Wood, the Undermaster, would have been chosen and the Town seems much disappointed on this account. All the Trustees attended and we are told that Mr Keate [sic] had 11 votes to Mr Wood's seven. Mr Keate comes most power-fully recommended and is said to be a very worthy man. As Mr Wood has been ten years Undermaster he had strong expectations.

Some wag wrote a ballad, which went:

> Some ill-natured Critics have foolishly thought,
> This age not so wise or as good as it ought,
> But it's all a mistake, as I'll prove by example
> Of what has just happened, a proof full and ample
> In the Tiverton Trust
> Oh! The rare Tiverton Trust.
>
> Honest Atherton tir'd with whipping and flogging,
> For many long years thinks it time to be jogging,
> And resolv'd to retire as it is but quite just,
> He makes known his desires to the Tiverton trust.
>
> So notice is give'n thro' the World to be sure
> In the papers of Country and Town to procure
> A Successor, worthy and clever, no Fool,
> To do the Trust credit and keep up the School.
>
> And now the Time comes, th'important great Day,
> That was fix'd, I'm told, for the middle of May,
> And in the fine Gentlefolk fail not to pour,
> In chaises, on horseback, in Coaches and four.
>
> Well, who's to be chosen? Why who do you think should?
> The whole Country and Town have decided for Wood.
> A fig for the Town – they're a parcel of Vermin,
> And their Honours' wise Heads can much better determine!
>
> 'What objection is made – weigh it well in the balance,
> Wood wants not in Conscience for Learning or Talents;
> He has wit and is sprightly.' 'But what is all that?
> We do not like sharp, who ourselves are quite flat.'
>
> 'Beside's the Man's tasty. They say that the Muses
> Are close to his elbows, whenever he chooses,
> And Apollo Musicians divine hold.' 'Enough!
> Apollo? The Muses? Don't talk of such stuff!'
>
> 'Then as for behaviour, you can say no less,
> He is courteous, polite in his manner and dress.'
> 'Oh! a mere Macaroni! ''Tis better, I vow,
> To prefer a plain Farmer just come from the Plough.'
>
> 'What! Discard a young man, who in faith, as appears,
> Is just now in his Prime and Vigour of Years?'

'All young Fellows are fools! We're determined to have
A man of three score that is sober and grave.'

'What! One ye ne'er heard of, when Wood has been true to ye!
Ne'er was known to neglect, or be slight in his Duty,
Who is perfect no doubt, for I am told he has made
A double apprenticeship now in his trade.'

'We care not for that', says the son of Old Nick,
His favourite Son, call'd on earth Jackey Quick,
And the wise Captain Barnard is in the same way,
Who most civilly swears what his Colonel will say.

So says Tommy Putt, with a face that, Good Lack,
Like his temper and heart is a little too black.
With the same to his tail he ties close a bundle,
Little Beavis, with Atkins, and each Master Blundell.

Then for want of enough there was joined to the crew
That steady, grave Gentleman, good Master Drewe,
Who is never addicted to gaming and drinking,
Speaks little or nothing, and ne'er without thinking.

Soon foolish electors Wood's merit agreed in,
And inveigh'd rather loudly against the proceeding,
Insignificant Fellows, you'll tell me at once,
Such as Bampfylde and Acland and Walter and Duntze.

With some other such gentry, mean names and no note,
That for sense and for Honour are not worth a Groat.
But the wise ones succeeded, and therefore you must
Applaud the rare choice of the Tiverton Trust.'

If Beavis Wood is right in his account of the voting, the 'poet' omits the names of four who voted for Keats, three of the seven who voted for Thomas Wood and the two abstainers. Beavis Wood soon turned against Keats, but we cannot but suppose that the judgement of the Feoffees was made on proper grounds. Both Wood and Atherton had been 'Old Boys' and perhaps they felt it was time for new blood.

Whatever the case it rankled with Thomas Wood for a very long time. The Feoffees minuted on 2 January 1788:

The Revd Thomas Wood, our Usher, having attended and informed the Feoffees that on account of his not receiving of their Order made the 17th of May, 1775 and of his ill state of health he requested the Feoffees to accept his resignation the twenty-fifth day of January instant.

The official length of notice as stated to both Keats and Wood when Keats was appointed on 17 May 1775, was a full six months. The Feoffees accepted Wood's resignation, reiterated the six-month rule and appointed the Revd John Ley as Usher, adding the strange injunction that he should always reside in the Usher's House. They also demanded that both Keats and Ley sign the Book to confirm their acceptance of the rule.

The meeting then proceeded to draft a letter to the Bishop of Exeter. Wood had obviously let slip that he intended to take pupils, so the Feoffees wrote:

To the Right Revd the Bishop of Exeter
My Lord,
We the Feoffees of Blundell's Foundation in the town of Tiverton whose names are hereunto subscribed consider it our duty to represent to your Lordship that the Revd Thomas Wood, Clerk, has this day been permitted to resign the place of Usher of this School on account of his ill health and having informed us of his application to your Lordship for a

licence to take scholars under his tuition in the said town of Tiverton, We think it incumbent on us to submit to your Lordship that such a licence may be very detrimental and injurious to the prosperity and interest of the said school. January 2nd, 1788.

All 17 Feoffees signed. The Bishop's reply came back from South Audley Street, dated 8 January, so the mail and the Bishop were prompt. He refused to grant Wood his licence. We have to jump over 150 years before we find the Governors wheeling in the heavy episcopal howitzer to discipline an Usher. In October 1946 they were informed by the Headmaster, R.L. Roberts, that the Revd R.A. Abigail, whom he had in effect driven out of the School, and who had now become Rector of Kentisbeare, was planning to write a 'History of the School, 1926–46'.

It was agreed that it was undesirable for such a document to be published in view of the leading part that Mr Abigail had taken against the Headmaster during the recent troubles of the School, and it was thought that the best medium of approach should be though the Bishop of Exeter to whom the Chairman [Sir John Amory] agreed to make the particulars known.

For whatever reason the book did not appear.

Thomas Wood is the first Usher whom we feel we can know. Firstly we have sightings of him from the outside adult perspective by the Feoffees and Beavis Wood; secondly we have evidence from his own accounts and miraculously we have evidence about him from the pupils he taught. The adult perspective shows him a competent man, expected by an informed and able witness, Beavis Wood, to be appointed Master and obviously considered capable of the office. Others, both the Feoffees who voted for him and the partisan author of the poem, considered him a worthy man. His father had been Rector of Bampton, and he was curate of Cadbury on behalf of his father, Rector of Poughill and sinecure chaplain of a regiment. Like Atherton he was a recipient of a few morsels from the Ryder-Duntze gravy train.

His accounts, which survive from 1763–66, give a nice picture of the life of a plodding pedagogue in an eighteenth-century backwater. He was a bachelor, whose sister kept house and catered for his boarders, for which he paid her a 'stipend' of a few guineas a year. In 1788, the year he retired, Dunsford says his successor took over '48 boys in the lower school', but in the years covered by his surviving accounts, 1763–66, numbers in the Lower School seem to have fluctuated from below to above 30, of whom less than ten were boarders. He kept his accounts from 'Xmas to Xmas' and they show that his incomings in 1763–64 were £163.19s. and in 1764–65 were £214.19s.10d. In 1765–66 he received the larger sum of £242.18s.11d, which he broke down into five income sources. As Vicar of Cadbury he got £23.5s.; from the Tithes and living of Poughill, £54.13s.9d; from Miscellaneous, £3.19s.7d; from 'my School', £68.16s. and from 'my boarders', £92.4s.7d. From the more detailed entries it is clear that his boarding fee was £14 a year, paid as a lump sum or half yearly, which would suggest he had seven boarders, which roughly fits the entry for 15 March, 1766: 'Paid Mr Knight for five boys sitting in the Church, 2 Beres, Bovel, Phelp, Sweeting, £1.5s.'

He had his stipend of £20 a year as Usher, which contributed to his income from 'my School'. The other £48 seems to have been made up of payments of a guinea or half a guinea, paid in January or at Whitsun from all pupils in the Lower School. In entering these payments he provides us with the first comprehensive list of scholars in the Lower School in existence. In the post-Whitsun list of 1766 there are 35 names; in the Christmas list 38. It was clearly a 'two-term year'. Punctuating the accounts as regularly as clockwork is a weekly entry: 'Dat Sor', or alternatively 'My Sister'. These are for sums that vary from one to two guineas, which were probably her housekeeping allowance for herself, her brother and the boarders. Every year the payments start in mid-January and continue until mid-April. When they stop in April, entries show him visiting Poughill, Cadbury and Bampton, so his cares in the Lower School have been suspended. The payments begin again in mid-May and continue with breaks in early June and August right through to mid-December.

The accounts show a man of regular habits, small pleasures and minor charities, the typical bachelor schoolmaster. He bought a fishing rod for 10s.6d and flies for 6d., but records paying his sister 1s.6d to buy a salmon. Almost every week, and sometimes twice a week, he played cards, usually losing such sums as 6d., but once as much as six shillings. He went to card parties regularly at the Athertons, and now and again hosted parties himself. He also frequented the 'Bowling Green' in the centre of town to play bowls or cards. He attended balls at the Three Tuns, once paying 4s.6d. for a 'turbot and venison feast' and he went to events at the 'Assembly Rooms'. He bought wine, brandy, malt for brewing beer, and in February 1766 a gross of tobacco pipes for three shillings. He bought play tickets and once he bought a lobster. He was probably musical as at one time he had a flute mended, and the references in the poem to Apollo suggest the same. Now and again he paid 'Old Charles' 1s.2d. a day to work in the garden. There are regular small gifts to debtors, families with seven children, beggars, soldiers and a 'poor woman at Cadbury'. He gave five shillings to a Welsh clergyman in distress and was a half-guinea a year contributor to a fund for clergy widows.

As he felt himself more settled, the luxuries crept in. In March 1766 he bought half a dozen silver spoons from Mr Skinner of Exeter for the grand sum of £6.15s.6d. Later in that month he bought a pair of silk breeches for £1 and stockings to match for 12s.6d. He had the luxury of six oranges brought from Exeter and he paid Mr Fursdon £2.8s. for three pounds of green tea, which Fursdon had fetched from London. He paid eight guineas for a horse he had bought from Mr Thomas of Bickleigh.

As far as one can tell he seems to have been a kind man. In October 1763 he gave two boarders, Bovel and Phelp, a shilling each for 'Tiverton Fair'. He regularly gave 6d. or 1s. to the 'Charity Children'. He allowed his sister four guineas for clothes, but often gave her more on special occasions such as March 1766, when he gave her an extra two guineas towards a 'new sack'. On 18 July 1764, he gave Miss Blundell of Collipriest 'a curious sixpence which I found'. In October 1765 he again gave the 'boys 7s.6d. to spend at the Fair'.

He also possessed scholarship and a witty father. It was Thomas Wood who was credited with the best translation of the elliptical verses that graced the gate of the School.

> Minerva, on her travels, sought to find
> Some hospitable seat to please her mind:
> She saw this School; struck with the stately dome,
> She cried with transport, – 'This shall be my Home!'

His father, it is told, was riding past the School gates in a chaise with the Bishop of Exeter, who asked him for a translation. Wood senior's translation was witty, but loose and probably refers to Betty Atherton.

> Within these walls two mighty monarchs rule,
> One in the Home, the other in the School;
> But see, My Lord, a sad disaster, –
> He rules the boys, but she the Master.

So it is strange that such a regular and mild man should have been the victim of a schoolboy rebellion in 1787. But then he was over twenty years older than the man in the accounts. He had probably been born around 1730, so was rising sixty by the time of the 'rebellion', and bitter at having been passed over for the mastership by a man for whom he probably had little respect. (Certainly, if Dunsford was right about the 48 boys in the Lower School in 1788, then Keats only had 34 boys in the Upper School.) Some schoolmasters mellow as they age, some get crabbier.

The little rebels certainly paint an unflattering picture of Thomas Wood. 'Swarthy', 'longshanked' and 'lantern-jawed' they call him, and quite shrewdly highlight the fact of his disappointed ambition, which must have become very naked for scraps mostly aged ten to thirteen to have become so aware. The wicked little urchins

Thomas Wood, Usher 1760–88, drawn by a naughty little boy in 1787.

Naughty little boys smoking. Blundellians no longer do this.

Naughty little boys destroying Usher Wood's plates and glasses.

The victory parade. A good illustration to show what eighteenth-century boys wore.

aroused Wood's wrath by smoking and sparked him into a typical schoolmaster's speech forbidding tobacco, not only where these boys were, but also 'in my other House' (so presumably he had more boarders now), and he proceeded to break their pipes.

> *We still continued to smoke and do everything that might offend the Haughty Tyrant, and now open war was proclaimed. From tobacco we proceeded to smoke assaphedita and swore to keep secret every design.*

From smoking they proceeded to vandalism. One of them, Eastcott, was suspected by Molly Woods of letting off gunpowder, and, for this crime and severe rudeness he was flogged, and so we have a description, with illustration, of what an eighteenth-century flogging was like. Another, Gandy, was flogged for blowing out Wood's candle. They had an anti-Wood procession, whose illustration of the event provides examples of 'school uniform'. They hissed Wood after prayers, they misbehaved at roll call, they cut bows and pretended to shoot him and they jumped out at him, making loud noises. But eventually their ink petered out and they drifted off to other things. Plus ça change. Not surprisingly Wood decided to call it a day and next year, as recounted, resigned and lived out the rest of his life in Washfield, marrying one of his sister's friends.

Boy being flogged. The victim was hoisted onto the back of a larger person and flogged with a birch called in schoolboy slang 'a plum pudding'.

Worthy of comment in the light of 'the rebellion' is that all the boys seem to have had penknives and access to gunpowder. All furniture from the Old School is covered with boys' names and all the walls of the School, accessible to penknife-wielding boys, has also been carved with their names, over 150 of which are still legible. A combination of the penknife and gunpowder enabled a 'winkey' to be contrived. The recipe was: cut a hole into a desk and keep the shavings. Deepen the edge of the hole and pack the deepened area with gunpowder. Place a low candle on the raised centre of the hole. Pack the whole with the shavings mixed with candle grease. Make sure you are doing your evening prep in another part of the room and, as the candle burns lower, await developments.

Keats introduced some novelties into the academic regimen. He was a bit of a character and had given every boy a sobriquet. He always carried a knotted rope called 'Discipline' which he swished at offenders, preferably unawares. He also introduced 'epigrams'; a topic would be announced at 8.30am and the epigram in Latin or Greek had to be produced by 9am. But he is remembered to this day for the invention of the Keats' Medals, two of which were awarded, one for Speaking, the other for Composition. Keats suggested the medals to the Feoffees in 1776, the idea was accepted in 1777 and the first medals cast in 1778, and awarded ever since. He is described as combining 'gravity with drollery' and as commanding respect yet having 'a constant playfulness of manner'. He certainly ran a happy ship. Snell quotes a boy who was removed from Keats' Blundell's and sent to Hyde Abbey, a school run by Richards' brother, where floggings were so regular that he begged to be sent back to Tiverton where he had never been flogged. This boy mentioned as plus points about Blundell's that they could rob orchards, bait badgers, climb in after hours, and keep donkeys, without Keats bothering to notice. It was still a small school, and probably fun, unless one was an elderly Usher with a grievance.

Part of the 'fun' were the special occasions, which had grown over the century and a half since the Restoration. From an early time it had been the custom to sally forth at dawn on 29 May to purloin greenery, mostly oak, to decorate the school-room in honour of Charles II's Restoration. Into the decorated room would come the Headmaster to sit in majesty under a large oak branch suspended from the roof. His duty was to hear each Blundellian 'spout' a certain number of lines of poetry. Later in that day it was the custom to have sports, which not only included running and throwing things, but such delights as 'jingling', 'treaclers' and donkey races. To take part in 'treacling' was to try to eat a bun, suspended above your head and covered with treacle and feathers, without using your hands. 'Jingling' consisted of a large number of blindfolded boys holding hands and attempting to arrest a sighted boy in the middle of the ring, who was armed with a bell.

Another immemorial custom was the 'P.B. holiday'. A typical 'P.B.' day can be seen through a schoolboy letter of 1818:

> There is a little stream here, the Lowman, which overflowed last night and inundated us all. The water was four inches deep in the Schoolroom and the hall, where we have our meals, and even made its way into the Master's drawing-room, so that there is a little bustle here just now. I mention this because it is an old rule of the school, that, when the water rises to a certain mark, the boys are to have a holiday, which is the case to-day.

Traditionally the holiday was occasioned when the stones '16PB04', set in the pavement outside the School gates were lapped by the flood waters.

The Keats Medal for Speaking and
Composition.

Just before Keats became Headmaster a Feoffee, Benjamin Incledon, gave
Atherton a register and so we know from 1770 the names of all pupils, their home
address, their age and how long they stayed at the school. From 1775 to 1791 Keats
admitted between 11 and 27 pupils a year, mostly under twelve and they stayed on
average about three years. Boarders seem to have outnumbered the day pupils by
more than five to one and the overwhelming number of fathers are described as
Esquire, Gent or Clerk and few of them came from beyond the West Country.
Numbers seem to have oscillated around 90. In his last years Keats saw entries rise:
from 1792–96 there were over 30 new pupils each year, which enabled Keats to hand
over a school of 106 to William Page Richards.

Not so much a development, more a resurrection under Keats, was the restarting
of Old Boys' Day in 1788. Tiverton historians talk of a gap of 'thirty years' as sepa-
rating the gathering of 1788 from its predecessors. It is probable that some who were
involved in the restart had been at the gatherings in the 1750s because the new meetings took the form that one can see in the frontispiece of Francis Fort's sermon of
September 1753: a sermon at St Peter's, a Feast and stewards to organise the whole.
Minutes and Treasurer's Accounts of these Old Boy gatherings survive from 1788
until their ceasing in 1850. At a meeting held in the Three Tuns on 25 September,
either before or after the 1788 Feast, they made three Resolutions: to hold an
'Anniversary' every year in the last week of August; to elect six stewards yearly to run
the subsequent anniversary; to allow admittance by ticket of half a guinea only and
money be subscribed for charitable purposes to be decided at the Feast. For the 1788
dinner 72 tickets were sold. That so many had come, from a school whose numbers
had for many years never been much more than 100, argues great loyalty and some
preparation. It must have been talked of for some time as on 20 September Beavis
Wood had written to the Ryders:

> Last night at a meeting in the Three Tuns, Mr Walker and Mr Pitman had a disagreement
> about a proposal for a meeting of the gentlemen educated at Blundell's School. The
> Trustees do not encourage such meeting and Sir Thomas Acland dislikes it. Mr Walker
> [Revd William Walker and a Steward] speaking a little freely of this baronet, Pitman
> [another Tiverton clergyman] began to talk in a high strain to Walker... would have
> increased had not Mr Dunsford [Henry Dunsford an OB and present at the 1788
> Feast] and some others intervened.

However the institution got off to a grand start. Until 1797 all the dinners had more
than 60 diners and in 1791 there were over 100. In 1797, a terrible year in the wars,
attendance fell to 47, but by the turn of the century numbers were again usually over
70. For the bicentenary of 1804, 89 attended. The event was publicised beforehand
in the London, Oxford, Sherborne and Exeter newspapers.

An Exeter paper, Trewman's Flying Post, reported the occasion:

> The Meeting was very fully and respectably attended. The company assembled in the
> School Green and for a while indulged themselves in those delightful feelings which the
> sight of friends and scenes of youth can inspire. From there they paraded to the Church,
> preceded by a Band of Music and numerous hopes of the rising years [i.e.boys], where a
> superior sermon was well delivered by the Revd Samuel Wells. After Church they partook
> of an excellent dinner at the Tuns, which was heightened by the liberality of Lord Rolle,
> with plenty of that favourite classic dish Pinguis Perena. The afternoon was exhilarated
> with appropriate songs and festivities and, to crown the whole, the various charms of
> numerous beauties at the Ball irradiated the evening of a day spent in unabused convivi-
> ality and friendship.

Most of those attending were clergy and gentry, the former usually making up a full
third of the gathering, but in 1792 they represented more than half the 74 who
dined. Many attended most regularly: both Keats and Thomas Wood attended every
year until their deaths. The Revd John Russell, father of the great 'Jack' Russell
attended every year from 1789 to 1813 – when the minute taker stopped recording
all the names of those who attended – except 1792, the year he got married, and the

two years after that happy event. He was a Steward in 1814 and in 1815.

Amongst the necessary accounts and administrative arrangements are some significant 'doodles'. Inside the front cover of the Minute Book there is a list of toasts. There is a false start with toast one as 'Our Old Friends' scored out and 'Church and King' substituted. 'Prosperity to this Meeting' with three cheers, and 'Success to Blundell's School' follow. Then came 'The Immortal Memory of the Founder' and 'The Memory of the generous Benefactors'. If anyone was still counting, toast number six or seven was 'Balliol and Sidney'. But there were still 13 to go: 'The Feoffees of Blundell's School; The Preacher and Thanks to Him; The Masters of the School; The Town of Tiverton and Trade; The Stewards and Thanks to Them; Prosperity to the County of Devon; The Knights of the Shire; The Mayor and Corporation of Tiverton; The Treasurer and Thanks to his Trouble; The Head Boy Present; The Stewards Elect; The President Elect; The Preacher Elect. Presumably before this they made their charitable bequests to the Porter's Widow and those of their fellowship who had fallen on bad times.

The whole event was a public statement. In their meeting of 1789 they decreed that they would meet at the School at ten o'clock and then process to St Peter's Church, the dinner to follow at three o'clock. Another of the 'doodles' in the Minute Book is the organisation of the procession. In front was Porter Warren in his rich blue gown, with his Staff of Office. The scholars came next, two by two 'as they rank in the School, Junior first'. Thirdly came the Upper and Lower Masters; then came the 'Band of Musick'. Next would come the 'Gentlemen educated at the School', followed by the Feoffees. Then in solitary splendour would march the Preacher, followed by the President. In the rear came the 'Stewards with White Wands'. They were to process up Bampton Street and when they arrived at the church gates the whole would stop and form a lane down which the Preacher and Stewards would march and the latter would conduct the former to the Reading Desk. The Feoffees would follow and the Old Boys and present scholars would then go in. After the service the procession would form up and return to the school via St Peter Street and Fore Street. In some years there is reference to the hiring of 'Rodmen' to accompany the procession, presumably to deal with any interferences.

Unlike the Feasts of the 1670s, so well recorded by Hume and Ham, we have no record of the bills of fare or the amounts drunk. Apparently the Band of Musick played at the dinner, held usually at the Three Tuns, sometimes at the Schoolhouse, and music has always been thirsty work. So it is no surprise to find the Stewards minuting in 1793:

Keats after the cares of the mastership. But he lived to enjoy the Rectories of King's Nympton and Bideford.

> *We recommend to our successor Stewards to have nothing to do with Tavern Bills for supporting the Band of Musick, but to agree to pay a sum not exceeding three guineas as our proportion of it.*

Three guineas was generous; annually the Treasurer entertained the tenants of the Prawle estates to 'cakes and ale' for less than £1. Regularly in the Treasurer's Accounts there was a handsome bill for broken glass and one is reminded of Evelyn Waugh's comment about 'the English County families baying for broken glass'; it was certainly the Tory Party at Prayer, Meat and Drink.

When Keats retired in 1797 he went as Rector to King's Nympton, where his tomb may be seen. He died in 1812 at the age of 81, last attending the Old Boys' Feast in 1806, aged seventy-five. After his death there was a subscription to provide an engraving from his portrait. Over fifty-seven years, from 1740–97, three humane Headmasters, Daddo, Atherton and Keats had created a happy school and a flourishing wider community of former pupils. Even the rebels of 1787 seem to have had 'fun'.

5
PRIDE AND FALL
WILLIAM PAGE RICHARDS, 1797–1823

Fun, however, is not a word one can associate with Richards, Headmaster from 1797 to 1823, product of a family that had had long links with Silverton. He became Master at the age of twenty-five and was only fifty-one when he retired in the wake of a scandal. His portrait breathes menace and a dark undercurrent of violence, but apparently he was one of the great Headmasters of the early-nineteenth century. His smallest annual intake was 35; regularly over 50 new pupils entered in a year and once, in 1814, there were over 70. By the end of the century numbers approached 130, by 1805 they were 150, where they remained steady until 1814 when for a period they leapt to just over 200, falling gently in the post-war depression back to 150.

His successor Alldersey Dicken, appointed in 1823 aged only twenty-nine, was an Old Blundellian and the son of an Old Blundellian, the Vicar of Witheridge. Dicken had a distinguished school career, winning a Keats' Medal and a Sidney Sussex Exhibition. He won prizes at the latter and became a Fellow of Peterhouse. He inherited Blundell's when its numbers had fallen to 149, and passed on 133 pupils to Henry Sanders in 1834, appointed also at the age of twenty-nine and numbers continued to dribble down towards 100, until the dramatic crisis of the 1840s when they fell to 31. The Feoffees in this period certainly had a 'Youth' policy.

It is difficult to get at an understanding of Richards, partly because the last fifty years of full boarding life at the Old School buildings were bathed in a glow of nostalgia and many details of life by the Lowman were so lovingly treasured that even the starkest details of Richards are softened with this penumbra. Partly he is difficult to grasp, because, to our eyes he was such an ogre, that we cannot comprehend how parents could ever have sent children to his charge. That they did so reminds us how much the sides of the triangular relationship of children, parents and schoolmasters have shifted and changed over the years. When the author was a Housemaster in the 1980s the 'possessive' behaviour of parents often made me cringe with shame on behalf of their sons. Yet their sons felt no shame, nor were they teased or bullied as 'Mum's boys' or milksops. It had all moved on from the 1940s and 1950s when my generation were sent to board at six or seven, with thirteen-week terms only punctuated by two visiting Sundays when one could be taken out from 10.30am to 6.30pm. However horrendous the bullyings or beatings, proper boys did not complain. Victorian schooldays seem to have been tougher still and in the Regency period, when children could be hanged for petty theft, school-days were tougher than tough. Yet as the previous chapter shows, the times of Daddo, Atherton and Keats may have been milder. A possible explanation may lie in a change of religious fashion; enthusiastic religion and enthusiastic flogging seem to go together, especially when the religion is based on some biblical fundamentalism. Richards' reign coincided with the first flush of the Evangelical Revival: 'Spare the rod and spoil the child.'

Yet a visitor to Blundell's in 1800 would probably have been struck by the continuities. The School's daily timetable was very similar to that decreed by Hayter for the Hanoverian princelings and there is no evidence that it was changed between the beginning of Keats' reign in 1775 and the end of Richards' in 1823. It was a day begun at 6.30am, punctuated by roll calls at 7.30am, breakfast at 9am, dinner at 1pm, 6pm supper and bedtime at about 8.30pm. Absence from roll call meant a fine of 2d. to be paid at the end of the week, when, if the money was not available, the

William Page Richards, Master, 1797–1823. Appointed at the age of twenty-five.

Opposite page: *The School Rooms just after Richards' time. They were quite unheated so that the ink sometimes froze. This view is from the Usher's room towards the Master's.*

culprit was flogged. (An invaluable lesson in the fact of life that there is one law for the rich and another for the poor!) In between there were three bouts of teaching in the schoolrooms, from 7–9am, from 10am–12pm and from 2–4pm. Walter Hook, a great Victorian divine, one of the great urban clergy of the century, who was at Blundell's in Richards' day described the place as providing 'indifferent teaching, the discipline severe and the food so scanty that he spent all his pocket money buying bread.' The Hook brothers, who had been attracted to the School from Hertfordshire, stayed only fifteen months. Abraham Hayward, 1811–17, later claimed his permanent ill-health was caused by the severity of school life, the cold and the poor fare. Incidentally, Hayward coined the phrase 'Eton of the West', to describe Blundell's though he perhaps did not mean any compliment to either. Blundell's under Richards, Eton under Keate, both meant 'Starvation, Bullying and Floggings'.

Another new boy wrote home in February 1818:

I went to school on Monday. There are two classrooms, one for the lower and one for the higher classes; but there is no fire in them and we are dreadfully cold while here. [The first heating in the classrooms was only installed in the 1830s, over 200 years after the founding and it is reported that work had sometimes to be suspended because the ink was frozen!] *I am in the higher school in the third class below the head class. We sleep two in a bed no bigger than my little desk-bed at home. There are about one hundred boarders here. We have for breakfast a penny roll and about a teacupful of milk and water. We are only helped once at dinner; sometimes we get a good plateful, and at other times scarcely enough to feed a crow, just as it happens. We have a small piece of bread and butter or cheese for supper and a teacupful of beer. These are our meals. You must not think, my dear mother, that I am unhappy here, for I shall be as happy as a prince when I have heard from you. I hope you will excuse the bad writing as I am in a hurry to send this letter by the evening post and consider that there are about a dozen boys playing and talking together.*

In another letter he described the work and some outline of life. He had to do 20 to 30 lines of Latin verse and write an English and Latin 'theme' (essay) a week. The books and authors mentioned were Caesar, Virgil, Horace, Cornelius Nepos and Xenophon. The gates were shut at three o'clock. They went to church at St Peter's twice every Sunday. They had to be sharpish getting into bed otherwise Richards would be 'very angry'. His needs were for a two-bladed penknife, a hone, and plenty of paper as they fill three sheets every week, also fine paper, wax and wafers for writing home. This small boy has a few kind words to say about Richards. On first arrival he:

… was shown to the parlour where he was, and after having sat a little while, he took me out and introduced me to a couple of head boys and desired them to take care of me. I breakfasted with him in the parlour on Sunday morning. He is a married man and his family consists of two little girls, the eldest only about four years old. He is of a very good disposition, and I like him very much. He is very careful of the boys, if they are unwell or have colds or anything the matter with them.

One wonders if this initial impression was soon corrected, for Richards is said to have regularly started the day by flogging half a dozen boys. In 1819 a rather precious and precocious boy, Robert Evans, 1818–19, aged fifteen, wrote to his school friend Charles Palmer who had left the School in December 1818 aged seventeen. It is the letter of a lad who sees himself joining the Church and discussing whether there are such things as 'innate ideas' and the problem of reconciling contradictory Biblical passages. Evans confesses the attractiveness of young women and the difficulty of getting up in the morning. The interest is in a postscript:

We have just passed that terrible epoch, vulgarly called 'Lines'. All the fellows did very well, not a single fellow was flogged. Richards was away from his house at his living on account of the death of his curate, by which means he was so far backward, that we did not finish our examination till Thursday last. On Monday too he was down in Teignmouth and stayed there till Wednesday evening. Mr Ley has been in a most desperate passion because the boys were not punctual at prayers one evening. He was just coming down after prayers when he met us coming up, upon which he stopped at the head of the stairs and

gave us one of his usual sublime speeches on our meanness and readiness to lick the spittle from under Mr Richards' feet. Some of the fellows have caught a good many fish, especially Stoneman [1810–19] and Napleton [1812–20]. Last week Richards sent out Sayers [1814–19] to catch some fish for a dinner party. Jack very cunningly bought a very fine trout and fastened it to the end of his line. He then pretended to play for a long time and at last drew the fish to the shore. Jack [Sayer] has no rival since Baillie was expelled, who it is said has gone to the West Indies.

One boy, whom he did flog, later to be famous as Parson Jack Russell, opined that he never knew anyone who hit as hard as Richards. And Russell, who was at the School from 1809–14, had been ferociously flogged by Richards with a riding crop for putting ferrets into a cage full of a monitor's rabbits. Another said of him that a 'blow was as good as a word'. Given the growing size of the School and the fact that Richards had at times over 80 boarders in his house, the 'system' must have been chaotic anarchy moderated by ferocious discipline. One comes back to those eyes.

A main attraction for the increased numbers of boarders, and the number of day boys seems to have been static and usually less than 50, were the scholarships. Income from Blundell's lands and investments had been rising. In one of the best of the early years, 1617, income had been £154.11s.3d. Between 1753 and 1761 total receipts were £1706.15s., giving an annual average of £243.16.5d. By 1839 the Charity's income was about £1100 a year. The greatest increase happened in the early-nineteenth century: in 1804 the rental of West Prawle was £244.15s.11, whereas in 1844 it amounted to £881.15s. As early as 1740 the Feoffees had sought the direction of the Lord Chancellor's Court about how to spend the growing surplus and had received the Order that:

> *Any such surplus may be disposed of from time to time either in Augmentation of the Stipends of the Blundell's Scholars at Balliol College in the University of Oxford and Sidney Sussex in the University of Cambridge or in the addition of new scholarships… to any College or Colleges in the said Universities.*

At the same time the Chancellor directed that the money bequeathed by Treasurer Ham in the 1680s, but only just become available should be laid out similarly. In Keats' last year as Master, 1796–97, the Great Account Book shows only three scholarships being paid totalling £39, on a Ham Exhibition and two Sidney Sussex scholarships. The Balliol Scholarships seem 'messy' in the 1790s – in 1794 a scholarship at Balliol was being paid to the Revd Philip Atherton, which must be 'wrong'. Everything is much clearer in 1822–23 when eight generous awards were made. In the meantime two benefactors, Benjamin Gilberd and Richard Down had added their bequests to the academic largesse, but these exhibitions were to be awarded by the Mayor and Burgesses of Tiverton and by the clergy of St Peter's respectively, so that they do not appear in the accounts. So the Feoffees awarded eight scholarships or exhibitions of £30 each and there were two more as well.

In the years between 1823 and 1840 income continued to rise and the Feoffees were able to add a further Exhibition, which was first awarded in 1832 so that nine awards were being awarded by the Feoffees. But one must not forget also that the Newte and Down awards were made by the Mayor and Burgesses and the Clergy of Tiverton and do not appear in the Great Account Book. Between 1810 and 1840 there were usually 10 or 11 undergraduates at the universities holding large Blundell's Scholarships. (In a prospectus of 1840 the then Headmaster, Henry Saunders, listed 12 scholarships, but that was in a 'prospectus'.) And by regulations made in the early-eighteenth century and repeated in 1788 the scholarships could only be held by boys

A document that illustrates the rising income from the Prawle lands.

₦o. 14.
RENTAL of the MANOR of WEST PRAWL.—1804.
LEASEHOLDS.

Lessees or Assignees.	TENEMENTS.	No of Lives	Ages in 1804.	Clear Yearly Rents.
John Edwards	Barton of Prawl and Little Walland	2	63 55	£.40 6 8
Ditto	Higher House, alias Seacombe	2	45 43	13 6 8
Elizabeth Prettyjohn	Goodshelter Tenement	2	69 37	0 6 8
Thomas Cornish	Heathfield and Spinstow Overland	2	63 55	5 0 0
Richard Heath	Hex's Tenement	2	45 41	0 13 4
William Kelland	Kelland's Cot, Orchard, and Little Field	2	77 72	0 6 8
James Torring	Tozer's Cot, Orchard, and Garden	3	57 58 26	0 5 11
John Payne	Ditto House and Garden in Kingsbridge	1	39	1 10 0
George Cary	One Third of Colridge Barton and Chillington Meadow	1	68.	6 0 0
	DEMESNE LANDS.			
James Edwards	Moor Tenement, let for 21 Years from Michaelmas, 1791	. .	. . . . .	63 0 0
John Stone	Sigdon Tenement, ditto 14 Years from Lady-Day, 1801	. .	. . . . .	24 0 0
Ambrose Patey	Sheath's Tenement, ditto 14 Years from Lady-Day, 1793	. .	. . . . .	10 0 0
Nicholas Hutchings	Initeart ditto, 14 Years from Lady-Day, 1801	. .	. . . . .	17 0 0
Samuel Goodyear	Blanche's, at Ford, ditto 14 Years from Lady-Day, 1801	. .	. . . . .	30 0 0
John Edwards	Great Walland ditto, 21 Years from Lady-Day, 1799	. .	. . . . .	33 0 0

Deduct Land-Tax out of some Rents £.244 15 11
                                    - 10 12 0

☞ Small Chief Rents paid and received to and from this Manor. £.234 3 11

✗ sold to redeem Land tax —

who had been at Blundell's at least three years, so it was worth your while sending your son to Blundell's. It was certainly worthwhile being the Master, or even the Usher, of Blundell's. Snell quotes Sir John Duntze, a Feoffee, as asserting in public that Richards made £60,000 out of the School. It is impossible to say with certainty whether Duntze was or was not exaggerating. Richards' official salary was still £50 a year, a pittance in 1800, so the profit came directly from fees. The Feoffees made no attempt to regulate what the Master or Usher charged for boarding fees, but Saunders' prospectus of 1840 gives the all-in sum for Board and Tuition as £50 a year, which probably broke down to £35 to £40 a year for boarding. If Richards had 80 boarders his gross income from that source would be almost £4000 a year. But it is clear that all pupils were also charged for tuition. By a strict interpretation of Peter Blundell's will, education in 'grammar', that is Latin and Greek, was free, but, it seems, extra tuition was on offer for a fee, and without that extra tuition it seems to have been surprisingly difficult to make progress up the School towards those scholarships. Moreover, all education, except in Latin and Greek, had its cost. In 1803 the Feoffees resolved to control and regulate those costs and passed the following Order:

That in future either of such Masters shall only receive yearly the sum of Four Guineas for the schooling of any Boy Boarding in either of their Houses and one Guinea additional to be received by the Upper Master for such time as any boy shall be under the care of the Usher in the Higher School. And that each Master shall receive only the sum of Six Guineas yearly for every Boy boarding out of their Houses. And that no further sums shall be taken or received without the express consent of the Feoffees. And that no charge be made for Schooling in future to any Boys whose parents reside in Tiverton.

In 1821 this last stipulation was amplified to refer only to those who had been 'born or for the most part under the age of six years brought up in Tiverton and not to the children of all such as shall happen to be resident in Tiverton.' In practice there were also extra charges for such things as writing and mathematics. Evidence shows that any wise parent, even a long-standing Tiverton resident, paid these fees. Francis Hole, Magistrate and Deputy Lieutenant and Tivertonian stated that:

> There are extra charges made to persons other than the Master of the School, with the sanction and under the direction of the Masters for education in writing, arithmetic, mathematics and French – I paid certain sums for my own son. The boys who do not receive education in such branches of education for which extra charges are made are prejudiced thereby with reference to the distribution and obtainment of the scholarships and Exhibitions attached to the said School, because marks of merit are given to the day boys who pursue such branches of education which are taken into account in their favour when the scholarships and Exhibitions are competed for.

George Coles, Cambridge graduate and a Magistrate, who had seven sons educated at the School between 1816 and 1835, and who resided in Tiverton, stated that:

> In or about the year 1820 £6 was demanded of me by Dr Richards, which said sum I sent to Dr Richards requesting him to consider it a gratuity, whereupon he immediately returned the amount to me.

Other parents, even Tiverton parents, lacking Coles' poise or position, tended to pay up in spite of the Feoffees' Order of 1803. Hornsey Gamlen, whose father, also residing in Tiverton, ceased paying, remembers Richards giving him a message to take home along the lines 'that if he wished his son to be educated gratis, he must take him to the Clerk of the Feoffees, Mr Wood, and have him registered as a pauper.' Another Tivertonian, William Fortescue Quick, 1813–17, and his father, also, a Tiverton resident, encountered Richards in the raw. He wrote:

> From the Masters, and particularly from Dr Richards, after my father discontinued paying, I received some hard treatment, such as I never have seen used towards the son of any parent who paid the Master well. For instance I was once at the head of my class and Dr Richards, as soon as I came up, struck me a violent blow under the ear and asking me what business I had there, ordered me to the bottom of the class and desired me to tell my father to send him the money. At another time when I was in the playground after school hours, Dr Richards called me to him and, without assigning any reason, gave me a box on the ear and said, 'Tch! Tell thy father thou knowest Greek better than Latin and to send me some money!' On another occasion, without giving any cause for so doing, he ordered me from a higher to a lower class and thus threw me back six months.

Quite possibly Duntze was right, Richards did make a fortune – by one means or another.

As for a few years following the Battle of Waterloo the numbers at the School reached 200, the majority of them boarders, some building was necessary. In 1802 the Feoffees minuted:

> Ordered that the additional Buildings be made to Mr Richards' House according to the Plan proposed at an expense not exceeding £80. And that the like addition be made to Mr Ley's House [the Usher from 1788 to 1824] at an expense not exceeding £60 and that the rooms so to be added be used solely for such boys as may happen to be sick or ill and for no other purpose.

Perhaps the little correspondent was right when he wrote that Richards was very careful of the health of the pupils, as after all nothing more discourages parents than deaths among the pupils. In 1806 the Feoffees ordered the:

> … laying out of any sum not exceeding £100 in altering the room now used for a Laundry in the Master's House into a Parlour and building another room over the cellar to be used as a Laundry.

In 1816 the Feoffees ordered:

> … that the sum of £80 be paid to Mr Richards upon his completing an additional

The rear of Old Blundell's where all those boarders were squashed in. A view from the town end.

Building to his House according to the Estimates now delivered in an expense of £124.17s. Also ordered that the sum of £30 be paid to Mr Ley for making an additional building adjoining the Parlour in his Dwelling house with a communication to the same.

Ley previously had had another new room in 1796. Nevertheless it is certain that conditions were cramped. In 1840 the then Headmaster, Henry Sanders, put out a prospectus, which emphasised that 'Each boy has his own bed.' Clearly in Richards' time this was not the case and boys were crammed in, two, three or four to a bed.

The greater numbers of pupils and the simultaneous growth of the Town's population also led to a problem of accommodation in St Peter's. In 1779 the Feoffees had ordered that 'all the scholars belonging to Tiverton School do sit together Sundays in the new gallery belonging to St Peter's Church.' (This gallery was built over the South Door of the Church.) By 1803 accommodation there was getting tight and the Feoffees set up a committee to buy up all the seats in the gallery, but:

> *... that in the meantime the Boys boarding out of the School be at liberty to sit in the Church where the persons they board with or their parents may think proper.*

This is a useful reminder that many 'boarders' did not live in the Usher or Master's Houses, but boarded with people in the Town. This committee continued its work until 1811, when presumably all the seats had been bought up, because in 1812 they ordered:

> *... that the agreement relating to the Gallery in the Old Church be confirmed and a faculty be applied for to vest the said Gallery in the Feoffees and that the proposed addition be made thereto at the expense of the Feoffees under the direction of the Committee before appointed.*

The bill for £117.18s.2d. was paid on 23 November 1813 and until 1823, when Richards resigned, the Feoffees paid a chief rent of £22 to the Church Wardens. In 1823 the Feoffees ordered that:

The Upper Master shall in future have the management and possession of the Gallery in the Old Church belonging to the Trustees of the school, but subject to the regulation of not charging more than four shillings a year for the sitting of any Boy and the Master also paying the Chief Rent of £22 to the Church wardens, and such Gallery to be repaired by the Trustees except as any willful damage which shall be made good by the Master at his expense.

Presumably, Richards had been charging the boys and the Feoffees paying the rent!

In Richards' time there is a first mention of a 'Speech Day'. The inauguration of the Keats Medal in 1777 involved a public-speaking competition. As the Feoffees paid for the Medals it is assumed that the competitors performed in the Feoffees' presence and the assumption becomes a certainty when at their 1820 Meeting they thanked:

… the Masters of the school for their great attention to the bringing forward the several candidates and speakers at the Meeting this day and for the handsome manner in which the candidates acquitted themselves in their examinations and in their speeches.

In 1824 they took the opportunity to lay down a procedure for 'Speech Day':

Ordered that in future the business of the annual meeting of the Trustees shall commence at eleven o'clock and in the following order:
1. The Speeches of such young Gentlemen as do not speak for the Medal.
2. The Speeches of those who do speak for the Medal.
Lastly, but not until half past twelve o'clock the examinations of the candidates for the Scholarships and exhibitions.

Soon after the inauguration of 'Speech Day' the regime of Richards and Ley ended with an unhappy incident. The family of a day boy, Houston, sued Ley for damages, alleging that Houston had been permanently injured as the result of a flogging Ley had administered. The court record says it began in the days before the Saturday afternoon of 7 February 1823, when John Houston, aged twelve, struck Henry Barne, aged ten in the face. But there had been a build-up. Henry Barne was a banker's son, who stayed at school until he was eighteen and was well connected, while Houston was the son of a surgeon and apothecary. Barne, although two years younger was 'head of the 3rd Form', of which Houston was a lowly member. On the previous Friday Houston had been heard to say he would cut school on Saturday and the following Monday, saying 'he would be coochy while other poor scrubs were

An early-1840s' engraving showing the end of the Master's schoolroom and the quarters for the Usher's boarders.

fagging at their [Latin] exercise'. As Head Boy, on Saturday Barne reported Houston's absence, with explanation. On the Saturday afternoon Houston, who had been told by another boy, Goss, that Barne had ratted on him, caught up with Barne, made his nose bleed and knocked out a tooth. Barne went back to Ley, who let it be known that he would flog both Houston and Goss. The court record states that Houston was a day boy and implies that the others were boarders.

Houston crawled unwillingly to school and, after breakfast on Tuesday 10 February was flogged. Houston's counsel described the event to the court:

> Houston was placed in that situation in which boys are usually placed for receiving punishment; two boys held his arms during the time, and it now became necessary to state the manner in which the punishment was inflicted. Not only were the clothes covering the lower part of his person taken down, but his clothes were also taken up, so as to expose the loins, the complaint was, that Mr Ley had punished the boy not in the manner in which boys are usually flogged at public schools, but that he applied the instrument to the loins of the boy, where, if punishment be unduly inflicted, great and lasting injury was likely to occur. He believed it could be proved that the boy was struck four or five times, that the rod broke and was again adjusted, and that other blows were inflicted. He was instructed to state that Mr Ley, more than once pushed the stumps of the rod violently against the loins of the boy.

Classroom furniture attacked by generations of boys.

Obviously a birch was being used. Later witnesses for the prosecution claimed to have examined Houston and found that blood had been drawn in 59 places.

Obviously a great fuss ensued, as on 12 February Ley asked his lawyer to write to the Houstons asking that Dr Kettle, or some other doctor be allowed to examine the boy, but the examination did not take place. However the evidence was not satisfactory. A number of boys, all boarders, stated that the flogging was 'normal' and that in the months after it had taken place they had seen Houston fishing, swimming and dancing. The contrary evidence all came from people too closely connected to the 'sufferer'. The case was extensively reported in the newspapers.

Before the case came to court in August 1824 both Ley and Richards had given in their notices, as was recorded in the Feoffees' minutes of June 1823. Unusually, but perhaps with the legal situation in mind, the Feoffees resolved:

> … unanimously that our thanks be given to the Reverend Doctor Richards for his great attention to the interest of the School during the many years which he hath been Master and which hath so materially tended to promote and uphold the Interest and Character of the said School during that time. The Reverend John Ley, the Undermaster, having given notice at this meeting of his intention to resign at the next meeting of the Feoffees, it was resolved unanimously that the thanks of the Trustees be given to him for the unremitting attention with which he has discharged the various duties of his situation during the thirty-five years that he has continued to fill the same, and that our Clerk do cause Advertisements to be inserted in the London and Provincial papers as usual for the election of an Undermaster on 29th June next.

They appointed Ley's son, Carrington Ley and followed that up with the following resolutions:

> The Trustees of the school, having taken into their serious consideration the necessity of maintaining and enforcing good discipline therein and supporting the Authority of the Masters in the due observance of them. Resolved that they will maintain and uphold the Masters in the proper exercise of their Authority.

The second resolution repeated their thanks and admiration for Ley.

The Court met two months later and found for Houston. They awarded him 6d. damages. But Richards and Ley were gone too.

DICKEN AND SANDERS

Exit Dr Richards for comfortable retirement at Teignmouth, where he became Perpetual Curate of the new East Teignmouth Church from 1824 to 1856. He had also been Rector of Stoke Abbas, in Dorset, a New College living, since 1811, drawing the stipend, but hiring a curate to do the work. He died in 1861 aged eighty-nine. As his successor the Feoffees appointed Alldersey Dicken, born in 1791, who had been at Blundell's from 1803 to 1811, but for some reason or another had been removed from 1806 to 1808. In fact his family was almost excessively Blundellian: his father, two uncles, a cousin, three brothers and two nephews also attended and the family had been moderately prominent in the area since the mid-seventeenth century, his father being Vicar of Witheridge for forty years. Alldersey had done well at School, winning a Keats Medal and an exhibition to Sidney Sussex, where he also shone, winning a university prize for composing a poem on the theme of 'Deborah' and graduating as 'Twelfth Wrangler'. He became a fellow of St Peter's College and had three sermons published in 1822. During his time at Blundell's he was a bachelor and his interest in mathematics led to his introducing the subject to the curriculum. A bachelor mathematician: it is difficult to think of a more sharp contrast to Richards. His portrait shows a nice, intelligent man trying to look stern.

On the other hand, continuity was initially the theme with the new Usher. Here Carrington Ley succeeded his father. Both father and son, like the new Master, were Old Boys. Carrington Ley had been born in 1789, and, whereas his father had won the Sidney Exhibition in 1779, he won a Balliol exhibition in 1806 and had become a Balliol Fellow. He remained Usher for only three years and was succeeded by the Revd Anthony Boulton, a contemporary of Dicken at Sidney, whose effectiveness as a schoolmaster was limited because he suffered badly from gout, but he stuck it out until 1844.

Dicken's successor in 1834, Henry Sanders, was a product of Westminster and Christ Church. He got a second-class degree, but stroked the College Boat, the first mention of any sporting attainment of a Blundell's Master. The editor of the Register describes him as 'a strict disciplinarian' possessed in a singular degree of 'the faculty for detecting and stimulating the abilities of those placed in his charge'. The former was a description to which he owned, for, when he left in 1847, in a speech giving thanks for the presentation of a silver kettle by former pupils, he said:

My boys, it is now nearly fourteen years since I took upon me the duties of Master, and ever since that time, as I have endeavoured never to pass over a fault, so I trust you will acquit me of the charge of punishing offenders too severely.

He inherited 133 pupils from Dicken, but only had 82 when the crash came. But some of those pupils were of high quality. In Sanders' time came Frederick Temple, 1834–39, and Richard Blackmore, 1837–43. Both of them were at the School for Queen Victoria's coronation in 1838 when the boys petitioned Her Majesty for a week's holiday and got it.

Like Richards, both Dicken and Sanders lived to be comfortably octogenarian, and Sanders' successor Hughes reached ninety-one. Longevity continued with A.L. Francis reaching seventy-seven years and Fusty Wynne, 1864–94, was a centenarian. The six successive Headmasters from 1797 to 1930 had an average age of eight-seven years.

Both Dicken and Sanders developed the facilities for boarders and updated the buildings. An enormous improvement in terms of comfort must have been the installation of stoves in the schoolrooms in 1828–29, costing over £100. Providing they worked, no more would the ink freeze on cold winter mornings. Regularly there are now bills for coal, which from 1840 was purchased from Goodlands, and which was

Alldersey Dicken, Master 1823–34. He instituted the teaching of mathematics for the first time.

Colin White

Henry Sanders, Master 1834–47. Distinguished as a strict disciplinarian.

Colin White

Frederick Temple, 1834–39, Bishop of Exeter, London and Archbishop of Canterbury.   Colin White

THIS TABLET WITH THE WINDOW ABOVE ARE A
TRIBUTE OF ADMIRATION AND AFFECTION
TO THE MEMORY
OF
RICHARD DODDRIDGE BLACKMORE, M.A.
SON OF THE
REV. JOHN BLACKMORE.
EDUCATED AT BLUNDELL'S SCHOOL, TIVERTON;
AND EXETER COLLEGE, OXFORD, (SCHOLAR)
BARRISTER OF THE MIDDLE TEMPLE, 1852;
AUTHOR OF "LORNA DOONE," SPRINGHAVEN AND OTHER WORKS;
BORN AT LONGWORTH, BERKS, 7 JUNE, 1825;
DIED AT TEDDINGTON, MIDDLESEX, 20 JAN.,1900.
"INSIGHT, AND HUMOUR, AND THE RHYTHMIC ROLL
OF ANTIQUE LORE, HIS FERTILE FANCIES SWAY'D,
AND WITH THEIR VARIOUS ELOQUENCE ARRAY'D
HIS STERLING ENGLISH, PURE AND CLEAN AND WHOLE."
"HE ADDED CHRISTIAN COURTESY, AND THE HUMILITY
OF ALL THOUGHTFUL MINDS, TO A CERTAIN GRAND
AND GLORIOUS GIFT OF RADIATING HUMANITY."
Cradock Newell.

Blackmore, 1837–43, the author of Lorna Doone, *another of Sanders' pupils.*

probably brought to Tiverton by the new canal, completed in 1823. In many areas of the School the walls were 'canvassed', presumably an early form of damp-proofing, and papered. The first mention of a water closet occurs in January 1834 when one was installed in the Master's House for £33.0s.6d with a new brick drain straight to the Lowman. But boys still used the privies, which were rebuilt and probably extended. In most years of the 1830s almost £100 was spent repairing the roof.

The push to improve the facilities reached a climax after 1836. The finances were extremely healthy and over £1300 lay in the hands of the Treasurer in ready cash, there was over £6000 in readily realisable investments and there was an estimated annual surplus of income over expenditure of about £300. The time had come to modernise. At their meeting on St Peter's Day the Feoffees dealt with a minor matter first. They ordered that George Folland, the Porter, known to generations of Blundellians as 'Old Cop', either because of his copper waterproof boots or because of his nose:

... to give up any concern in the sale of spirituous liquors on or before the twenty-ninth of June next as being incompatible with his present situation.

But the last three items on their agenda were of great importance:

A Plan with Specifications and Estimates having been produced by the Revd Henry Sanders for certain Alterations and Improvements in the house and premises now occupied by him, the expense of which will amount to about £500, it is ordered that the same be approved of and that such alterations be forthwith made and that a sum not exceeding £500 be allowed to the said Henry Sanders and he agreeing to pay the residue of such expense out of his own pocket.

They went on to pass a similar resolution for developments to the tune of £160 for Mr Boulton's House.

On St Peter's Day 1837 Henry Sanders showed the Feoffees the new work 'performed under the superintendence of G.A. Boyce, Architect'. They were told that the work had cost much more than £500. They then proceeded to inspect the developments in the Usher's House and authorise the release of their £160 and were assured by Boyce and Boulton that the work had cost more than that sum. Their tour of inspection must have left some of their desire for improvements unsatisfied because they minuted that:

... at the next meeting the propriety of laying out a sum of money for improvement of the rooms for the accommodation of the boarders in the Masters' houses be taken into consideration.

In this period of much building and improvement they took a decision that as much work as possible should be done in the vacations. Amidst their important deliberations they had time to revert to Folland and they:

Late-nineteenth-century view of the new buildings for boarders.

Ordered that in case G. Folland shall renew his License to sell beer and spirituous Liquors he cease to continue to hold the situation of Porter from that day and that he immediately give up possession of the Porter's Lodge.

In 1838 The Feoffees ordered that:

Plans, Specifications and Estimates for improving those parts of the Masters' Houses which are used by the Boys to include flooring the Hall and improving the sleeping rooms so that Each boy may have a separate bed and that these Plans be produced at a special Meeting of the Trustees to be held at the Castle in Exeter on Friday in the Sessions week at 12 o'clock.

It seems clear that the Trustees did approve the 'each boy having a bed' plan because of Henry Sanders' 1840 prospectus, but they did not actually get round to minuting their approval. The only relevant entry in the Great Account Book may be 'To Messrs Becks and Garth for New Campanile, Buttresses, new Privies and other works ordered at the last meeting of the Trustees: £300', which was paid on 20 May 1840. The Buttresses and new, lighter Campanile certainly altered the appearance of the old buildings. The beds Sanders chose were curious box-like things so constructed that all the bedding could be folded into the 'box'. Their construction enabled a boy to read secretly at night by using his blankets to create a tent like arrangement. Early Trade Directories assert that there was now room for 100 boarders in the Master's House and room for 40 in the Usher's.

The privies were always a problem, once noses became more sensitive. In 1841 the Feoffees had some very serious thoughts about them:

They were of the opinion that the new privies, if completed in their present position would be very objectionable. They ordered that new privies be erected 'as far upstream as practicable to avoid the present inconvenience arising from floods, but taking care that there shall be a sufficient supply of water always flowing underneath to remove the soil.

Eventually in 1855, because local residents complained so much, they had a wooden channel made to swish the water underneath where the soil fell, and the Porter was thereafter paid to ensure that soil did get taken away by the long-suffering Lowman.

The reforming urges of the Feoffees and the Masters were not exhausted by their admonitions to Folland, or by their exertions in bringing the buildings up to date. (And repairing and updating the fabric of the School in the 1830s must be seen as the equivalent of a nineteenth-century church restoration.) They also set about

A drawing by a boy of those fold-away beds.

Sanders' prospectus. Each boy has a separate bed.

A Prep Room, drawn by the same boy.

Cricket on the Green. The drawing by Mrs Boulton, the Usher's wife, is before the buttresses were built in 1840 and probably dates from Dicken's mastership.

improving the School in many other respects. For the first time they made some official arrangement for recreation. The 'Green' in front of the School was already used, mainly by the boarders, for 'games'; the part on the right was devoted to cricket and that on the left to football. Fives were played, sometimes inside the Lower School, sometimes against the outer wall. When the buttresses were built in 1840 and made Fives difficult, the Feoffees allowed £20 for building a Fives court in the southeast corner of the Green. In 1834 they asked the 'committee of Management', an inner core of hard-working Feoffees who met regularly in this period, but whose minutes have not survived, to investigate the possibility of buying some land for a cricket field and to provide a bathing place.

The Feoffees then moved on to the curriculum. To introduce some objectivity into the choosing of scholars, in 1834 they invited a Fellow from Balliol and Sidney to join them on St Peter's Day to examine the candidates and assess the merits of the boys in the various classes. In 1836 they thought of appointing a French Master at £25 a year, but did not do so; therefore all teaching beyond 'grammar' remained a matter of fee paying outside the Great Account Book. But through the later 1830s the reforming intelligences of the Feoffees moved towards a comprehensive updating. Eventually at their meeting at Exeter Castle in January 1839 they unanimously approved an 'Application by Petition' to Chancery seeking formal approval to apply the growing surplus in the following ways:

To raise the salaries of the Masters so that charges for tuition would become unnecessary.

To make some additions to the present scholarships.

To make provision for instruction in Mathematics.

To increase the numbers to above 150.

To make better provision for boarders.

To seek a ruling as to how to apply Peter Blundell's stipulation that the consent of the ten highest Subsidy payers was needed before a 'foreigner' could be admitted.

To increase the Porter's salary [which was only £2.15s., but he did get paid for a whole lot of extras, such as winding the clock, lighting the fires and tending to the oil lamp that hung at the Gate].

The troubles then began in earnest, and, like a storm long expected, were all the more protracted and furious. It had been apparent for years, even to the Feoffees, that the Trust was breaching Peter Blundell's will in important particulars. His stipulation that it should be a 'Free School and not a school of exaction' and that the Masters should 'hold themselves satisfied and content with that recompense for their travail (i.e. £50 a year and twenty marks respectively) without seeking or exacting any more either of parent or children'.

Blundell had even gone on to make the shrewd point that fee paying encouraged favouritism and discrimination against the non-fee payer. He had also made it clear that the school was primarily for Tivertonians and that foreigners were only to be admitted if there was a 'want' and if there were not 150 suitable Tiverton boys. Blundell had also insisted that non-Tivertonians, or foreigners, should only be admitted:

> ... with the assent and allowance of such ten Householders of the said town of Tiverton aforesaid as for the time being shall be most in the subsidy books of our Sovereign Lady the Queen's Majesty and not otherwise. And my meaning and desire is that they from time to time will make choice of the children of such foreigners as are of honest reputation and fear God, without regarding the rich above or more than the poor.

For many years all these stipulations had been ignored.

In 1802 the Feoffees had become anxious about the question of fees and sought a comparison with what was paid at Eton, Harrow, Westminster and Winchester. After they had digested the results of this inquiry, they decided to authorise what was probably already a practice, that tuition fees could only be charged to boarders and non-Tivertonians. However, the evidence given above shows that even Tivertonians were pressed into fee paying whenever possible.

In 1822 the consciences of the Feoffees twitched again, this time over the twin issues of the admission of 'foreigners' and the awarding of the scholarships. In September 1823 they paid £37.12s.4d for having obtained an opinion from a London lawyer, Mr Bell, 'as to the proper mode of admitting foreigners into the School.' They had asked him to comment on their current procedure, which was to let in any foreigner, even if there were already more than 150 boys in the School, without seeking any consents. If a boy were a candidate for a scholarship the assent of any ten householders was obtained a day or so before the election. They also asked if they were bound to prefer a Tivertonian candidate for a scholarship over a foreigner. The clerk sent the summary of their case to Mr Bell with a fee and on the cover a note 'Expedition herein will be esteemed a particular favour.' So it was seen with some urgency. Mr Bell's answer gave the Feoffees food for thought, and, in retrospect, they did not chew on his unpalatable advice hard enough. His advice over the issue of scholarships confirmed that the Feoffees had discretion and that foreigners and local boys could be chosen on equal terms and that the only criteria were sound learning and financial need. But his advice about the admission of foreigners must have been a bombshell. It was basically that foreigners had to get the necessary permission before admittance; that necessary permission could not be given by any ten householders; and that, as there were no more subsidy books, there was no one able to give the necessary permission so 'that in strict law the right of foreigners is now in abeyance, so that they can only be admitted under the direction of a Visitor', i.e. Peter Blundell's legal heir or the Lord Chancellor himself. Further correspondence with Bell during the winter of 1822–23 elicited the further advice that they should apply to Chancery to seek a means of regulating the admission of foreigners. If Bell's interpretation of the law was right, here was a bomb waiting to go off.

The Feoffees kept worrying at the problem and in 1825 approached another lawyer, Mr Shadwell. Gnawing at the bone from a different angle, they put to him that the admission of foreigners seemed to have been unregulated, at least as far back as the Book of Orders (1663), and that without boarding fees from foreigners the Master and Usher could not survive. They mentioned that recent increases in Tiverton's population as a result of the prosperity derived from Mr Heathcote's lace factory had led to

---

Cricket in 1844

Woolmer's Exeter & Plymouth Gazette.
September 14th, 1844, 3e

On Saturday [September 7th, 1844] a cricket match was played between the Tiverton Cricket Club and the gentlemen of Blundell's School on the Town ground which terminated in favour of the former by 15 runs. On the side of the School Mr.Bartholomew batted, bowled and kept wicket in such a manner as to deserve special commendation, as also did Mr.Lewins on the side of the Tiverton Club.

TIVERTON CLUB

	1st Innings		2nd Innings	
Kirwan	b Fowler	35	b Fowler	0
Amory	c Edyvene	2	c Harding	0
Lewins	b Fowler	0	b Bartholomew	14
Spurway	b Fowler	3	b Fowler	4
Marsh	b Fowler	0	b Fowler	2
Thierens	b Fowler	8	hit his wicket	8
Dunsford	b Bartholomew	4	b Fowler	5
Burne	c Bowden	0	c Leigh	1
Rowcliffe	c Harding	1	c Edyvene	2
Teschemaker	not out	4	c Harding	0
Spurway, H.	b Bartholomew	0	not out	1
	Byes, 7; wide balls, 1 ...	8	Byes, 4; wide balls 0 ...	4
		57		37
		65		41

BLUNDELL'S SCHOOL

	1st Innings		2nd Innings	
Manley	b Lewins	4	b Lewins	11
Bartholomew	b Lewins	7	run out	0
Fowler	run out	1	b Thierens	7
Pearse	b Lewins	6	b Dunsford	7
Earle	c Lewins	6	b Lewins	6
Bowden	not out	9	b Lewins	0
Borlase	c Lewins	2	b Kirwan	1
Harding	b Kirwan	0	b Kirwan	0
Dene	b Kirwan	0	b Lewins	9
Leigh	leg before wicket	0	b Lewins	1
Edyvene	b Kirwan	2	not out	0
	Byes, 1; wide balls, 7 ...	8	Byes, 4; wide balls 0 ...	4
		37		42
		45		46

The return match will be played to-morrow (Saturday) in the School Green.

The earliest yet discovered score card of a Blundell's match. The author is grateful to Jeff Stanyer for drawing it to his attention.

demands for 'free' education, even from foreigners who had backed up their demand with the consent of ten householders. To protect their ability to offer free Grammar education and to provide 'good and godly preachers' for the Church of England, the Feoffees reckoned they needed to be able to charge fees and to prevent the entry of foreigners who could not pay. Shadwell's answer was as hard as Bell's. If there were 150 natives suitable for Grammar education they had to be entered without fees; if foreigners were to be admitted they must have a proper consent, which might be that of the ten highest tax payers, but Chancery would have to rule if this was an acceptable procedure; and that if these conditions meant that the school could not flourish then 'application must be made to Parliament for relief' as Chancery could only execute the will as it stood. This was also a poser that the Feoffees ignored.

Finally in 1836 the Feoffees asked yet another lawyer, Sir W. Follett, for his opinion whether they could legally spend some of the surplus, currently running at £300 a year, on the provision of a French teacher at £25 a year. In their submission to Follett they said a French Master had been going into the school one day a week for some years to teach those boys whose parents paid the relevant fee. Almost in an aside they also mentioned that local boys were educated free, 'although some gratuity is expected and usually paid.' (See above!) Follett's reply was that Chancery would almost certainly approve of the broadening of the curriculum, but that the Feoffees could not use the surplus except under the Chancery Scheme of 1740, (which decreed that the surplus should only be used to endow more scholarships and exhibitions) without petition to Chancery, and he advised that such a petition should be wide-ranging enough to cover all the likely surplus.

Hence the seven-point petition to Chancery of January 1839. But in the previous twenty years the world had changed. Since the accession of George I the politics of Tiverton had been 'arranged' first by those whom history calls Whigs, then after the accession of Hayter's pupil, George III, by the Tories. Only the 24 members of the Corporation had the right to vote and for many years they had elected the nominees of the Ryder family and their local allies, the Duntzes. Regularly Tivertonians claimed that all householders had the right to vote; as regularly they were rebuffed. Long traditions associated the Church of England with the Tories, but it is difficult for us to appreciate the passions with which both Tories and Church of England clergy were hated in the 1820s and 1830s.

Eventually the mounting tumult for 'reform' achieved the appointment of a Whig government in 1830, whose Reform Bill, giving the vote to urban householders whose properties were worth £10 a year, failed and an election was called in 1831. In Tiverton the Corporation, loyal to the Earl of Harrowby, a vehement opponent of 'Reform,' elected Mr Ryder and Mr Spencer Perceval, the son of the Prime Minister assassinated in 1812. Harding wrote:

The election was conducted amid riot and disorder. The church-wardens refused to allow the bells to be rung, and in the evening the effigies of both Members were paraded round the town and afterwards burnt in Fore Street. When Mr Perceval attempted to address the world from a window in Fore Street, his discourse was halted by a bombardment of fish heads, 'cod' the reporters said.

No Tories were elected in Tiverton for another forty years. In 1832 John Heathcoat became one of the two MPs elected under the new franchise and after 1835 Palmerston was the other.

Meanwhile in Parliament another Reform Bill had been passed by the Commons, but thrown out by the Lords in October 1831. Analysis of the voting showed that 21 out of 26 Bishops had voted against reform. Rioting followed in Tiverton. Throughout the country the Church of England was 'a special target of popular abuse, the soft underbelly of Old Corruption' [Evans]. The Bishop of Exeter needed police protection, the Bishop of Bristol's palace was burnt down, the Bishop of Bath and Wells stoned and Bishop Ryder of Lichfield was threatened with being thrown into a pond. Great Days! The hatred of the Church of England mounted even higher when a Unitarian, Wade, published the *Extraordinary Black Book* in 1831, an updating of a book first published in 1820. It pilloried the clergy, reckoning their revenues exceeded the state budget of Prussia, showed that over 60 per cent of the Church of England's parish clergy were pluralists, non-residents or both, and that the Bishops were grossly wealthy. Scared Tories feared the tumbrel and the guillotine and were gripped with panic. Mr Perceval, MP, rose in Parliament, took his Bible in one hand and:

> ... for an hour and three-quarters denounced the nation and the Parliament in the name of Jehovah, prophesying that the land would be desolate, that pestilence would be loosed on it, that the Church would be laid low because she had corrupted the way before God, played harlot with the state and forsaken the doctrines of the Lord [Chadwick].

He regularly called for the Government to call a Day of Fasting so that the nation might have a chance to repent of its unreadiness to obey its King and priests. He punctuated his orations, usually with Bible in hand, with cries such as, 'To thee, Oh God, I cry aloud! To thee, Oh God!' He animadverted against the wicked French, who had just got rid of Charles X, whose last Prime Minister Polignac governed in the light of advice given by the Blessed Virgin, and replaced him with King Louis Philippe. What worried our Perceval was that Louis Philippe was King not 'By the Grace of God', but 'by the will of the People' – and this Perceval called blasphemy. In January 1832 he filled seven columns of Hansard and would have achieved more if the exhausted scribes had not often given up with the comments, 'The Hon Member then read extracts from the Bible to the same effect.' Or 'The Hon Member then read the proceedings respecting Nineveh.' At one point he screeched at his fellow Members:

> You are all infidels! You sit there like a race of infidels. If you reject me you reject God, in whose name I appear.

John Heathcoat, MP, the Liberal opponent of Sanders and the Earl of Devon.

The attitude of this last product of the electoral power of the unreformed Corporation of Tiverton to reform is easy to sum up. In the Commons he thundered: 'The rotten boroughs constitute a great and valuable part of the whole.' It is not surprising they threw fish heads at him.

When the Reform Bill duly passed the Lords and new elections took place in October 1832, the identity of Anglican with Tory was complete in the public mind. In the campaign Whigs asserted that 49 out of 50 Anglican clergy supported the Whigs. The liberal *The Times* thundered against political clergy, but with great impartiality praised those few who worked for the Liberal cause. In Tiverton John Heathcoat and James Kennedy were elected. Kennedy was replaced by Lord Palmerston in 1835 and the Liberals kept the Parliamentary seats for a generation.

The Old Corporation lasted until it was swept away by the Reform of Municipal Corporations in 1835. In order to inform itself of the nature of its task, the first Parliament after the Reform Bill sent Commissioners to investigate the operations of the existing, unreformed Boroughs. Their report on the Tiverton Corporation was peculiarly damning. They found corrupt practices involving the Duntzes, Ryders and members of the Corporation going back over fifty years. They reported that the Corporation was an engine for directing patronage to its members and their connection. They praised George Coles, one of the principal supporters of the Town against the Feoffees, for his efforts to limit the activities of the Corporation. An analysis of the Corporation Members of 1835 shows that all the Capital Burgesses had either been pupils at the School, or had sons at the School, or both. The Feoffees' men of business, their Clerk and Treasurer, were the Tiverton solicitors George Owen and Frederick Patch; one was a Capital Burgess, the other an Assistant Burgess. The Parliamentary Commissioners ended their description of the unsavoury practices of the Tiverton Corporation with the damning words:

> In no place we have visited do the pernicious effects arising from the connection between a Corporation having the right to return MPs appear to be more clearly displayed than in the Borough of Tiverton. The management of public affairs by the Corporation has neither deserved nor obtained the confidence of the inhabitants.

TIVERTON DISTRICT

CONSERVATIVE CLUB.

SIR,

The First Quarterly Meeting of this Club, will take place at the ANGEL HOTEL, on MONDAY the NINTH of JULY next.—DINNER on TABLE at 4 o'CLOCK.—You will be pleased to signify at the Inn, at least Three Days previously, whether or not it will be convenient for you to attend.

I am Sir,

Your obedient Servant,

FRED: O. PATCH,

Secretary and Treasurer.

Tiverton, 16th June, 1838.

The Feoffees' Secretary and Treasurer, Fred Patch, Tory.

The Municipal Corporation Act swept away the Old Corporation and probably created more local antagonism than the Reform Bill. Parliament was far away, but the prestige of running the Town was local. Tories were prickly and aggressive; Liberals were triumphant and crusading. It was not likely that they could work together to achieve a harmonious reform of the School. By 1839 the School was the last untamed bastion of the former Tory stronghold of Tiverton. A curious survival is a set of three documents stuck together by sealing wax, folded as if they had come out of a small envelope. Two of them are receipts, dated 19 May, 1838, in the hand of Frederick Patch, the Feoffees' Treasurer. The receipts are Henry Sanders' and Anthony Boulton's Poor Rate. The third is a circular from the 'Tiverton District Conservative Club', an invitation to a 'Quarterly Meeting' and dinner at the Angel Hotel on 9 July, 1838, signed Fred O. Patch, Secretary and Treasurer and dated 16 June, 1838. The conclusion is obvious: Patch was the organiser of the local Conservative Party and Sanders and Boulton active members.

By 1839 the last bastion of Toryism in Tiverton was Peter Blundell's School. And how did a Liberal or Whiggish townsman see Blundell's in 1839? They thought their School had been hijacked. The will stated that new Feoffees should be heirs of Feoffees or should be 'near inhabitants', but the majority of Feoffees now came from 'away'. Between 1807 and 1839 27 Feoffees had been elected, but only Benjamin Dickenson and John Were Clarke are entered as from 'Tiverton', and in Clarke's case this was an error as he came from near Uffculme. Perhaps John Worth of Washfield, elected in 1823, might be regarded as a courtesy Tivertonian. Fourteen Feoffees signed the minutes of that meeting in 1839, which decided to petition Chancery; their Chairman was the Earl of Devon, along with three baronets, Kennaway from Escott, Duntze from Kenton and Acland from Killerton. The ten Esquires included Clarke and Worth, and the others came from Fulford, Crediton, Newton St Cyres, Peamore, and Pynes. If on no other grounds, local patriotism demanded that the Town intervene. Into the minds of more Radical townsman loomed *Carthago est delenda*.

Moreover to townsmen who had sent their sons to Blundell's, it was notorious that the place was run unscrupulously for the boarders and that their sons had been mistreated there. And should the evidence be disbelieved, the novelist, R.D Blackmore in *Lorna Doone*, who was a boarder at Blundell's from 1837 to 1843, described the treatment of boarders in the following terms. They 'kick the day boys out, with words of scanty compliment.' And again:

> *According to custom we drove the day boys in a brave rout down the causeway, from the school-porch even to the gate where Cop [the Porter] had his dwelling and duty. Little it recked us and helped them less, that they were our founder's citizens. For it had been long fixed among us, who were of the house and chambers, and these same day boys were all 'caddes', as we had discovered to call it, because they had no groat for their schooling, and brought their own commons with them. In consumption of these we would help them, for our fare in hall fed appetite: and while we ate their victuals we allowed them freely to talk to us. Nevertheless, we could not feel, when all the victuals were gone, but that these boys required kicking from the premises of Blundell. And some of them were shopkeepers' sons, young grocers, fellmongers, and poulterers, and these, to their credit, seemed to know how righteous it was to kick them. But others were of high family, as any need be, in Devon – Carews, and Bourchiers and Bastards, and some of these would turn sometimes, and strike the boy that kicked them. But to do them justice, even these knew that they must be kicked for not paying.*

Elsewhere he would describe them as, 'Helots for whom no treatment was too bad.' Blackmore's plot is set in the 1680s and he wrote it in the 1860s, but the Blundellian scenes portray life by the Lowman in the 1830s. In the legal disputes of the 1840s the following testimonies, although open to the charge of being unrepresentative and biased, confirm Blackmore's picture. Thomas Hurley, the son of an innkeeper, who joined the School in 1829 aged fourteen deposed:

> *I left the School on account of my having received ill-treatment from the boarders… I was always punished by the boarders if I refused to go errands for them. The ill treatment for which I left was, that having refused to go on an errand for a boarder, I was placed before the fire until the*

skin of my face was very burnt and afterwards a boarder threw a cricket bat at me with so much violence, as to break the bat and injure me so much that I was kept in bed for several days... I think the Masters encouraged the boarders to use the day boys ill. If any parent complained, the Masters said they could not interfere as it was a schoolboy's trick. I can say that the native boys day scholars in the said school besides myself were ill-treated by the boarders and that in particular a native boy of the name of Fisher was held with his head through the hole of the seat of the privy with his heels just above the seat until he was nearly suffocated.

Theodore Parkhouse, bookseller and printer, deposed that his son, Thomas 1838–40, was removed from the School on account of the boarders' ill-treatment. In particular he quoted the occasion when Thomas had been set upon by two boarders, who had smashed his fishing rod, beaten him up and filled his mouth with horse dung. Parkhouse had the Mayor summons the two boarders and they were fined. Witness after witness came out with signed statements that 'the boarders ill-treat the day boys', with details of stone throwing, name calling, clothes tearing and book ripping. It is difficult to know how to treat this evidence. Clearly day boys were harshly treated by boarders, but then small boarders were abominably treated by large boarders. Little boys who could not swim were tossed into deep pools in the Lowman in terrible fear, not knowing that the current always would take them to safety. Little boys were severely pummelled by 'bolstering': tied down to beds and hit repeatedly by 'bolsters' of bedding folded into tight bundles, rather like a rubber truncheon in consistency. Their sleep was disturbed by 'crimping', that is tying fishing line round their big toe and passing the line through the keyhole of a locked door and hauling away so the sufferer would spend a cold night with his foot wedged against the door. Fights, like the one described by Blackmore between Jan Ridd and Robin Snell, were part of a regular and accepted pattern, ignored by the Masters.

Above all, at the time the Feoffees were preparing their petition to Chancery, the liberal townsfolk wanted a school that was focused on the educational needs of their sons who were going to have careers in trade and commerce and the new professions of engineering and accountancy and the like. They wanted less emphasis on the impractical Classics, they agreed with the Feoffees on the provision of instruction in modern languages; they wanted science and all the branches of mathematics.

But the words of Lewis Owen, an Old Blundellian and Balliol Scholar, on the crises served only to pour oil on the fire in a letter in early 1839, in which he sneered:

Those who really believe that our existence as a nation will greatly depend on an advanced knowledge of mathematics and chemistry had better find funds to found a rival school.

With such as Owen no realistic dialogue was possible. Townsmen also wanted education to be free and the Masters to be paid sufficiently well that they did not need fees. And they did not want the substance of the school's finances to be wasted on the provision of buildings for boarders. A particular complaint was the bias of the Feoffees towards the awarding of scholarships to foreigners. They could not let the Feoffees' petition to Chancery go unchallenged.

Let the last bastion of Old Corruption in Tiverton fall. The struggle in Tiverton between the Earl of Devon, an 'old' peer, representing the School and John Heathcoat, a 'new' industrialist, representing the Town, was the struggle for the Reform Bill in ferocious miniature. Henry Sanders was not a man who could have worked with Heathcoat to achieve a compromise. The tenor of his background can be seen in a letter he received from his father in 1817 on the occasion of a Tory victory in the Devon County election of 1817 when the Tory, Sir Thomas Dyke Acland, a Feoffee since 1813, defeated Viscount Ebrington. Sanders' father wrote:

Nothing could be more gratifying to those who feel as I do and as I trust, for your own happiness you always will. Let 'Church and King' always be in your heart and as a toast always on your lips. Never let me hear of your being tinged with Radicalism or ever of associating with those that are – avoid them as you would a dog with hydrophobia!

It was to be war to the knife.

NEMESIS

The rumbling discontent of the townsfolk first expressed itself in a petition to the House of Lords in 1837. It had 150 signatures, the vast majority of whom were lesser tradesmen and householders who were under the £10 qualification for voting set in the 1832 Reform Bill. The Feoffees ignored it. Things went further when a public meeting was called on 26 December, 1838, when obviously the Town's representatives had got wind of the Feoffees' determination to present their bill in Chancery. This meeting decided to appoint a committee to communicate with the Trustees, comprising the Mayor, Thomas Rossiter, Dr Kettle, John Heathcoat, four clergy and 13 others. It worked fast and sent a letter on 3 January to the Earl of Devon and Sir Thomas Dyke Acland, the leading Feoffees, both of them Tories.

It was a very polite letter. It made the points that they were interested in broadening the curriculum and in emphasising that the institution was founded for Tivertonian day boys, rather than foreign boarders. As can be seen in the last chapter the Feoffees paid no attention to this letter and, at a meeting attended by Devon and Sir Thomas on 8 January, 1839, endorsed their own plans for upgrading the boarding accommodation, easing the regulations for admitting boarders and only slightly broadening the curriculum. The minutes of this meeting go out of their way to state that the Feoffees' decisions were unanimous, and they make no mention of the committee's letter. The snub to Heathcoat and the Town Committee was glaring. Harding, an Old Blundellian and complete Tory, asserted that Devon wrote to Heathcoat a conciliatory letter on 28 January, 1839. But such a personal letter could in no way be interpreted as a formal response to the committee's approach. Throughout the conflict, from now on, fierce Tories would accuse Heathcoat of dishonesty, 'glozing' or dissembling.

The townsmen met again in the Guildhall on 31 January. They appointed a further committee to oppose the Feoffees' petition to Chancery and made a further resolution deploring the 'fact' that there had been no reply from the Feoffees to their letter. They were quite right in this assertion. Incredibly, at their meeting of 8 January the Feoffees, who included Devon and Acland, did not even mention the letter from the Town Committee and there is no minute in the Book of Orders mentioning any reply on behalf of the Feoffees. With unbelievable 'hubris', the Feoffees were pressing ahead with their petition to Chancery, without taking into account a committee, which had the support of the local MP, whose colleague was Lord Palmerston, the Foreign Secretary. Those whom the Gods wish to destroy, they first make mad. Even the Feoffees' counsel thought it rash to be increasing accommodation for boarders.

The Vice Chancellor heard the Feoffees' petition on 4 June, 1839. In court the Feoffees' counsel objected to the inhabitants' agent, Samuel Amory, being heard. So the Feoffees pressed on, fine-tuning their petition. At one point it was even suggested that a group of five Feoffees should be set up to approve the admission of foreigners. At this point a counter-petition was presented by a group of 16 townsmen led by the fiery Dr Kettle. This petition wanted the surplus income to be spent on providing instruction in science and general literature. More and properly salaried staff should be appointed. The School should be geared to day boys and the present Feoffees dismissed.

In February 1840 the Vice Chancellor dismissed Kettle's petition with costs. The School community and the Tories gloated and were heavy with ribaldry, some amusing, and some infuriating. Quite amusing was a rollicking poem, entitled 'The Chapter of Rads!' It may well have been composed by Boulton, the Usher.

The Tories in Tiverton once had sway,
But Johnny's reforms swept them all away;
Then the Radicals soon came tumbling in'
And as quickly about their reforms begin.
Chorus: Yet barring all pother of this, that and t'other,
They shall all be great men in their turn.

The Ryders soon from their asses were thrown,
And the Rads quickly made their seats their own,
The Corporate body went out en masse,
For they could not retain a single ass!

Still Blundell's School was a sore to their eye,
That nest of good Tories and loyalty;
They could not get rid of all their disasters,
Until they turned out those Tory Masters.

Then followed two awful verses describing the setting up of the Town Committee, before the versifier described each leading 'Rad' by turn:

First stands Dr Kettle a Scholar bright,
Who says for his Townsmen's rights he'll fight:
Their system is bad he will vow and swear,
His son is a proof they can teach nothing there.

Frank Hole is the next, of great civic fame,
Then follows the other who bears his name
And next with humble and glozing mien,
The humble and glozing Heathcoat is seen

George Coles is the next, who, a wily wight
Seems blest with the power of second sight;
He foresaw that the School would soon be free,
So for eight of his sons de'il a sou paid he.

We wish that the next had not been there,
You will see that we mean the Rector of Clare;
He probably too may now think the same,
And wish to the Rads he'd not lent his name.

Ambrose Brewin comes next, who, whenever he can,
Lends his great name to a Radical plan;
Beer of Colliepriest now comes before ye,
Whose greatest delight is to worry a Tory.

Next Gamlen that meek and modest young man,
Tho' he cannot do much will do all that he can.
And if he should feel at all worse for the service,
He'll apply to the next, Esculapius Gervis.

With such Worthies as these, there can be no doubt
Of turning both Feoffees and Masters all out;
The Rads will then manage all things their own way,
For the devil a Tory in Twyford will stay.

Insulting and infuriating was a handbill with a mock Scheme, supposing what 'the Rads' would set up if they won. It started off with a rather heavy early-Victorian preamble, which is only amusing if you are totally convinced that the be-all and end-all of all education is the study of the Classics and that those who know no Latin or Greek are a species of yahoo. It then lists 27 new Feoffees with their 'profession'. Almost all of them are 'Lace Makers' or otherwise involved in local manufacturing, including John Heathcoat and his son-in-law, Ambrose Brewin. Among the Masters listed is the 'Lecturer on Alchemy, Chemistry and the Abstruse Sciences in general William Kettle.' Even more wounding was the deliberate insult to the distinguished Minister of the Congregational Church in St Peter St., 'Lecturer on Divinity!!! – Revd!!! W.H. Heudibourck.' The last paragraph of this convection ran:

> As it will be proposed to educate every boy suitably to the profession, trade, or calling he may wish to follow, it is suggested that competent Masters be appointed to superintend the HIGHER departments of the Arts and Manufacture – such as Breeches-making, Carpentering, Glazing, Tailoring, Bricklaying, Shoemaking, etc. and that the apartments in the Masters' houses hitherto appropriated to the use of boarders, will be no longer wanted for that purpose, they may be fitted up as small shops for the accommodation of such respective professors.

Meanwhile, amidst increasing acrimony, the Feoffees pressed on with their Scheme. The Town Committee was preparing a Petition of Appeal against the decision of February 1840 and was applying delaying tactics until it could be heard. They also filed an 'Information' against the Feoffees and Masters in March 1840, which meant that, if accepted by the court, there would be a judicial investigation of facts and first principles. The Lord Chancellor tried the appeal on 18 January 1841 and his decisions marked a turning point in the case. He 'discharged' (cancelled) the Vice Chancellor's decision of February 1840, costs were to be reserved, proceedings of the Feoffees' Scheme heard on 4 June 1839 should stop, and the process of the Information should go ahead.

There was now gloom in the Tory camp and elation among Liberals. Both camps should have done well to heed the court's words:

> I think it right in all cases to abstain from expressing any opinion upon matters not directly before me for judgment, but in the case of a charity in which continued litigation, whatever be its result, must greatly exhaust the funds otherwise applicable to objects the most desirable, I cannot but express a wish that both parties would consider, whether that which both have in view, may not be obtained without further expense.

But in the heated party atmosphere the obvious compromise, that the Town would concede on the boarding issue and that the School would concede on the syllabus issue, seems not to have been considered. The case moved with awful deliberation. It took from January 1841 until 1844 for both sides to agree on the basic facts, or in legal terms 'admissions', on which the case could be based. These were such things as the will, the deeds with Sidney Sussex and Balliol, the Chancery Judgment of 1740, the Book of Orders, etc. They then had to decide on the questions to ask witnesses. The years 1844 and 1845 were spent interrogating witnesses and writing down their answers to the 31 questions that had been agreed. Collation and preparing briefs followed and it was not until 2 May 1846 that the Vice Chancellor, Lord Lyndhurst, eventually heard the case. The court did not rush. Verdict was given on 29 October 1846 and to the Feoffees and Masters it was crushing:

> There were to be no more boarders.
> All education was to be free.
> Only free scholars could be eligible for scholarships and Exhibitions.
> A Scheme was to be drawn up for the payment of salaries and for the spending of the surplus.
> All costs were to be paid by the Defendants, i.e. the Feoffees and the School.

Between 1847 and 1852 various details of the new Scheme were spelt out. Provision for the admission of foreigners meant gaining the signatures of ten of the following: the three Rectors, the Lord of the Manor, this year's and the previous year's Mayors, the Aldermen and the Magistrates. The School was not to contain more than 150 pupils and they were all to be Grammar scholars. Latin and Greek must be taught freely, but charges could be made for instruction in French, maths, writing and arithmetic. The Master was to be paid £400 and the Usher £100, but could not take boarders. The Assistant Masters would be paid £50, but could have up to ten boarders in their houses.

The consequences of the Vice Chancellor's decision were dramatic. The financial costs were crippling. The fees to the School's lawyers were £2670 and those to the Masters' lawyers were £998. The Town's fees amounted to £3239 and there were miscellaneous court fees of £96. In all the Feoffees had to find over £7000 to settle the costs. Some of this could be paid out of the surplus cash in hand, which in 1842 stood at £2302. But when the bills of Samuel Amory, Heathcoat's solicitor, came in they amounted to over £3000. This could only be met by selling off most of the Feoffees' Consols and South Sea Annuities and over £3500 worth were duly sold. The sum of £7000 represented an amount that would have bought the Horsdon Estate and built the new School thirty years later.

The Feoffees were as generous as they could be to the Masters, who had now lost most of their income with the departure of their boarders. In 1847 and 1848 they paid Sanders £328, and Hughes, who had replaced Boulton as Usher in 1844, £67 in compensation for this loss. Sanders decided he would no longer struggle on and resigned in December, 1847. The Feoffees appointed Hughes in his stead. When he took over, the exodus of boarders had left the School with only 31 pupils; when he retired in 1873 there were 90. Sanders did not starve. Immediately it was known he was going, Henry Philpotts, the Bishop of Exeter, wrote to him with the offer of the Rectory of Sowton.

Another casualty was the regular parade of the Old Blundellians, which had restarted in 1788. Numbers had fallen since the early days, but from the end of the Napoleonic Wars until 1846 the average number who had processed and sat down to dinner had been a respectable 60. In 1847 after the defeat in the Vice Chancellor's court there was a burst of defiance and 116 Old Boys turned up, much the largest number at any dinner since 1788. This Old Boys' Day, which took place on 25 August, came after the boarders had left. Numbers were so great that the dinner was held in the National School Rooms in St Andrew Street. The full extent of the defeat then sunk in and numbers attending OB Day fell to 24 in 1848, 29 in 1849 and only 22 in 1850.

They decided that this would be the last parade. The President, The Revd H.F Yeatman, 1797–1804, declared that the Vice Chancellor had reduced their School to the status of a 'charity school'. Yeatman fulminated against their enemies:

> … 'the mistaken inhabitants of the town of Tiverton… men of little minds, of contracted understandings or ungenerous dispositions, whose object has been to pull down to the humble level on which they themselves are placed.

When proposing the toast of the Masters, Yeatman returned to the attack, describing the present day boy pupils as:

> … retiring and betaking themselves to the alleys and back streets of the Town and to companions of a lower grade, companions of perhaps sensual and immoral habits.

These were the entrenched attitudes that had bedevilled the previous thirty years. Yeatman ended his third and last speech of the evening:

> Some of these ardent Spirits [OBs] have gone forth to the battle field, periling their lives in defence of their native soil, the religion and the laws and liberties of England. Have I not seen others sitting in high places riveting the attention of the listening senate, administering the laws, upholding the public morals, protecting the public rights of property and of person, and so maintaining for high and low… equal privileges and equal rights and an equal enjoyment of our unparalleled and parental Constitution? Whilst lastly I have seen another and a larger class of my friends and fellow students, humbler no doubt as to rank and degree but not less necessary to the wants and necessities of their fellow men, standing as 'Watchmen on the Towers' of our modern Zion, raising the Cross and preach-

ing the great truths of the Everlasting Gospel and to aid in the fulfillment of that blessed prediction 'That the knowledge of the Lord shall cover the Earth as the Waters cover the Sea'… In conclusion I will only say that I hope for better things, for better days and for more felicitous opinions: hoping as I also do, that we shall soon be met by the inhabitants of Tiverton in a spirit of greater kindness, and with an earnest desire to restore again the faded honors of this once great establishment. And now Gentlemen, in approaching the bitter moment of separation and estrangement to take a last, a fond and lingering look at the 'Stamp and Impress' of our immortal Founder; let me finally say this: that if for the present we are to meet no more till the dark cloud on the horizon above us is happily dispelled, if we are here to raise for the last time our mingled voices in grateful praise of that generous and beloved Philanthropist; and here to entwine our hands, uttering one last affectionate adieu, then I most earnestly implore every son of Blundell to let one prayer be offered at this last flitting moment for the prosperity of this School, and the eternal repose of our generous and distinguished founder; so that it might be said of each and every one of the sons of Peter Blundell, in his dying moment, that he loved his immortal Founder to the last, and that like the stricken warrior of old when closing his eyes for ever, Coelum, Aspicit, et Dulces Moriens Reminiscitur Argos! [Continued and repeated Cheers.]

Yet fled was that music.

E. PROFUNDIS

It says much for the strength of Peter Blundell's Free Grammar School in Tiverton, that in spite of the 'doom and gloom' consequent on the Vice Chancellor's decision, it was never in any real danger of succumbing to these adversities. The legal costs were rapidly paid, the boarders within the walls departed and when Henry Sanders grumbled away to Sowton, numbers fell to 31. John Bickley Hughes, Usher since Boulton's departure in 1844 was appointed Master and took the occasion to get married to Elizabeth Middleton at St Peter's on 8 January 1848. She was the sister of one of his pupils, Sholto Middleton, 1845–53, who became a Balliol Scholar, and returned as Usher to the school in 1859, leaving in 1864 to become Head of King's, Bruton. Hughes was perhaps the most prolific of Headmasters, hence his nickname 'Daddy', his wife bearing nine children in the Master's House, who all survived. All four sons, Robert, Henry, Walter and James were educated at the School, also probably a 'record'. Life went on, but it was different.

One difference that the Feoffees would have noticed is that their annual dinner at the expense of the Trust now ceased. At their first St Peter's Day meeting after the Vice Chancellor's decision, they minuted to that effect, thus ending a tradition of feasting that had lasted for almost 350 years. When the finances improved they voted themselves a five-guinea luncheon. They met again in November 1847 to accept Sanders' resignation and to appoint Hughes in his stead. The minutes of this meeting fill the last pages of the Book of Orders, which had been begun in 1663. Literally a new page in the School's history was to begin.

A line drawing of the bearded Hughes in his schoolroom.

The Porter's Lodge. Note stumps and bat to the far right of the picture.

Unlike Sanders, the Feoffees did not resign, but they did have serious financial problems to face. The 'Old' School had to a certain extent paid for itself in that the salary bill was very small. The Master only received his £50, and £10 for an Assistant in the Upper School and the Usher only got £20 a year; they made their living through fees that did not go through the accounts. Until 1843 the total cost of the salaries was only £80. In 1843 the Feoffees allowed another £60 for a Mathematical Instructor, but that only put the 'teaching' bill up to £140. The 1852 Scheme laid down that the Master, who would of course have no income from boarders, should receive £400, the Usher £100, and the three Assistant Masters teaching modern languages, mathematics, and writing and rudimentary arithmetic would receive £50 each. The total new salary bill would potentially be £650 and it could not be paid out of the traditional sources of income, which had been diminished by the costs of the Chancery case. Financial health would depend on the income from Head Money, which, by the 1852 Scheme, was paid by boys taking the extra subjects taught by the Assistant Masters at the rate of £4 for one subject taken, £5 for two and £6 for three subjects. The devisers of the Scheme themselves envisaged problems as they added Clause 31 entitled 'Salaries to abate rateably in case of deficient income.'

The Feoffees had to take advantage of this Clause 31. Throughout Hughes' headmastership the Feoffees minuted at every St Peter's Day meeting that the teachers should have half their salary paid to them, but that the payment of the other half, or proportion thereof, would depend on the availability of sufficient income. Initially things were grim. In 1854 the Feoffees were only able to pay Hughes £210 and the Usher only £52 and the poor Assistants £26. Only after 1858 were all salaries paid in full, and only in the 1870s did the Feoffees stop passing their annual motion that only half of the salaries be paid before the annual audit.

One reason why the salaries were paid in full in 1858 was the descent of a curious windfall. In June 1858 the Clerk reported that he had been approached by the Ebbw Vale Iron Company who offered £200 for the right to prospect for iron ore and other minerals at Dictor's Cliff on West Prawle Barton.

Nothing much came of the prospecting, but the School moved steadily towards a new financial basis: that of relying on Head Money to defray the running costs of the teachers' salaries. In the first full year of the new 1853–54 Scheme, Head Money receipts were only £133, a drop in the ocean compared with the salary bill of £650. In 1858–59 the Head Money total was £250 and five further years later, in 1863–64, it was £493. It rose to over £600 in the early 1870s. A new solvency had been achieved and the Feoffees were very frugal about it. Whenever they could snatch a surplus they squirrelled it away into Government Bonds, £1700 between 1862 and 1876.

The provisions for foreigners being admitted into the School caused a few problems. The 1852 Scheme allowed the Assistant Masters to take up to ten boarders in their houses with the assent of ten named local officials and allowing the Headmaster rights of admission and inspection of the houses. But this and other parts of the 1852 Scheme were deemed too inflexible and in 1865 the Feoffees petitioned Chancery to accept a new Scheme. The 1865 Scheme allowed any person to apply to the Feoffees to become a 'licensed boarding house' and only boys living in such licensed boarding houses or with their parents could be admitted into the School. A levy of £4 a year per boarder was imposed on the boarding-house keepers. Some boarding houses so licensed had just one or two boys, but the Revd R. Duckworth, appointed Mathematical Master in 1866, had a house that was licensed for up to 50 boarders. (Duckworth had been recommended to the Feoffees by Hughes in 1858 as a Mathematical Master, but not appointed as, given the low numbers of pupils, it was deemed that the Usher could do the work.)

Other flexibilities of the 1865 Scheme allowed the Feoffees to appoint extra Masters and to widen the curriculum. Head Money was also increased to £5, £6 and £7, and, if they did add new subjects, they could charge an extra £1 per subject. They could also adjust salaries.

Most remarkable about the 1865 Scheme is the impression of goodwill between Feoffees and Town Council. In June 1859 the Feoffees contemplated five vacancies in their number and elected Sir John Taylor Coleridge, the Hon Mark Rolle, Thomas Dyke Acland, William Carew Rayer and John Heathcoat Amory into their places. This John Heathcoat Amory was the grandson of 'glozing' Heathcoat and the son of Samuel Amory, the solicitor who had run the Town's legal assault on the Feoffees' Petition in Chancery of 1839. At all stages of the 1864–65 Petition to Chancery proposing the new Scheme the Feoffees wrote courteously to the Town Council and both sides listened and co-operated. The meat of the 1865 Scheme could have been achieved in the 1840s if the then Masters and Feoffees had not been so cavalierly obscurantist.

To implement the Scheme the internal regimen of the School had to be developed. At their first meeting after the new Scheme became 'law', in July 1865, the Feoffees appointed six of themselves as a School Committee to explore 'the best method of applying the provisions of the New Scheme.' The committee reported to a full meeting at Exeter Castle on 22 December, making 15 recommendations. The first was to split the job of the Usher and Mathematical Master, raising the Usher's stipend to £150. Secondly they sacked the Writing Master, who was the son of that bibulous Porter, George Folland, as they wanted the new Writing Master to be able to teach arithmetic, English grammar and composition, as well as writing; also that mathematics and modern languages as well as Classics should count towards the gaining of the university scholarships; that improvements should be made in the School fittings and that more classrooms be provided. In fact desks increasingly became normal, rather than forms and some of the old boarding accommodation of the former Usher's and Headmaster's Houses was used to carve out classrooms. Most interestingly the Headmaster was ordered to draw up a timetable and there was to be a new emphasis on punctuality. 'Interesting' because up to 1866 the School 'ran' without a timetable! Another staple of the modern school had already appeared in June 1859 when £1.3s. was paid 'for a blackboard and carriage of the same'. Ten years later 'wall maps and sundry registers' were purchased. In May 1870 'E. Dunn, Bookseller', was paid £3s.11d. for 'printing Examination Papers, Quarterly Reports of Conduct and Sundry Registers'. Timetables, blackboards, wall maps and reports, all introduced within ten years! A curiously modern touch is the bill for the printing 'of circulars to parents' in connection with the 1865 Scheme.

In so many other ways the period between 1850 and 1870 was a hinge between old and new. In 1850 Peter Blundell's School was run as two virtually separate establishments under the Master and the Usher. By 1870 there was a staff of six, rising to seven in 1874. Hughes was Headmaster now earning £500. Ingram, the Usher, earned £200. Highton, called the Assistant Classical Master, earned £150, Herr Lehfeldt, the French and German Master earned £100, as did Clough, the Writing, Arithmetic and English Composition Master. R. Duckworth, the Mathematical Master, was paid only £50, but he had a boarding house with 40 boys in it that year.

Only 1d.

There had been rather a lot of changes to this little band in the years of Hughes' mastership. His first Usher, Buck, had died in office in 1859. His second, his brother-in-law, Middleton, had left in 1864 to go to King's, Bruton. Prideaux had then only lasted until 1867, when he had been replaced by Ingram. The big problem seems to have been finding and keeping Modern Language Masters: Arlington 1853–54, Tavernier 1854–58, Galindo 1859–60, Bruning 1861–64, Rouge 1865–69 and Herr Lehfeldt after 1870 show that there were 'shortage subjects' even in the 1860s! In 1869 they began to buy chemicals and chemical apparatus, but there is no clue who taught the subject, until G.H. Spring was appointed as Third Form Master and Natural Science Teacher in 1874. After the move to Horsdon he built North Close.

By the end of the Hughes' era the School was renting a cricket ground from John Heathcoat Amory and the Porter was being paid extra to maintain a properly organised swimming place through which water from the Lowman flowed. Both the ground and swimming place were where Medland Twose is now. The boys were also involved in the Volunteer Movement, which had grown up as a patriotic response to the perceived aggressive intentions of Napoleon III. Much of the Cadet Force work in connection with the Volunteers seems to have involved 'drilling' and in 1865 the Feoffees sought the opinion of parents whether such 'drilling' should include 'gymnastics' or not. The parents were only clear that they objected to the expense involved in providing their young Hectors with the Cadet Corps uniform. A sad sign of the looming imminence of the vast waste of money over the next 150 years is that in 1869 the Feoffees started talking about the provision of a 'Covered Play Shed', the primitive ancestor of our grandiloquent 'Sports Hall'. 'Covered Play Shed' does seem a better description.

In the 1860s the schoolboy population of Blundell's was very much alive. One example of this is that little gangs of boys got together to produce hand-written news sheets, which they called the *Blundellian*. From them we can see their sense of humour and pick up little bits of information, such as that the staff had their own classrooms by 1861. One may perhaps assume that there was a continuous series of these hand-written *Blundellians* until in 1869 four boys, including T.U. Cross, produced a printed *Blundellian* that sold for 6d. When Cross and co. moved on to University the *Blundellian* hibernated to reawaken when Cross returned as a Writing and Arithmetic Master in 1877. Since 1877 the *Blundellian* has been continuous.

Illustration from the Blundellian of 1861. Peter Blundell and the editors.

In praise of the captain of cricket.

An early cricket team.

The earliest hand-written sheet is from 1861, but otherwise undated. The editors hoped it would come out 'every Saturday morning', and as No 2 is dated 21 September 1861, the first was probably 14 September. It tells that 'the captain of the Blundell's School eleven last year, viz the famous leg-hitter L.B. Wells, has been appointed Captain of a well-known eleven at Ley [Lea?] near Blackheath, London.' On his first match he astonished the natives by a leg hit for 7, a thing almost unparalleled in the annals of cricket. Obviously occurring in what we would regard as the Michaelmas Term are accounts of two cricket matches, one against Crediton Grammar and the other against Uffculme School. 'We' beat Crediton by over a hundred runs. 'W. White played remarkably well, scoring in the second innings 39 off his own bat. The fielding of Jukes was universally admired.' The following is the account of the Uffculme game, the first fully described game in the history of the School, on Saturday 14 September 1861.

The Uffculme XI won the toss and sent their opponents in. Messrs Jukes and Hill took the wickets, but the latter gentleman soon got out with one run and the former soon after followed. Mr White went in and was soon running up a most magnificent score when he hurt his arm and Mr Rendell took his wickets. This gentleman played in a most splendid way and carried out his bat. Mr Baker made some runs in a dashing way, but no more runs were made after him until Mr J. Gribble took the bat and made several runs in a most MAD style, but was run out. The whole side was out for 73 runs. The 22 then went to dinner, after which the Uffculme went in, but came out pretty quick for 11. A second innings then took place in which Mr Gribble made the largest score and carried out his bat. The match was unable to be finished owing to the state of the weather. The Uffculmites in the evening went home in a brake and two horses.

The surviving 1866 editions of the *Blundellian*, which were produced in April and May, start off hand-written, but later editions experimented with lithographing, not very successfully, but raising the cost to 1d. In their first issue the editors refer to the fact that one half of the green was used for football, the other half for cricket, which shows that renting a cricket field was necessary. The captain of the XI hoped that team members would practice on half-holidays and later that the numbers of good cricketers in the School would allow of a second XI. They describe a Sports Day held on the green to the strains of the Militia Band. The events were 'throwing the cricket ball', hurdles, the donkey race, the flat race, the pole vault, putting the weight, the mile, high jump, the sack race and three-legged race. Sadly treacling had died, but jingling survived until after 1869, so there were still some fun events. The major saints' days were still holidays. In the period covered by the 1866 *Blundellian* St Marks' Day fell in term and was a whole holiday; the boys fished, bathed or played cricket.

The printed editions of the *Blundellian* start and stop in 1869 and begin again permanently in 1877. We learn the Headmaster Hughes' son had been captain of cricket in 1868, and that the boys paid subscriptions to the cricket club, graduated from one shilling in the First Form to four shillings in the Sixth and the 1st XI players paid ten shillings and the 2nd XI 7s.6d. The green was to be reserved for the Junior Elevens and the top teams would use the 'Town Ground'. Accounts of a Games Committee show that pupils not staff ran the whole games programme. A boy committee was also set up to enlarge the bathing place. Fourteen cricket matches were played and eight won. Those against Exeter G.S, Wellington, Exeter Training College, Brampford Speke, Dulverton, the South Western Cricket Club, Taunton College and 'Twenty-Two Tiverton Tradesmen' are recorded. In the latter game H.G. Sweet got 11 wickets in the Tradesmen's innings. Most teams were played twice and in the return match against the Twenty-Two Tiverton Tradesmen J.P.A.

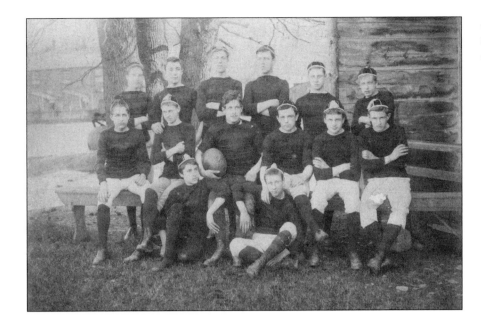

An early 'football' team. The setting is probably West Exe Rec. Note the colours caps.

Murray-Aynsley took 15 wickets in their first innings and 11 in the second, 26 wickets in the match. Great days.

In the last few pages of the 1869 edition there is a description of a game of 'Football' between the School and the Old Boys. It was played with 12 on each side, but quite what was going on, the author leaves to you:

The ball was kicked off at 3.15pm, by the Old Blundellians from the Lower Goal, but was soon returned, but for some little time kept down the green. Soon, however, the superior weight of the Old Blundellians began to tell, and School were driven back to their own goals. The Old Blundellians made several good tries at goal, and at last Rendall [OB] succeeded in kicking one during the absence of the goalkeeper. The School began with one man short, and the loss was not repaired before the first goal had been kicked. In the second game Murray-Aynsley and Sweet played back and E. Hardy was in goal. The ball was driven back to the School goals, where a fierce struggle commenced: but at last, while Murray-Aynsley and Sweet, who had received severe shins, had left the field, Hill [OB] gained a second goal. After a short interval of rest the game was resumed, and for the rest of the time was played more evenly as the Old Blundellians were getting fagged. Several attempts at a run were made by Murray-Aynsley and Manley, who were always collared before they could get any advantage. The match thus ended in a victory for the Old Blundellians by two goals. E. Hardy kept the goal very well for the school and several times saved it. A dispute unfortunately arose early in the game about picking up the ball, which at first caused some little unpleasantness, but was soon amicably settled.

While the boys were playing their cricket and football, their elders were discussing more 'changes'. No sooner had the ink dried on the 1865 Scheme than all was thrown into the melting pot by the Appointment of a Royal Commission to investigate all the Endowed Schools in the country. The Commission resulted in The Endowed Schools Act of 1869 which contemplated the reordering of all educational endowments, including Peter Blundell's so as to provide a nationwide network of 'First Grade, Second Grade and Third Grade schools. To preserve Blundell's great endowment for the benefit of Tiverton became a key issue, and Feoffees and Town entered into urgent and anxious negotiations. Key points related to whether a First School could be established on the Lowman Green site or not, and if not whether the site could be used for a Second Grade School and how many schools of what grade Tiverton could get out of the new system. As A.L. Francis had such an influence on the outcome of these negotiations they will be dealt with later.

Meanwhile development and change were also the themes of the School's relationships with Balliol and Sidney Sussex. During the 1850s Parliament set up a

Body of Commissioners to inquire into the affairs of both universities and make recommendations for reforms. These recommendations were incorporated in Acts of Parliament, which abolished closed fellowships, so that the senior Balliol and Sidney Sussex Scholar could no longer become automatically a Fellow. Nothing could change the Ham, the two Gilberd and Blundell's scholarships, whose holders had to find their own places. After long and hard three-sided negotiations between the Feoffees, the Colleges and the Parliamentary Commissioners a complicated new arrangement was hammered out. At Balliol there would be five scholarships, each tenable for five years, so that on average one Blundellian a year would receive a scholarship. With Sidney the arrangement was for three scholarships. In order to ensure high standards the candidates would be examined by three examiners, one appointed by Balliol, one by Sidney and one by the Feoffees. The examiners were to come to Tiverton and conduct examinations in the days before the main Feoffees' meeting on or near St Peter's Day. They would classify the candidates and the Feoffees, advised by the Master, would then nominate. They were allowed to take other qualifications into consideration apart from the strict classification of the examinations. This system began in 1861.

Ten years later Hughes made the 'mistake' which brought his career as Headmaster to a shameful close. The Feoffees' minutes of June 1871 gave no hint of the coming crisis:

> *Thomas Hodge Grose, Esq., MA, the examiner appointed by the Master and Fellows of Balliol College, Oxford, the Revd John Rundle Cornish, MA, the examiner appointed by the Master and Fellows of Sidney Sussex College, Cambridge and the Revd Osborne Gordon, MA, the examiner appointed by the Feoffees of this School report that they have examined the candidates who have presented themselves for election to one of the five scholarships chargeable on the corporate revenues of Balliol College and that they have elected to one of the said scholarships Francis Henry Carew, son of the Revd Robert Baker Carew of Bickleigh. The said examiners further report that no duly qualified candidate has presented himself for election to one of the three Exhibitions now chargeable on the corporate revenues of Sidney Sussex College.*

'Daddy' Hughes, 1847–74.
From the Register.

A hint that all might not have been well is an 'unnecessary' paragraph at the end of the meeting:

> *Mr Hughes then made a statement to the Feoffees respecting certain circumstances connected with the late examination in* Horace *for the Balliol Scholarship, informing them also that he had laid the whole matter before the examiners. The Feoffees requested the attendance of the examiners and conferred with them on the subject, after which they informed the Headmaster that under all the circumstances they declined to express any opinion on it.*

Sundry matters then began hitting the fan. At their next meeting, on 5 April 1872, it was reported that Grose had reported certain irregularities to the Master of Balliol, who had passed the matter on to Sir Stafford Northcote, a distinguished Feoffee, who had been Secretary of State for India in Disraeli's first Ministry, was MP for North Devon and a former member of Balliol. Grose reported that there had been something wrong about:

> *… the proceedings of the Headmaster on the occasion of the Examination in* Horace *for the Balliol Scholarship in June last. Mr Hughes having been heard thereon it is ordered that he be requested to prepare a written explanation of the matter to be laid before the Feoffees at a meeting to be held at the castle of Exeter on Friday next, 12 April at half past 11 o'clock.*

Hughes produced his written report, but the 12 April meeting postponed a decision until their meeting of 24 May. On that date the Feoffees may have grasped the nettle, but their minutes seem a fudge:

> *That regard being had to the fact that a new Scheme will be adopted for the School, application be made to the Charity Commission for leave to grant a retiring allowance to the present Headmaster of £200 per annum, in the event of his resignation, he having*

occupied his present position for twenty-seven years. And that Lord Devon be requested to communicate the above resolution to Mr Hughes.

So things might have ended except that Highton, the Assistant Classical Master wrote a letter to Sir John Kennaway alleging further misconduct against Hughes and that Clough the Writing and Arithmetic Master wrote to the Earl of Devon accusing his colleagues of pursuing a vendetta against Hughes. At their meeting on 19 June 1872 they appointed a sub-committee of Sir Stafford Northcote, Mr Popham and the Earl of Devon to investigate and report.

They did so on 11 October 1872. The Feoffees had to wade through statements, mis-statements, half-truths and economies with the truth. Originally, at the June 1871 meeting, Hughes had told them that he had by mistake told the boys the passage in *Horace's Epistles* in a way that allowed them to discover it. He had told them it because to some of them it might have come as an 'Unseen' as they had been absent with whooping cough when it had been prepared as a set book. And he claimed that he only told them to mark their *Horace* 'Unseen' so that they would not be penalised. For this 'indiscretion' he had been duly rebuked in June 1871. (Although the rebuke was not minuted!)

But it became clear that Hughes only admitted part of what he had done to Grose, the Balliol examiner, after Grose had heard of it from other sources. Initially Hughes had told Grose the 'half-truth' that to some of the boys the *Horace* should be treated as an 'Unseen'. Mr Ingram, the Usher, however informed them that Hughes had definitely ordered him to prepare Carew in the *Epistle* immediately before the examination and that Hughes had actually told Ingram that he was to prepare Carew because the *Epistle* had been set in the exam. It was also reported to the sub-committee that Duckworth had assisted the candidates in following up Hughes' hints and finding the relevant passage. Further accusations came out of the woodwork when allegations were made that the exams of 1867 and 1869 had also been fiddled. Highton had received evidence from a former pupil, Winchester, that they had been crammed overnight to prepare them for questions set in the next day's papers. The sub-committee dodged any conclusion except:

> *… throughout this investigation we have found the Assistant Masters generally ready to place the worst construction upon the acts of the Headmaster, while he in turn has imputed their proceedings to a spirit of personal hostility to himself. It is impossible to lay the blame exclusively on either side, but it is clear that such a state of things is highly detrimental to the interests of the School.*

It was time for a change. But the Feoffees were in a bind. They could not sack Hughes without scandal, and scandal would be most unfortunate when negotiations for the future of the School as a 'First School' under the Endowed Schools Act were so delicately poised. With his nine children, 'Daddy' Hughes was holding out for his pension. In February 1873 the Earl of Devon informed his fellow Feoffees that the Charity Commissioners would accept a request that the Trust, 'upon full considera-tion of the circumstances', be allowed to pay Hughes a retiring pension of £200. The 'request' was made; the Charity Commissioners duly approved the pension. But Hughes still needed to be pressed. At their June meeting in 1873 it was minuted:

> *Ordered that Mr Hughes be informed that the Trustees request him to send in his resignation at Michaelmas next with a view to the completion of his retirement at the Christmas of 1873.*

His resignation letter was read out at the October meeting and they moved to the election of his successor from among the 64 applicants. However, Hughes did not go quietly. The Feoffees had to call a special meeting in November 1873. The Earl of Devon read to the meeting a letter from the Revd J.B. Hughes:

> *… enclosing a communication from Mr J.C. Clough, Writing and Arithmetic Master, complaining of the conduct of the Assistant Masters in the School. Resolved that the Feoffees do meet tomorrow morning, Saturday, 8 November, for the purpose of investigating*

the statements contained in the communication. Ordered that our Clerk do give notice accordingly to Mr Hughes, Mr Ingram, Mr Duckworth, Mr Clough and Mr Highton and to desire the boys named in such communication may be in attendance.

On 8 November they minuted:
The Chairman [the Earl of Devon] afterwards stated to Mr Duckworth the several charges against him and informed him that the Feoffees would be ready to receive any communication which he might desire to address to them thereon.

It then at last seems to have fizzled out. Letters were written to Duckworth and Clough, but we do not know their contents.

For the guidance of those Feoffees who were interviewing the seven candidates shortlisted for the mastership, the Feoffees drew up six criteria. They may have had the sad events of the last three years in mind when they drafted four of them:
That he should possess adequate self-control as regards temper.
That he should love his work and be earnest in discharging it.
That his manner, age, habits and appearance should be such as to win the confidence and affections of the boys.
That he should be a man likely to act cordially with his Colleagues and harmoniously with the Governing Body of the School.

The Feoffees asked the Revd William Johnson of Repton to be Master. He refused the appointment. So they offered the post to Mr Augustus Lawrence Francis MA, Composition Master of Dulwich College, who accepted and took up office from Christmas Day 1873.

Old Boys' Day in the later 1870s. A.L. Francis is standing modestly in the back row next to the man in a top hat. Rooper, Spring (with mortarboard) and Cross, who respectively founded Westlake, North Close and Old House, are sitting together on the right behind the portentous chap with the whiskers. Parson Jack Russell is seated behind the right shoulder of the man in imposing academicals and mortarboard.

HAIL TO THE CHIEF!

Augustus Lawrence Francis started work in January 1874 at a salary of £500 p.a., or less if the income to the Trust was inadequate. There were great changes in his first five years. He immediately regulated the teaching of science by bringing in G.H. Spring, from his old Cambridge College, Jesus, who had been a colleague at Dulwich and who had a Natural Science degree to teach the subject throughout the School and to do general teaching in the Third Form, including Classics. Spring later founded North Close and retired in 1912, a stint of thirty-eight years. Thomas Uttermare Cross came to be the Arithmetic and Writing Master in 1876 and later founded Old House. E.P. Rooper, the founder of Westlake, joined in 1877, as Assistant Classical Master, a few months after Cross and retired in 1910. G.H. Norman soon followed in 1879. He was later to found Petergate and he left at the end of the summer term of 1913, thirty-four years later.

To illustrate this point about A.L. Francis, it is worth anticipating the move to Horsdon. Cross died young in 1892, but Spring's thirty-eight years, Norman's thirty-four years and Rooper's thirty-three years were not unusual in Francis' head-mastership, which itself lasted forty-three years. He gave loyalty; he received it in

OB Day 1880. A. L. Francis is now in the front row, second from the right. Rooper is behind him wearing a mortar board. Jack Russell is on ALF's right. Newly arrived G.H. Norman stands behind the seated man with the white beard. Cross is in profile behind the Mayor. G.H. Spring in a mortarboard is on the far left.

return. His first appointments after moving to Horsdon were the Classicist Henry Tatum, 1884–1917, who achieved thirty-three years' service, and Joseph Thornton the great mathematics teacher also appointed in 1884, who died in harness in 1916, thirty-two years later. Francis Herring was appointed in 1885 and retired in 1921, thirty-six years later. Spring, Rooper, Norman, Tatum, Thornton and Herring all worked alongside Francis for thirty years or more, seven of them in a Common Room of a dozen or so. These affectionate relationships must have been a breath of fresh air after the aggravations of the Hughes' regime.

After he had been at Blundell's for three months, Francis presented the Governors with some sweeping suggestions. First he asked for an extra Master to cover the Classical teaching in the Third Form and to do science, recommending Spring. He then reviewed the Boarding House situation. Robert Duckworth had a large Boarding House of over 40 boys, two other Masters, Highton and Clough, had six or seven each and there were a gaggle of boarding houses with only one or two pupils. As he put it 'the chief difficulties arise from the small boarding houses where much greater latitude is permitted than is consistent with good order.' He pressed for and got greater powers of visitation and inspection and greater controls of the hours for evening work and the regulation of 'leaves'. Some of them have a 'modern resonance', e.g. there would be no absence from evening work (prep) without the Headmaster's sanction. The Headmaster would decree times of 'Lock Up'. He planned for a greater restriction in the use of the cane and he pressed for the abandonment of the tradition of organising the School's year into 'quarters' and for the adoption of the 'Three-Term Year'. Later in 1874 he and Duckworth established two 'Boarding Exhibitions' so that the School could attract good incoming pupils. When Spring started up a boarding house for ten pupils, Francis was able to insist that all 'boarders' resided in the houses of members of the teaching staff.

When Cross returned to the School as a Master, he immediately restarted the *Blundellian* and its first issue came out in March 1877. It shows a vigorous little community. There had been talk of a School Library in the 1860s, but one was now in existence with all of 500 books. There were plans for an end of term concert. To encourage cricket and to fill up the space at the end of the Lent Term the Games Committee had decided to remove Sports Day from its traditional Oak Apple Day of 29 May and place it in the middle of April, which was then the end of the first term of the year, where it stayed until the 1980s. The Games Committee had also just inaugurated an annual steeplechase to be run on 24 March 1877 and named it after a famous Old Boy, 'Jack' Russell. It is clear from team write-ups that 'Colours' had been introduced. The old buildings at the back of the School built to house the early-nineteenth century boarders were knocked down and there was talk of new Fives courts being built. A.L. Francis held Shakespeare readings in his house on Mondays. During the year 1877 the School played 14 cricket matches and 12 football matches, descriptions of which show that it was now clearly an early form of rugby football. Some of the games played within the School were fun. On 13 November 1877 the Sixth Form took on the Rest and the game was a draw, though the Sixth were greatly outnumbered, as were the 1st XV who took on 25 of the Rest. A correspondent mentioned that as many as five Masters played cricket with the boys and contrasted that favourably with the lack of Masters playing a few years previously. A hockey club was started in 1878. Extracts from three plays, one Greek, one French and one English were performed on Speech Day. In 1879 there was a tennis knock-out competition. Every year there was a well attended OB Day, in the preparations for which the Revd T.U. Cross acted as a proto-E.R. Crowe and 'Organiser-in-Chief.' There was no OB Day recorded in the 1869 *Blundellian*, but it seems there may have been one in 1876, since when they have been continuous.

This was a happy school, but not yet a numerically flourishing one, in spite of the fact that there was every incentive for Francis to increase the numbers. In 1877 he moved to a new type of salary. On 17 December 1876 he received the last half-yearly payment of £250 and in June 1877 received a proportion of his new salary of only £200 a year. But this was made up by a 'Capitation Fee', which allowed him between £3 and £6 per boy per year. He did in fact get £3s.10d. per boy, paid termly, and received over £400 from this source in 1877, when there were about 120 boys in the School. Nevertheless when the School marched out of the old buildings to the new home at Horsdon he had barely 80 pupils.

This serious fall was due to the cloud of uncertainty that hung over the School, darkest in the later 1870s, but growing from 1869. The modified Scheme of 1865 was soon superseded by the Endowed Schools' Act of 1869. This was a very sweeping measure and reflected the determination of Gladstone's Government to introduce a thorough-going reform of the whole of English education to back up its flagship measure, the provision of universal primary education for all children, the 1870 Forster's Act. This measure might have been introduced twenty years earlier if the various Churches had not wrangled over the type of religious education to be provided and over whether the non-Anglican taxpayer could be asked to pay taxes to support existing schools, most of which were Anglican and run by the village parson, and often, as in most Devon villages, sited at the rectory gates, or next to the Anglican parish church. One of Blundell's most distinguished sons, Frederick Temple, since 1860 Bishop of Exeter, negotiated the famous Cowper-Temple clause, which allowed freedom of conscience in schools and enabled the 1870 Education Act to be introduced without interdenominational Armageddon.

The 1869 Endowed Schools Act took the bull by the horns. It defined 'Endowed Schools' widely as almost any school that had an endowment more than fifty years old. It set up a body of Commissioners to draw up Schemes 'most conducive to the advancement of the education of boys and girls.' In drawing up those Schemes the Commissioners could basically do what they liked with existing endowments and the Trusts administering them. Trusts could be split or amalgamated. Governing bodies could be dissolved or given more powers. The Act laid down that any Educational Trust with an income of over £1000 a year could pre-empt the actions of the Commissioners by preparing its own Draft Scheme for submission within six months of the Act coming into force. There would then be a three-month pause for interested parties to make comments. The Commissioners could then hold an inquiry at the end of which they would prepare a Scheme for submission to the Privy Council Committee of Education. There was going to be no delay. Local people had to get their act together or the rich educational endowments of Tiverton – Blundell's, Blagdon's Blue Coat School in Castle Street and Chilcott's School – could be lost to local control. As guidance in drawing up Draft Schemes the Commissioners laid down a template of First Grade Schools, Second Grade and Third Grade Schools. A First Grade, or County Boarding School would prepare children for university, the armed services and the learned professions. A Second Grade School envisaged its pupils leaving at sixteen years old and aiming for a commercial career; a School of the Third Grade would lose its pupils at thirteen. A First Grade School would teach Greek as well as Latin. A Second Grade Boys' School would offer book-keeping, but not Greek. A Girls' Second Grade School would not tax the little dears with mathematics, but they would do needlework and domestic economy. There seems to have been countywide agreement that Blundell's was the obvious choice for the County Boarding School of the First Grade.

But there is only one word that can describe the Feoffees' response to this challenge and opportunity: 'Pathetic'. The matter of the Endowed Schools Commission appears from time to time on the Feoffees' agendas. In April 1871 a Mr Fitch, one of the Commissioners, attended:

> ... with a view to learn from them what were their views respecting the application of the Endowed Schools Act to the reorganisation or improvement of this foundation.

Incredibly, they gave none. In April 1872 they appointed a sub-committee to discuss with the Commission an 'Outline of Proposals' for a Tiverton Scheme. In May they had no comments to make except to raise the question of the propriety of being able to pay the pension necessary to get rid of Hughes with the minimum of fuss. In June they decided to ask five of their number to discuss the Educational Scheme put forward by the Town Committee. In November they had twice to be prodded by the Commissioners to comment on the proposed Draft Scheme. By this time the question of a site for Tiverton's First Grade School was a hot issue. The Feoffees' contribution to the debate was that moving would be expensive and that it would be preferable to spend £7000 on the present site. Later in the same November meeting, the Feoffees said it 'would be better to move to a new site', though that might cost £15,000. An important meeting in April 1873 lacked a quorum. At all later stages they reacted and reacted weakly rather than taking any initiatives.

The Earl of Devon was a loyal Feoffee from 1852 to his death in 1888, but it is hard to see that he had any vision or drive. The Endowed School Act came at a difficult time, a time when the Headmaster and the staff were a sackful of squabbling ferrets, a time when a Headmaster, who had instigated cheating in an important examination, had to be removed, but the Feoffees cannot be absolved from the charge that they totally lacked drive and vision. Devon was not a good Chairman.

The drive and initiative came from the Town not the School and the driving visionary was William Partridge, a solicitor who lived in St Andrew Street. The ball started rolling when a group of citizens presented a petition to the Mayor in November 1870 asking that he call a public meeting:

> … with a view to discuss the provisions of the Act and adopt such measures as would be most likely to secure the establishment of Schools of the Three Grades contemplated by the Act.

Every attempt seems to have been made to get signatures that crossed party lines; there are the names of Anglican Clergy, Hughes' name is there, as are the Liberal establishment. Simultaneously Partridge brought out a pamphlet, though he presented it as a joint effort. The frontispiece was signed by seven men. John Heathcoat Amory, one of the MPs, was a Blundell's Feoffee; Francis Dunsford was an Old Boy from the 1830s and from a family with Blundell's connections going back to Atherton's day, and a member of the County Committee, as was W.R. Noble. The other signatories were Robert Duckworth the Boarding House Master, Mackenzie, an Old Blundellian and up-and-coming Tiverton doctor, F.O. Patch the Feoffees' former man of business and William Partridge himself, also an Old Blundellian of the 1830s, whose son would come to the School in 1874.

The pamphlet is divided into four short sections. The first reviewed the sweeping powers of the Act. The second summarised the strong claims for Tiverton and Blundell's being the County First Grade School and made claims for the Town having schools of the seconds and third grades, based on the extent of the Blagdon and Chilcott endowments. Section III was the nub of the pamphlet. It pointed out that the present numbers at Blundell's, about 100 pupils, made it twice as large as 'any other School of note in Devonshire.' It reviewed the School's extensive connections with the universities, mentioning its fourteen closed awards. It went on:

> As to the Establishment of such First Grade School, it may be considered in the opinion of some, that the locality of Blundell's School renders it ill-adapted as a site for a boarding school, from its low position and its proximity to the River Lowman, but the want of sufficient area and the space to adapt it to the requirements of modern times, would be held by others to be a stronger and perhaps insuperable objection to its selection as a site for a Boarding School of the First Grade.

BLUNDELL'S SCHOOL, TIVERTON.

TO THE
INHABITANTS
OF
TIVERTON.

We, the undersigned being as well for ourselves as others, deeply anxious for the welfare of Tiverton and its neighbourhood, and taking a lively Interest in the prosperity of the Schools at Tiverton, have drawn up the subjoined Statement for your consideration, in the earnest hope that a first grade School may be established at Tiverton, under " The Endowed Schools Act, 1869," and the large existing Educational Endowments here reorganized into three Schools of the Grades contemplated by the Commissioners; and further, we beg to suggest, that at no distant period, it will be most desirable that a public meeting of the Inhabitants should be called to consider and discuss the whole matter, and decide upon what measures should be adopted to secure the object in view, which meeting we doubt not, the Mayor on a requisition would readily call.

J. H. AMORY, ⎫ Members of the
F. DUNSFORD, ⎬ Devon County
W. R. NOBLE, ⎭ Committee.

R. DUCKWORTH,
F. MACKENZIE,
W. PARTRIDGE,
F. O. PATCH.

The Partridge pamphlet of December 1870 that may have saved the School.

As Tiverton must have, in any case, a Second, as well as a Third Grade School (as stated in various Commission Reports), the present School buildings would be found available for this purpose.

A new site for the school of the first grade would therefore have to be provided, and may be considered a necessity. The Commissioners (in defining the qualities of a First Grade School) suggest:

The mere fact that it is possible to get a good playground in a new site and not possible in an old, is, in itself, quite a sufficient reason to justify removal if there be not stronger reasons against it. The Governors ought therefore to have the power of 'Removal' and 'to raise money on the property of the Endowment for that purpose'.

The importance of a healthy site and good buildings cannot be overrated, according to the opinion of the Commissioners:

Next to a good Master, there is nothing more important for a school than a good site and buildings. Health, order, dignity, good teaching are all intimately concerned with the aspect and accommodation of the School itself, and that a Grammar School may occupy its right place in the respect of the inhabitants, it should occupy a worthy position among the buildings of the Town.

In the last section the author went into ways and means, concluding that the moving of the School to a new site was financially possible. He even suggested that Masters would find it profitable to build a boarding house adjacent to the new site. He ended with a clarion warning about 'the necessity of taking immediate steps', a fantastic contrast to the doziness of the faffing Feoffees:

The present suspense and uncertainty as to the future of all schools in Devon will inevitably injure their prospects, and is at present undoubtedly affecting their interests. And to show that all scholastic enterprise is being paralysed at present, we need only call attention to the unmistakable fact that Devonshire boys are repairing to those more favoured schools, where new Schemes are already in active operation. Let us then take active measures, and promptly, in order that New Buildings for a school of the first grade may be provided and erected on a new site.

Because of the bumbling Feoffees it would still take ten years. The Mayor called a meeting on 3 December 1870. It was attended by both MPs and was well attended by about 100 people. It passed four resolutions, of which the most important were that the points of Partridge's pamphlet were endorsed and a committee set up to pursue the matter with the Commissioners, with Partridge its Secretary. The Committee produced its first report on 17 December, recommending the purchase of the Horsdon Estate and recommending that the buildings of 'Old' Blundell's should be used as for a school of the second grade. In fact the removal of Blundell's to another site was the key ingredient of the Town Committee's thinking. The vacation of the old buildings unlocked the path to the Town's plans for two Second Grade Schools.

In the spring of 1871 Mr Fitch was sent down by the Commissioners for discussions. As already related he had a rather unsatisfactory meeting with the Feoffees, Hughes and the Assistant Masters, from whom he learnt that, whereas the Feoffees and Hughes did not want to move to a new site, most of the Assistant Masters did. From discussions with Partridge and his Committee, Fitch would have learnt that they wanted to move Blundell's to Horsdon and, use Old Blundell's, the Chilcott School's buildings in St Peter Street, the Blue Coat School buildings in Castle Street, to set up two Second Grade Schools and two Third Grade Schools in the Town.

As a result of his visit Fitch wrote a memorandum revealing the nub of the problem: The Feoffees and the present Headmaster, Hughes, did not want to move from the old site, believing that it could be adapted. In response to this the Commissioners were minded to leave the decision about the site to the Governing Body appointed under a new Scheme. The Town wanted Blundell's on a new site, a Second Grade Boy's School at 'Old Blundell's', a Second Grade Girl's School somewhere else, and Third Grade schools for boys and girls, in the Chilcott and Blue Coat premises. The Commissioners, on the other hand, were thinking of leaving the Blundell's problem to the future and only establishing two hybrid Second-Third Grade Schools in the Town.

In response Partridge wrote a 16-page pamphlet, and summoned the Committee to discuss it and Fitch's Memorandum on 17 May 1871. Out of this meeting came the Committee's own Scheme, which was outlined in the previous paragraph. Partridge backed it up with a report signed by seven medical men asserting that:

> … *on sanitary grounds it is undesirable to adopt the present site of Blundell's school for the enlarged buildings contemplated by the Endowed Schools Commission for the reception and education of a greatly increased number of pupils.*

This in turn was backed up by a report by Dymond, a surveyor, written in April 1872, which ended damningly:

> *It needs no argument to show that the site of Blundell's school, shut in as it is by hills and buildings and on an incurably damp sub-soil cannot compare as regards salubrity with the site suggested by the Committee [Horsdon], nor does it in our opinion present any point of superiority except the prestige belonging to an institution, which has become venerable by age and valued from the association attaching to it as the place where many leading men of Devon have been educated.*

William Reginald Courtenay, 11th Earl of Devon, Chairman of Governors 1857–88, who laid the Foundation Stone of the new School.

Nevertheless, faced with the Feoffees' unwillingness to consider moving the School, the Commissioners produced a Draft Scheme in January 1873. The Scheme left the question of site open for the new Governors. It laid down the new way of paying Headmasters by means of a small salary and the prospects of a large sum of 'Head Money'. It laid down that tuition fees should be between £15 and £25 a year and that boarding fees should not exceed £60 a year. The Headmaster would be given much more control over the appointment of staff and of their rates of pay. It laid down the standards for an entrance examination. A candidate for admission should:

> … *never fall below the following standard: reading, writing from dictation, the first four rules of arithmetic, the outlines of the geography of England.*

The School should teach English, Latin, Greek, arithmetic, mathematics, history, geography, natural science, at least one foreign language, drawing and vocal music. An outside examiner would inspect the efficiency of the school annually. The Draft Scheme enshrined a parental right to remove any child from any religious worship or religious instruction, and specifically outlawed any discrimination by the Masters against any child so withdrawn.

The Commissioners only produced the Blundell's Draft Scheme in 1873 and, as the Committee pointed out, this prevented any useful discussion of the provision of education for the Town as a whole. It was reissued as a 'final' Draft in August 1875, the only important adjustment being that fees should be between £12 and £24. The majority of the Committee were now exhausted and prepared to accept the Scheme even though it would make it impossible to achieve proper Second Grade Schools in Tiverton if the County First School stayed in the old buildings by the Lowman. Partridge differed and at this point he resigned as the Secretary of the Committee. They begged him to reconsider and he was still Secretary when the Committee wound itself up in October 1876.

The 'Tiverton: Blundell's School' Scheme received the Royal Assent in August 1876. There were to be 18 Governors, nine of whom were to be nominated by such local bodies as the JPs, and the MPs of the Town and County, by the Town Council and the other Tiverton schools. One was to be elected by the Headmaster and Assistant Masters and seven were to be co-opted. The remaining Governor was to be the Lord Lieutenant of the County or his representative. The first meeting of the new Governing Body occurred on 15 December 1876. The Lord Lieutenant, the Duke of Somerset, nominated William Partridge as his representative.

Partridge lost no time. On 10 January 1877 the Governors met again. He brought the following motion before the Governors:

In view of the enlarged prospects before the School under the present Scheme the Governors are of the opinion that a new site and buildings for School purposes should be provided at as early a period as may be found practicable.

The Earl of Devon, still Chairman of the new Governing Body, had not changed his spots. Although all the arguments for and against had been being made for at least five years, the motion was adjourned until the April meeting.

In April Partridge proposed his motion and Sir John Heathcoat Amory seconded it. Lord Coleridge and Frederick Temple, the Bishop of Exeter then carried an amendment to refer it to a sub-committee to report on practicalities. Its membership comprised Devon, the Bishop of Exeter, Amory, Bere, Dunsford and Partridge.

The meeting of June 1877 began by appointing a young Balliol Fellow, Henry Herbert Asquith, later Prime Minister, as external examiner for the year. The sub-committee then reported that the resources of the foundation, when compared with the costs of starting up Clifton College, were in their opinion adequate for the move to a new site. The Governors accepted the report and reappointed the members as a committee to find a new site. In October the Governors accepted that part of the Horsdon Estate would be suitable. There was some disagreement in that the majority wanted the present site, while a minority wanted to build nearer the Town, between the present Headmaster's House and Horsdon Garage. To pay for it and the new buildings the Governors resolved to sell large parts of the historic South Devon endowment. Their sale in October 1879 realised £9168.

Those who have ever followed the tortuous, nay tortured, ways of Tiverton politics know that steadiness of purpose is not a quality for which its local government is renowned. As soon as it was known that the move to Horsdon was decided the Town protested. At their meeting of 10 August 1878 a Governor nominated by the Tiverton Middle Schools, Mr Payne, proposed that the Governors name a day for a special meeting to discuss the Town's objections to moving the School and that in the meantime 'the proceedings in reference to the purchase of a new site at Horsdon be suspended.' Partridge jumped in with an amendment that the Town's objections be discussed 'today'. Twelve Governors were present, ten voted and the vote in favour of the amendment was six to four. Partridge then proposed 'That the matter had been fully discussed and decided and should not be altered'. This was carried. Striking while the iron was hot, Partridge then proposed 'that the Governors do proceed to obtain plans for such buildings as it may be found expedient to erect', which was carried by a majority of eight. Such plans had to be submitted by interested architects by the end of September 1878. Finally the Chairman was empowered to sign the purchase documents for the Horsdon acres.

Payne, however, had not given up. Using Clause 13 of the Scheme, which allowed any two Governors to call a special meeting of the Body, he forced the Chairman to call the Governors together on 9 September. He drew their attention to Clause 26, which stated that any new site had to be within 'easy access' of the Town, and to clause 66, which stated that in cases of doubtful interpretation they were bound to appeal to the Charity Commissioners for guidance. It was all unavailing; the Governors voted 9–3 and 10–3 against his stopping proposals.

> # TO THE GOVERNORS OF BLUNDELL'S SCHOOL, TIVERTON.
>
> My Lords and Gentlemen,
>
> The fact of my probable absence from the next Meeting of the Board (fixed for Wednesday, 4th April) and consequent inability to move in person the Resolution of which notice has been given by me " That in view of the "enlarged prospects of the School under the present Scheme, " the Governors are of opinion that a new Site and Build-"ings for school purposes should be provided at as early a "period as may be found practicable," will, I hope, be deemed my sufficient excuse for submitting the following as some of the grounds on which the resolution is based, and by which the motion is to be supported. Perhaps this mode is preferable to their mere oral communication, as giving fuller opportunity for consideration. Should I not be present at the meeting the resolution will be moved for me, and I hope will be found to commend itself to the approval of the Governors.
>
> Yours obediently,
>
> WM. PARTRIDGE.
>
> Tiverton, 19th March, 1877.

The Partridge pamphlet of March 1877 that persuaded the Governors to move to Horsdon.

An architect's impression of the new School.

The move continued. By March 1879 Messrs Haywards' plans had been chosen. In November tenders were opened. At first Veale's tender was accepted, but, when he wrote saying that there had been a £1000 error in his arithmetic, it was dismissed with ignominy and the tender of Langdon and Pool accepted. Work started in 1890.

But the move was not without casualties. Duckworth decided that he would resign and did so in 1879, starting up his own private school in the Town. As 40 of the 100 boys in the school boarded at Duckworth's House this was a potentially devastating blow. In his report to the Governors on the year 1879 Francis was alive to the dangers.

> *The year was on several accounts a very anxious one. The strong opposition raised to the moving of the School in the autumn of 1878 did serious harm in more ways than one. The delay which it caused was in itself very damaging and spread a feeling of uneasiness at the prospects for the School, coming as it did at a time of general depression [economic] it must have gone far towards determining Mr Duckworth to resigning his mastership...*
>
> *I invite their [the Governors'] most serious consideration to our prospects as a Boarding School. It is well understood that a new site has been chosen because the present one is unsuitable for a First Grade Boarding School. For many years past the question has been raised. If then we are in two years time to open our new buildings on a site less convenient for Town boys without offering accommodation for a single boarder nearer than half a mile off it will be a grave misfortune.*
>
> *I believe it to be essential to our prosperity that boarding houses, capable of containing not less than 60 boys, be opened on or near the new site at the time when the move takes place, and that no time should be lost before letting the public know that this will be done. Nothing less than this will restore the public confidence, which the School apparently once enjoyed, but which has been seriously injured by the mistakes and delays of the last thirty years. In any case, surrounded as we are by other Schools, who have obtained a start from us, we cannot hope for a success so rapid or so great as would have been possible if the move could have taken place ten or even five years ago. Still, with good buildings and with good boarding accommodation I feel no anxiety as to the future of the School and I feel confident that it will continue to take a leading place among the Schools of the West of England.*

Building proceeded apace. Arrangements were made for boarders. The Charity Commissioners gave permission for the Governors to raise a mortgage of £1500 to extend the Headmaster's House for boarders. It would be paid off at the rate of £100 a year and the Headmaster's salary would stand as security for the loan and interest payments. T.U. Cross took a similar, personal, financial risk in getting a mortgage of £2250 to rent a part of the Horsdon 'campus' and build Old House,

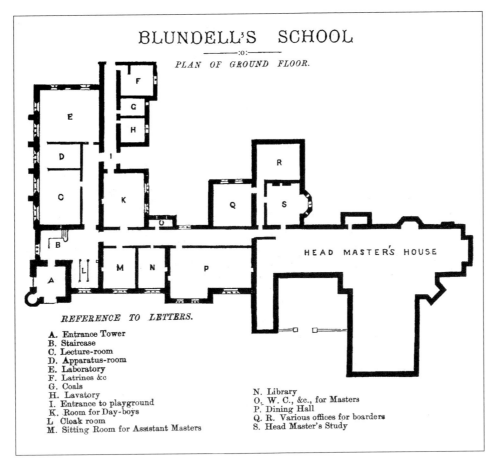

The ground floor.

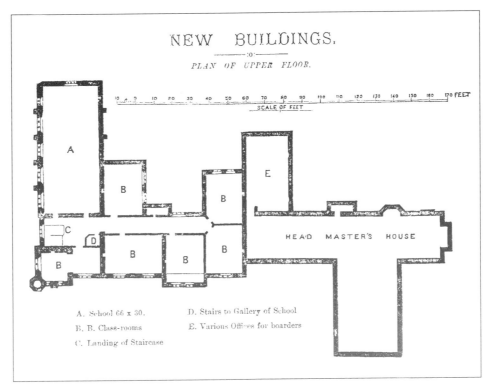

The first floor.

being specially allowed to join up the drains of the House to the school's drains. Spring started plans for what would become North Close. In the first half of 1881 decisions were taken to sell a quarter of an acre to a separate Trust, on which to build a chapel. To emphasise that the Chapel would not be part of the School the Charity Commissioners initially stated that it should be surrounded by railings to mark it off, but in February 1882 they relaxed their conditions and allowed it to be kept apart 'by walks and boundary stones instead of an iron fence.' The cost of construction was met by a great burst of private giving. It is still a matter of legal fact that the Chapel is not technically part of the School.

In March 1882 the Headmaster requested the Governors:

... that a Committee be formed to arrange for the removal to the new School and to decide on the fittings necessary to be procured and the following Governors were appointed to act: the Revd H. Venn, Messrs Fisher and Snell.

As the March 1882 edition of the *Blundellian* put it:

... the new buildings are nearing completion, the grounds are in great measure laid out, and the cricket field is being leveled. The Chapel is already above ground, and it is to be finished at the end of July. This is the last time we shall address our readers from within those ancient walls, which we have inhabited for nearly three centuries. In a few short days all will be over, and we shall bid the dear old buildings an everlasting farewell. Blundell's School is on the eve of a new existence. May its future be no less glorious than its past!

Adieu to the home for 278 years.

HORSDON, 1882–1914

BUILDINGS AND STAFF

As promised in the Editorial of the April 1882 issue of the *Blundellian*, the School moved into the new buildings for the Summer Term. In the June issue it was reported that the builders had almost moved out and all was well. The new school, designed by Messrs Haywards and put up by Langdon & Poole, looked well. Building had started in 1879, in early 1880 it had been decided to add a Headmaster's boarding house onto the main School buildings and to allow Mr Cross to build Old House. In October 1880 it was realised that the Town water supply did not extend to Horsdon and the Clerk was instructed to write to the Town Clerk to ask when they proposed to extend the mains to the School. In December the Governors were told that the Town had no plans to extend the water mains towards Horsdon. Luckily the wells that the builders had dug to provide water for mixing cement were found to be safe for supplying drinking water. A cistern was placed in the Tower just below the clock and water pumped from the well near the foot of the Tower. Naturally, this extraction caused the ground to shrink, which caused cracking to the Tower, necessitating expensive underpinning in 1896. The Town water supply, which reached the School in the later 1880s, was sadly deficient in dry summers and the Governors wrote a furious letter in 1896, full of phrases like 'grave scandal', 'immediate remedy' and 'manifest duty' scorched the page. Water remained scarce until the 1940s.

The Porter's Lodge and the gates, the latter a gift from Sir John Amory in 1891 and the first of many gifts to the School from that generous family.

Initially, sewage was another problem. Tacking on two boarding houses at quite a late stage in the development had some pretty obvious consequences. As early as November 1882 the Governors were faced with complaints about 'the smell'. After two requests the architects produced the plans of the drains. During the building, permission had been given for the OH drains to join the SH drains. In the summer of 1883 the Governors hired a sanitary engineer, Mr Row, to give expert advice and

Big School about 1910. The present Library.

a sub-committee investigated and found the drains to be totally defective. In August 1883 the architects and builders were sacked and Mr Row asked to furnish a solution, which he did by extending the pipes to the Ailsa Brook, to the dismay and alarm of the downstream neighbours of the School, who for many years were bitter in their complaints, until the Town extended the sewerage.

But overall, the move was a great success. The buildings are what you see and they cost £13,137s.2s.8d., paid for on the nail from the accumulated assets of the foundation, without selling the historic estates of South Prawle. The numbers tell the successful story. In May 1882 the school reassembled 87-strong. By January 1885 numbers had soared to 190 and by January 1890 had moved up to 249. A peak of 272 was reached in the Summer Term of 1890 and 280 in the Summer Terms of 1891 and 1892.

This phenomenal threefold increase within ten years triggered further building. An emergency measure was the partition of the Chemistry Room in 1894. More fundamental was the building of an extension from the north-south axis of School House in an easterly direction. The plans were regularly changed, but in 1887 it was finalised as a three-storeyed extension, with a mix of classrooms, studies and bedrooms. It was completed soon after 1890 at a cost of £1138, of which Francis paid £635 from his own pocket. Before its completion, a 'Covered Playground' and Workshop had been built for £500 on the site of the former Modern Languages Block. The Governors only agreed to contribute £100 of the cost, the remainder being guaranteed by the staff. Levies from the pupils paid for the first Fives courts, which used one of the 'Covered Playground's walls. To the east soon appeared the Old Pavilion with its clock presented by the North Devon Cricket Club. In 1887 the Tower clock was presented by Mr Frank Morrison of London, who was neither an OB, nor the father of an OB.

Between 1889 and 1892 the Sanatorium was conceived and built, again financed jointly by Governors and staff. The biggest piece of joint financing was the conception, planning and building of a Library, the present Staff Common Room, the staircase and the rooms beneath between 1894 and 1897. The Governors only contributed £300 to this project; the staff guaranteed and paid for the rest, over £1000. The other major additions before the First World War were the science laboratories. The first was the laboratory built largely with a donation from a Governor, Mr Coles of Washfield, who had made his fortune in insurance. This is now the physics lab. The present Chemistry Block was completed in 1911, also with the aid of a large gift from Mr Coles. He also endowed annual prizes for science.

The old Chemistry Room with E.G. Peirce in charge of a tidy lab. It is now the main geography classroom where Jerry Salter presided. Sadly, the column, to which boys were chained, is gone. Notice the door to the Monitors' Room; it was the Chemistry Store. Charles Hamilton, former denizen of OH, now teaches there.

A generous OB, Charles Billyard, donated workshops in 1890. He was only at Old Blundell's for eighteen months in 1873 and 1874 and only thirty when he made the gift. The Billyard Workshops were built between the east end of the Chapel and the Old Pavilion, containing a room 38 feet by 15 feet for carpentry, with two smaller rooms for lathes and a forge.

Extra accommodation for the swelling numbers became urgent. Both Francis and Cross pressed for extensions. The building of North Close by Spring, who had had boarders at his St Aubyn's Villas residence in the 'old days', relieved some of the pressure. The *Blundellian* of October 1882 reported a start to the building works. The December issue reported the roofline as being reached. The rapid schedule was

The Coles Laboratory.

maintained for, in June 1883, the magazine reported that 'Mr Spring has begun his migration from St Aubyn's Villas to 'North Close'.'

Westlake and Petergate soon followed. Rooper had started with a few boys in 'Redlands', and in November 1885 it was reported that:

Mr Rooper intends to build a boarding house more suited to his requirements, as his number of boarders is so rapidly increasing, and has chosen a piece of ground between Redlands and Mr Spring's house.

In the Autumn Term of 1886 G.H. Norman also opened up a house at Redlands. Somewhat optimistically the School Roll of January 1887 entered Rooper and Norman's houses as Westlake and Petergate, but it took a few years for them to fill their respective establishments.

It was all so very optimistic. When the builder, William Grater, had completed Petergate in August 1887, George Norman not only wrote him the following letter, but he had it specially printed:

Dear Grater,

As, after all I cannot come to the dinner – which I just could have done if it had been at three – I should like to express to those whom you have employed on my house my best thanks for all the trouble they have taken on it.

And to the men I should like to say that I appreciate their work and their conduct; for, from the time the house was begun (a year or more ago) till now, when it is finished, I have rarely heard a bit of bad language, and in all my dealings with them I have met with nothing but civility and a wish to do whatever they could to please me.

You may tell them with my compliments, that such well-regulated behaviour comes from having such a man as yourself and brother at the head of affairs, and that as long as they take their copy from you they won't go far wrong.

Lastly I would congratulate you all, and each one in particular, on having completed this job without any serious accident, and for my own part it ought to be more than just a matter of congratulation, it ought to be a matter to thank God for. I dare say familiarity

A view of the newer buildings taken about 1900, which shows the progressive extensions from SH to the Old Pavilion. The section with the roof lights was the Covered Playground. The Old Pavilion with the Tuck Shop extension and the Billyard Workshops can be seen. Behind the Tuck Shop is the new Library and its bow window. Careful research could date the photo as two new windows are being inserted into the Chapel. The military figure addressing the group near the right is Sergeant Ayres ('Czar') in the Corps from 1909–29, who then ran the Tuck Shop until 1937.

Petergate unveiled, 1887. Windows open to dry out the plaster. Norman's dream of service to God's Glory.

An early OH group. A more interesting composition than the boring serried ranks of modern House photos!

Westlake in 1888. Mr and Mrs Rooper are surrounded by some rather hard-boiled looking boys. Rooper had a reputation for finding discipline difficult.

with danger breeds contempt – and there is not such recognition of God's care as there ought to be – but, when any bad accident does occur, do we not feel that we are nearer the danger than we allow ourselves to remember?

If you will I will take it kindly if you will wish from the bottom of your hearts that this house, which was begun in God's name, may long be continued to His honour, and that the boys who are brought up in it may grow to the glory of His name, which is my own great wish.

Yours very sincerely,

Geo. H. Norman.

And this brings us to the Chapel. When the foundation stone of the Horsdon buildings was laid by the Earl of Devon on OB Day 1880, the assembled throng repaired to the Old School and held a meeting to discuss the erection of a chapel, an issue first raised by the Revd T.U. Cross at the OB dinner the previous evening. Devon took the Chair and the Bishop of Exeter, Frederick Temple, proposed that:

… it is essential to the well-being of the School that due provision should speedily be made for the erection of a chapel as part of the School buildings.

The Chapel as a building site.

Chapel interior. Note the ornate pew ends, later removed by Gorton, also the organ with its painted pipes, played from the north side, and the newly built Victoria aisle.

The second resolution named a Committee made up of the Earl, the Bishop, the Headmaster, a Governor, F. Dunsford, and the Revds T.U. Cross and Owen, to prosecute the work. Cross and Francis became the Committee's Secretaries and they sent out letters asking for subscriptions. By the end of 1881 over £1500 had been subscribed and the Committee was confident enough to go ahead and accept Grater's estimate of £1627.11s.1d. In December 1882 the *Blundellian* reported that 'the Chapel is approaching completion, and will, we hear, be opened next term.' Small delays led that opening to be postponed until the Summer Term and it was consecrated on OB Day 1883. Such was the press to join the congregation that the service was by ticket only. In his sermon Temple said that nothing so affected the nature of a school's influence as a school chapel, where the boys would love a service which was their own, and would listen to teaching directly intended for, and especially suitable to, themselves. At schools where a chapel had long existed it became the life and spirit of a school, and it was to the Chapel that the thoughts of former pupils turned instinctively as to the real centre of the School.

Building the Chapel was not without problems. Subscriptions continued to be sought for a variety of purposes. Seating and heating cost a further £400. Various groups of well-wishers contributed stained-glass windows. The Balliol Scholars contributed one; another was from the Old Boys, the funds collected by the former Headmaster, J.B. 'Daddy' Hughes. The Peter Blundell Memorial window was almost entirely paid for by Cross. In 1900 Temple, now Archbishop of Canterbury, dedicated another window to OB Sailors and Soldiers. Generous gifts of furnishings were given by many staff. Norman gave a patten and bibles for the whole Chapel in memory of his wife, who died in 1892, Herring gave a window in memory of a boy who died at school and there are over 50 gifts of one kind and another recorded in the Chapel Minute Book by 1914. Although given later, the most interesting of these gifts must be the 'May Chalice', a silver cup of 1573 given by G.O. May, 1889–91.

The rapid growth of numbers made the original Chapel inadequate and the northern, or Victoria Aisle was dedicated in 1887. Work had started in Easter 1887 and was finished in time for Harvest Festival on 16 October at a cost of £800. Simultaneously, subscriptions had been sought for an organ, which was installed in the summer of 1888 and dedicated in September. Francis Herring had become in charge of School music and the Choir. In addition he ran the Tuck Shop, Games Club finances, the football (i.e. rugby), as well as a full teaching timetable. In 1892 a choir vestry room was built as a 'lean-to' against the west wall. A spire and pulpit followed as a memorial to T.U. Cross who died in 1892.

Francis Herring with the School Orchestra of 1911. Herring came in 1885 and retired in 1921; School concerts usually ended with 'Three Cheers for Mr Herring.' He and Rooper played half-back for Devon and, with his shock of ginger hair, he was known to the vulgar as 'Red Herring'. In the middle row, Norman (flute) and Tatum (violin) look tired: it had been a strenuous thirty years. In the rear, with moustache and trombone, is the great Exelby, School Porter, from 1906–41, and possessor of a wonderful voice.

Early drama. In the background the Cross memorial spire is being built.

The *Westminster Gazette* in a review of Public Schools in 1893, a sort of proto-league table, placed Blundell's 17th. The basis of the 'table' was the number of scholarships won in the previous seven years, a measure that took no notice of the size of the schools. If size had been taken into account Blundell's would have been 8th. The new School had 'arrived'.

In a report to the Governors in 1903, A.L. Francis estimated that staff had raised over £11,000 either from their own pockets or by organising fund-raising subscriptions. He was writing at a time of deep trial as numbers had fallen from a peak of over 270 to a trough in 1902 of under 200. Staff had accepted a five per cent cut in salaries, and old 'Daddy' Hughes had agreed to a cut in his pension from £200 to £150, the income from the South Devon property having fallen in these years of agricultural hardship from over £750 to under £500. In September 1902 the entry had been only 13 boys. In writing his report Francis made some telling points about the inadequacies of Tiverton as a place to which moneyed people might like to retire and live; a particular point was the extraordinarily poor stock of housing the Town had to offer, a situation that has not improved as field after field has been gobbled up by bungalows and unimaginatively designed estates. He referred to the lack of local amenities and opined that Blundell's prosperity must always depend on its rising above its local handicaps.

He reviewed the past. He pointed out the savage destruction wrought by the Judgement of 1847:

> It is hardly too much to say that, but for the personality of Mr Duckworth, the School, for all its past, would not have survived as a First-Grade foundation. At the time of my appointment, though the old Public School spirit survived, there was nothing material or tangible to embody that spirit. So depressing seemed the prospect of the foundation that the Headmaster first appointed by the Feoffees in 1874, after a brief survey, resigned what appeared to him a hopeless task without putting his hand to it.
>
> The stock-in-trade, if I may use the phrase, which came into my possession, consisted of a few pictures, a dozen volumes of classical books of reference and a register dating back only to the year 1770. The very building, hallowed as it was by grey antiquity, had been formally banned by all the medical men in the Town as standing on a site quite unsuitable for a Public School. Yet strangely enough a strong party in the Town in the face of this public condemnation deprecated any change on sentimental grounds.
>
> If the Governors were now to make a careful inspection of our New Buildings, room by room, they might well wonder at the change which so short a time has brought about... In addition to furnishing the School, the following sums have since been expended on

enlarging and completing its equipment, without any cost to the Governors:

Chapel and Fittings	£5540
Workshop and Fittings	£480
Gymnasium and Fittings	£750
Bath and Supply	£800
Fives Courts	£200
Pavilion	£450
Tuck Shop	£350
Levelling Playground [Big Field]	£330
Library and Day Boys' Rooms	£1500
Books	£500
Cups	£120
Museum and Rifle Corps	£100
TOTAL	£11,120

The total liability left on these accounts is £665.

In a later paragraph he referred to £20,000 as the costs incurred by himself and his Housemaster colleagues in building their houses. Luckily the fall in numbers was only temporary. By 1906 numbers moved above 250 and always stayed above that level. But the years since 1882 had been very hectic and Francis reminded the Governors that the strains had told:

> Some twenty years ago we had five boarding houses each in the charge of a young married man. It is sad to think what havoc has been made in our ranks by sickness and death. We lost Mr Cross and Mrs Norman to our deep regret, my own wife's health has for years made her unfit for an anxiety which only her courage enables her to bear at all. Mrs Rooper has quite broken down. And both Mr and Mrs Spring have both suffered seriously from the strain of this life.

In case modern readers are tempted to suggest that the staff of 1903 did not have the modern pressures of examinations, it is worth noting Francis' list of the exams which his colleagues had to prepare boys for: Classical, mathematical and history

An heroic crew: the Common Room in 1886–87. Front row: G.H. Norman, T.U. Cross, A.L. Francis, G.H. Spring, A. Bristowe, E.P. Rooper. Standing: F. Herring, W.H. David, J.M. Thornton, H.F. Tatum.

scholarships to Oxford and Cambridge; exams for special scholarships, the Dyke, the Huish Responsions at Oxford and the 'Little Go' at Cambridge; exams for Woolwich, Sandhurst and the Indian Police; Naval Clerkships and Cadetships; preliminary Examinations for Law, Medicine, School of Mines, Banks, Societies of Architects and Chartered Accountants. There was no bursary. Each Housemaster did his own accounting and Francis held the central accounts for tuition fees and paid the assistant staff, sometimes, in years of deficit, from his own pocket. Rooper supervised the building repairs with some help from a new Science Master, E.G. Peirce.

It was an heroic crew. We shall not see their like again. They put up their own money and they deserved their reward. Francis' salary was only £200 p.a.; the rest of his emolument was in the form of a capitation grant. In 1881 his income was only £561, in 1887 he received his £200 and £1047 capitation money, in 1892 his capitation money had risen to £1151. The figures were similar in 1897, but in 1902 his capitation money had fallen to £697 and the School was heavily overdrawn at the bank. By 1907 the School was again in surplus and Francis' capitation money was again over £1000 a year. By then the hard decision had been taken to sell off most of the historic South Devon estates in 1905 for £12,000. In the sad days for agriculture their rents had dwindled and there were better ways of using the money. 'Penera', a private house next to North Close, was purchased for £3600 for use as a Junior House. The Junior House had started at Redlands under Revd P. Hunt in 1899 and in 1906 his successor, the Chaplain C.G. Lowe, moved into Penera with 16 boys. Another important step had been to seek recognition as worthy of a Government Grant from the Board of Education within a scheme to encourage the development of science teaching in schools. In 1903 the first grant was received and by the outbreak of war the grant was worth over £550 p.a.

This Grant-aided status involved the School in regular inspections and from them we learn Francis' real stature. In 1908 the Inspectors wrote:

He has the faculty of gathering around him a staff of masters, who, like himself, have the welfare of the School most at heart, the result being that they have all been ready to put themselves to any trouble and to undertake any personal responsibility if the good of the School demanded it… The headmaster has been at the School for the past thirty-five years. What the School owes to him cannot be overestimated for in its present condition it is very largely his creation. It is during his tenure of office that the activities of the School have been so extended as to make Blundell's so well known today. The School as it is to-day is a splendid monument to a life of devotion on the part of its Headmaster.

He also had a national reputation as a man of wit and letters, a regular contributor to *Punch* and other magazines, hymn writer and man of many mots, as when in his London Club playing Bridge, a worse-for-wear oaf asked where the lavatory was, Francis replied, 'Along that corridor and the door marked 'Gentlemen', but don't let that put you off…'

But academically the School was not a one-man band. Francis Tatum, like his 'Chief', had been educated at Christ's Hospital. He was a Balliol Scholar and won the Ireland Prize, and was regarded as the best Classicist of his year. His recruitment in 1884 was a great coup for Francis. As Francis had taken a First Class degree at Jesus College, Cambridge, for over thirty years the Blundell's Classical VIth must have had arguably the best teaching team in England. They both retired together in 1917. Also arriving in 1884 was another remarkable teacher J.M. 'Joey' Thornton. Six years younger than Tatum, graduate of St Catherine's College, Cambridge, and 4th Wrangler, he began his career implausibly as Mathematical Lecturer to Newnham and Girton, a post somewhat wasted on a lifelong bachelor. He communicated his brilliance to a number of superb pupils. P.E. Marrack, 1892–1900, became a Senior Wrangler and Tatum's *annus mirabilis* was when Knox-Shaw, 4th Wrangler and later Master of Sidney Sussex, A.V. Hill, 3rd Wrangler and later Nobel Prize Winner, and J.R. Marrack First Class Degree in Natural Science, all went into residence at Cambridge together and all had university careers of the greatest distinction. In a loving tribute A.V. Hill tried to put his finger on 'Joey's genius'. He thought it was

A.L. Francis, 'The Chief'. 'What the School owes to him cannot be overestimated.'

Joey's hatred for carelessness, looseness and inexactitude of thought, diction or habit, which he saw as not only foolish and unprofitable, but also despicable and wrong. Joey Thornton died in harness in 1916, aged only fifty-seven, and left all his property, including his house, to the School. It is now a Girls' House, oddly fitting in with his Newnham and Girton days. What a fantastic 'top end' to a Staff Common Room that never numbered more than 15!

The facilities for games were so much better at Horsdon, and with over 200 pupils to choose teams from, it is not surprising that games flourished. The first printed *Blundellian* of early 1869 refers to a 'Football VI', so presumably one existed in the winter of 1868–69, but that is no reason to suppose that this was the first season of pseudo-rugby football at Old Blundell's. What is clear is that the first game played by OBs was in 1882.

In 1870 the School dropped its strange local rules and adopted the full rugby code of laws. When the *Blundellian* restarted in 1877, there was a fixture list of 16 First XV matches spread through the two Winter Terms, mostly against adult club sides. There was also a 2nd XV. In the Season of 1890–91 the First XV played 17 games and the schoolboy opponents were United Services College at Westward Ho!, Newton College at Newton Abbot, Allhallows, West Buckland and Queen's, Taunton, – the rest were Club sides, Tiverton, Wiveliscombe, South Molton, Torquay, Heavitree, Wellington, Heathcoat and Exeter Teachers' Training College. Twenty years later the fixture list was very much the same, though Clifton had joined it. When Newton College was in decline some scores were stratospheric, 146–0 in 1900 and 107–0 in 1899. Until the turn of the century staff often played in the first XV matches.

A peculiarity of the early seasons was that the team played nine forwards and three three-quarters. The first season when they played eight forwards and four three-quarters was 1895.

In the pre-war period Blundell's produced four England 'Internationals', R.S. Kindersley, 1868–73, C.H. Harper, 1889–95, T.S. Kelly, 1895–98, who was captain of England in 1908, and H.A. Archer, 1896–1903. Kindersley, Harper and A.D. Sloane 1892–1900, were Oxford Blues. H. Mainprice, 1895–1902, was the sole Cambridge Blue, playing for four years 1902–05, the last two as captain.

Rugger continued until halfway through the Lent Term, when it gave way to the Russell and athletics. The Russell, begun in 1877, was run every year until 1917, when it had to be cancelled due to an epidemic of 'Boche Pimples'. It remained as

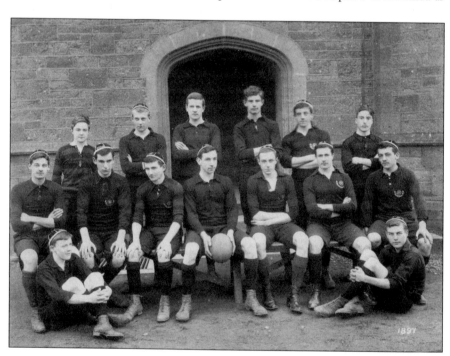

The XV of 1897–98. One of them is T.S. Kelly, who later captained England.

it had started an individual competition, into which individuals entered themselves; there was no 'compulsion'. In the 1890s the course became recognisably what it would remain until the 1990s, out to Pileywell, to Chevithorne and back along the Lowman. In 1894, as there were more boys in the School, a Junior Competition came into being and an Intermediate Competition was added in 1895. There was never any namby-pamby nonsense about calling it off because the Lowman was in flood. The 1913 Russell was described thus:

> *The runners were sent away in three divisions, the Open at 3.00 as usual, the Under 16 at 3.14 and the Under 14 at 3.30, and the wading or swimming of the river was watched by a crowd of interested and anxious spectators. The water rose a foot between 3 o'clock and 3.30, but ropes were stretched across the river and ready helpers were at hand in case of need, with the result that all got across in safety.*
>
> *Bad as were the conditions at Gornhay, they proved to be far worse at Crazelowman, where the Lowman had to be crossed four times by the Open and Under 16 runners. The mill at Crazelowman was not working and all the floodwater was diverted into the old river. It was a raging torrent that no one could jump or cross with impunity, and almost everyone was swept from his feet. Some tried swimming and some tried to abate the flood by swallowing it. Some, more wisely, followed the directions of our good friends the farmers, who had turned out to see the sport and to give help if wanted, for which, as well as their permission to use their lands, we owe them many thanks.*

The 'Open' in those days was genuinely 'open' and from 1907 to 1911 R.A Rendall won it every year of his School career.

Athletics followed the Russell and used up the last weeks of the Lent Term, which then ended in early April. Sports Day was usually in the last days of March. In 1884 the sports took place over two days and most of the old fun events had fallen away, though there was a 200 yards three-legged race, but that soon dropped out. Similarly, at the end of term, a Gymnastics Cup was competed for, in which entrants tackled the bars, rings and the horse. The best two gymnasts were entered for the National Gymnastics competition at Aldershot in June. R.S. Owen, who joined the staff in 1888 and retired in 1912, took over the gymnastics in 1895. Sgt. Leigh assisted with the training and between 1900 and 1912 the School gained one first, and four thirds.

There was some boxing but not enough for Norman Clark, 1907–11. In his autobiography he tells of bouts arranged by Bert Hughes, a Tiverton fishmonger and well-known sportsman, to provide Clark with extra practice before the Public Schools' Boxing Championships for which he was entered in 1910. One late evening in the Gym, long after lock-up, Hughes was refereeing a bout between Clark and a local fairground boxer called Sam McKeown; many boys had sneaked in to watch. In the middle of a round a tall figure entered and advanced into the pool of light:

> *… he was recognised to be none other than that of the Headmaster, the August 'F' himself! Paralysis ensued, and we waited for the heavens to fall. But, after glancing around, the 'Head' turned on his heel, and walked out as quietly as he had entered. The lights were extinguished and we all crept away with our tails between our legs. What was to happen to me now? Expulsion? Or twelve strokes of the birch? Or both? Every moment on the following day I expected the porter to bring the fatal summon. But none came. In the street, two days later, I met the 'Head' coming straight towards me. When within a couple of paces he stopped, looked down on me from his lordly height and heaved a half-sigh, 'Clark, Prizefighter,' and moved on.*

When Clark's anxious Mother wrote to Francis asking if it were safe for her wee lamb to box, Francis replied that 'judging from an exhibition I have been privileged to witness, I have more fears for his opponents than himself'. As Clark wrote:

> *It was difficult not to be conscious that in both scope and technical ability Francis was a cut above the ordinary type of Headmaster.*

The Summer Term belonged to cricket. A Games Committee resolution of 1885 stated that no one could play tennis if they were needed for cricket. By 1900 Big Field

The unbeaten XI of 1889. Won 7, drawn 3. The coach is Sgt Leigh.

C.T.A. Wilkinson, Blundell's and Surrey.

was level and one of the better wickets in Devon, the Old Pavilion was built and the limes were becoming statelier with every passing year. Blundell's staff have always been keen cricketers. The Chief himself took 8 wickets against the School in 1884 and 6 wickets the following year. Staff played in matches, but until about 1900 the captain of cricket ran the teams, assisted by a professional, Shaw, who did some coaching. The first member of staff to 'take' the 1st XI was the Revd O.F. Granlund, sometime after 1908. Fixtures were still controlled by the necessity of travelling everywhere by train, but the fixture list was abundant; as many as 25 games were played in the course of a term that would go from early May to the end of July, with no A-levels. And some games were of the two days, two innings, variety against touring sides like the 'Welsh Rabbits'. In 1909 the Rabbits scored 125, Blundell's replying with 225. The Rabbits reached 333 in their second innings, leaving 234 to be got in two and a half hours. The School won by three wickets. In these years the mule that pulled the roller was called 'Bendigo'.

The first unbeaten side was that of 1889, who, during the season scored 2613 runs, averaging over 27 runs per wicket. Their opponents scored 1323, average just over 9 per wicket. Two of the 1889 side, B.H. Drury and C.W. Brabant played for Devon while still at school. A third member of the 1889 side, C.J. Francis, later played for Gloucestershire. C.T.A. Wilkinson who was in the XI in 1902 and 1903 later captained Surrey, when Hobbs was in his prime, and played for the Gentlemen in the company of W.G. For the average Blundellian the exciting cricket of the term was the House Matches, timeless two-innings affairs in a knockout competition. In 1888 S.H. scored 593 in their only innings, with C.J. Francis, son of the Chief, scoring 282 and sharing in three century stands. They beat N.C. by an innings and 453 runs. In a similar game in 1919 Considine scored 343 for Westlake. More usually, the games were tense, nail-biting affairs. Their demise in recent years is a great loss.

Every Summer Term came to a June climax and a July climax, OB Day and Speech Day. Once the Chapel had been built it was no longer necessary to march to St Peter's, but the old custom of the Procession, which dated at least as far back as

Temple at OB Day 1882. On his right is Jack Russell. This was Russell's last OB Day; he died in 1883.

1725, was kept up every five years. The Commemoration Service was followed by a dinner and a concert, sometimes also a ball. Francis Herring created 'School Music' and the early concerts usually ended with 'Three Cheers for Mr Herring'. He also started the Chapel Choir and led the fund-raising for the organ, which was installed in 1905–06. An OB Society was started in 1891, the OBCC in 1892 and the 'London Dinner' came into being.

And then there were the special occasions. In October 1900, Frederick Temple, the Archbishop of Canterbury visited his old school. He brought with him his son, who would also become Archbishop of Canterbury and would also visit the School to meet Gorton, when his bishopric of Coventry was in the offing. 'Granite on fire' was how they described the old man. He was brought to School in a horse-drawn carriage for chapel at 10am, the newly formed Cadet Corps presented arms, and the procession, which included almost twenty OB clergy and the two chaplains, formed up and the service began. He preached on the effect of good and

On his way to preach a memorable sermon.

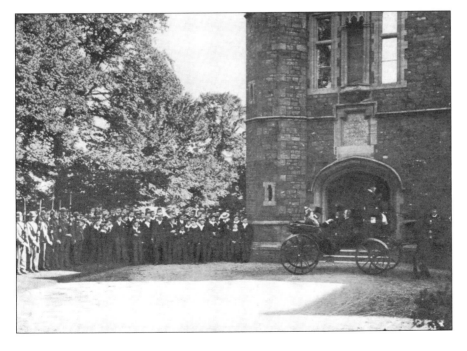

The Archbishop's arrival. The Corps presents arms.

The Tercentenary Invitation displaying High Victorian polish.

Gold Street en fête.

Francis and Spring lead the staff towards the arch, June 1904.

bad in a school community and he exhorted them to live lives that would bring honour to the school, to which he was proud to belong. The occasion moved him; one onlooker wrote:

> *I shall never forget the touching words of the end of his sermon; and to see the tears rolling down the rugged cheeks as he talked of days long past would have moved a heart of stone.*

His carriage then conveyed him townwards, followed by most of the School and the great man stopped at Old Blundell's to relive his experiences in 'The Ironing Box', to find his name carved on the wall and to relive his cricketing feats. Then on to the Town Hall to receive the Freedom of the Borough and make a very witty address of thanks. And so to Tiverton Station to catch the 12.57 to Exeter. A good morning's work for a seventy-nine-year-old.

But the grandest occasion was the Tercentenary in 1904. It was celebrated on Wednesday 29 June, beginning with the usual procession from the Old School to St Peter's. In addition to the staff, Governors and boys there were the Masters of Balliol and Sydney Sussex, the Bishop of Crediton and the Mayors of Tiverton, Exeter and South Molton. During the service the Chief's newly composed hymn 'Great Lord of wisdom, life and light' was sung. Three hundred Old Boys sat down to the dinner. A concert followed in the evening when the School was en fête with fairy lights and Chinese lanterns from the Tower. On the two successive evenings there were balls and there were three successive days of cricket. On 30 June the Old Boys played the Gentlemen of Devon, then followed a two-day match Past v Present. Most of the organisation had been done by the indefatigable Francis Herring.

It would be wrong to end an account of these years without touching on the contribution Blundellians made to the Empire. They were everywhere. In the years before 1904 many had gone to fight, and to die, in the Boer War and their memorial is on the north wall of the Chapel. They accompanied the columns into Southern Rhodesia, led troops against the Dyaks, accompanied the expedition into Tibet, administered large chunks of West and East Africa, and were to be found in Hong Kong and the Malay States. All eight Halifax brothers served in the Indian Civil Service, Police or Army. An Old Blundellian conquered large parts of Burma

The Boys enter St Peter's. Clare House in the background.

The Tercentenary Luncheon.

Outside the Palmerston.

This is OB Day 1912, but it shows how the Blundellians would have been dressed. Porter Exelby is leading. Our present Porter will head the 400th anniversary parade!

The tercentenary turnout of Old Boys.

Colonel W.P. Dicken, 1845–48, who did much to conquer Burma for the Empire.

and was inordinately proud of his achievements. The foremost expert on China and adviser to the British Forces in Peking was also an Old Blundellian. When wearing his 'showman's hat', the Chief often wondered if it was not the 'Blundell's Empire'.

In the early 1880s Francis had refounded the School at Horsden with a band of stalwarts, Spring of North Close, Cross, Rooper, Norman, Tatum, Thornton and Herring. Others had contributed and then left. Cross had died, but in 1910 they were all still in harness and rarely can a group of schoolmasters have looked back on such years of toil, but such years of achievement. Rooper and Spring soon retired. Norman retired in 1913 at fifty-eight. In 1914 Francis was sixty-six and had been Head for forty years; Tatum, Thornton and Herring were all either side of sixty and had been at the School for thirty years or more. Any thoughts of retirement had to be postponed; their last work would be to struggle through the dreadful years of war.

Envoi: the Chief and his men in 1909. Front Row: Norman, Rooper, Francis, Spring and Thornton. Middle Row: O.F Granlund (1907–35 Chaplain and Petergate), Herring, Tatum, Peirce, H.H Batterbee (1906–46 and thirty-two years Housemaster of OH), unknown. Back Row: On the left is C.G. Lowe (1903–25 Chaplain and founder of the Lowe Medals). The other three, along with the unidentified man end of middle row, are Paddison, Wheeler, Owen and Roberts.

BLUNDELL'S AND THE GREAT WAR

On 12 June 1915, the Governors' meeting minutes record that the following resolution was passed, moved by the Chairman (Mr John Coles) and seconded by the Mayor (Mr Gregory):

The Governors of Blundell's School desire to place on record their high appreciation of the patriotism and self-sacrifice of more than six hundred Blundellians who are now serving in the Naval and Military Forces of the Empire. They also desire to send their hearty congratulations to all those who have won such well-merited distinctions in that service and lastly to express their deep sympathy with the relatives of those Blundellians who have suffered or given up their lives for their country's sake.

And the response of Blundellians to the outbreak of war had fully merited that resolution of the Governors. The declaration of war had been the occasion of scenes of wild delirium in Tiverton, fully reported in the *Gazette*. There were meetings at the Electric Cinema where citizens not only joined up but also volunteered for rather futile duties in the Civic Guard to protect key points against possible attack by small raiding parties of Germans.

The Corps 1902. Our earliest photograph. On the path is Captain Clarke who was Clerk to the Governors 1888–1929. The other officers are E.G. Peirce, science teacher from 1899, Housemaster SH 1906–12, Spring's successor as Housemaster of North Close 1912–39, Bursar 1930–41 and later Governor 1948–70, when he died aged ninety-six. Behind Peirce is Lt Hooke 1901–03.

Bisley 1905. A very academic team. Seated in front of Peirce (third from left, back row), is Nobel Prize Winner A. V. Hill, DB 1900–05 (front row, third from left), and with glasses behind is T. Knox Shaw (back row, second from left), later Master of Sidney Sussex. Both Hill and Knox Shaw won the MC and Shaw also won the Belgian Croix de Guerre and was three times mentioned in dispatches. Farley, front left, also won the MC.

This enthusiasm to join the colours was not just engendered by the atmosphere of July and August 1914; Blundellians, and the class from which most of them had sprung, had for many years been preparing themselves for war. It is a complete myth that the outbreak of war in 1914 had caught people unprepared. The occasion, the murder of the Archduke Ferdinand at Sarajevo, may have been unexpected, both in itself and in its consequences, but war against the Central Powers had long been on people's minds. The Blundell's Officer Training Corps had been formed in 1900 and the Governors inspected it on parade in Big School, the present Library, in December, when it already consisted of two Officers, Captain Clarke and Lt Pierce, 6 NCOs and 100 Cadets, all in khaki and carrying Lee Matford rifles and fixed bayonets. In 1907 Lord Clifford inspected an OTC of 150 cadets.

There was a wide-ranging reorganisation of the Army in 1908, and Captain Peirce, as he now was, summed up the role of the OTC in the new frame of things. The Corps' aim was to get as many Cadets as possible through Cert A. To qualify a cadet had to be physically fit, be regular in parade attendance, to be proficient at musketry and to be present at an Annual General Inspection. He had to pass a written exam on the Drill Book and show proficiency in drilling a squad and a Company, to show ability in the tactical handling of a Section and to be able to care for his arms.

Peirce's pre-war attitude, which is relevant to illustrate why so many Blundellians and others endured the Somme, can be seen in a telling exchange of letters in consecutive editions of the *Blundellian*.

Sir, May I be permitted to encroach upon your valuable space, in order to suggest a means whereby the efficiency of the Corps might be improved? It was noticed last term that B Company, of which about 30 per cent were recruits, during the whole term went through only one company drill. The remaining parades were entirely made up of firing work or work in the Ailsa field. Surely it would be better to give recruits some experience in close order company drill before entering into more advanced work requiring great steadiness. Also would it not be advisable that the Sergeant Instructor should be allowed to put in more time with the junior company?
B COMPANY

(A very good suggestion, which we are sure will meet with approval if it comes to the notice of those in authority. – Ed.)

But Captain Peirce's riposte in the next issue, July 1912 was:
Sir, I was considerably surprised to read 'B Company's' letter in your last issue. I hear indirectly that the author is no longer a member of the Corps. If he were his letter could

only be regarded as a flagrant breach of discipline, which, in the "Service", would be punished with a severe sentence. But, as he has left the Corps, all I can do is to suggest to him that his letter is very bad form, is characterized by sheer ignorance and that the School Magazine is not the place to criticize the officers of the School Corps.
Yours truly, E.G. Peirce.

Whew! There are regular reports of the OTC going on camps and being inspected. The camps were usually at Aldershot or on Salisbury Plain and were treated very seriously by the powers that were. The 1910 camp at Aldershot was called the 'Public Schools Brigade Camp' and in the middle of the Summer Term Peirce penned a letter to all parents. Its first paragraphs covered administrative points, the dates (28 July to 6 August), the inclusive cost (£2.5s.) and that the cadets' luggage would go by goods train. The final paragraph went:

In conclusion I would point out the great importance to the State and to the School of the attendance of every available Cadet at camp. The School Cadet Corps are practically the backbone of the future citizen Army in that they are destined to supply the Officers, and the training of a Cadet is incomplete without attendance at camp.

In the term before they went to this camp the Blundell's OTC had paraded on May 20th to mark Edward VII's death, and the next day, as usual, on Big Field to celebrate 'Empire Day' when the contingent was addressed by Admiral Sir William Acland who asserted that 'every man has the duty to defend his country by keeping himself healthy and ready.' At the 1910 camp the Public School Brigade was inspected by Lord Kitchener and HRH the Duke of Connaught and visited by Field Marshall Lord Roberts of Kandahar.

Off to camp at Tidworth in 1909. An excellent view of the Billyard Workshops and the Cross Memorial Spire.

Lord Kitchener inspecting the Blundell's lines, Farnborough Camp 1910.

Keep this Card by You and Read it from Time to Time.

In joining your School Corps remember that you are of your own free will taking upon yourself a responsibility. By so doing you are privileged to wear the King's Uniform, and you must do your best to live up to the privilege.

The object of the School Corps is to help to make a man of you,—a man who can command and also obey. To be able to command you must first learn to obey, and that is what you have got to do in the School Corps. Accept the discipline because it is good for you ; obey the most junior N.C.O. as readily as the senior Officer : do not criticize your superiors : above all things do nothing that is "bad form" or ungentlemanly. Bear in mind that each action of yours, big or small, that should not have been done, is a falling off from your undertaking and a bad mark scored against the reputation of your School.

Wear your uniform as a sign that you have undertaken this responsibility. Your training will then do much towards making you a helpful and good citizen, will assist you in after life by strengthening your character, and will help to make you useful in case your country requires your services.

One of the greatest soldiers of to-day has said that there are five things essential to the making of a good soldier.

RELIGION.
PATRIOTISM.
EDUCATION.
PHYSICAL FITNESS.
PHYSICAL COURAGE.

Keep that saying before you.

GOD SAVE THE KING.

The OTC card to be kept beside you at all times.

Lord Roberts reappeared to inspect a Field Day organised jointly by Blundell's and Clifton at Lydford in 1912. Roberts followed this up with a letter to the *Blundellian*:

You boys are about to take your places in a larger life... I would like to remind you that you must never forget that you owe a duty to the Country and the Empire of which you are members.

You have had great advantages... What do you mean to give your country in return?... Your personal service is needed to persuade your fellow-countrymen of the great necessity there is for every able-bodied man being trained to defend his country in time of need... As you know some of our fellow-countrymen across the seas have already adopted this principle that it is the duty of every man to be trained in the use of arms; believe me, boys, you can give no greater service to your country than by doing your utmost to procure the adoption of the same noble principle in the Motherland.

Yours etc, Roberts, F.M.

This was the world and the Zeitgeist that led to the issuing of the card issued to all ranks of the OTC (see illustration), and when Lord Kitchener issued a 'letter' to all soldiers leaving for France in 1914 which ended:

Your duty cannot be done unless your health is sound. So keep constantly on your guard against any excesses. In this new experience you may find temptations both in wine and women. You must entirely resist both temptations, and, while treating all women with perfect courtesy, you should avoid any intimacy. Do your Duty bravely, Fear God, Honour the King.

In the 1913 camp the Blundell's OTC was inspected by General Rawlinson, whose tactics on the first day of the Somme would be responsible for many of their deaths. The 1914 camp was interrupted by the outbreak of the war itself. The young Lieutenant Hotblack, who had recently joined the staff was given a lift back to Tiverton by Captain Batterbee in his Ford 'Fliver' and later wrote:

All along the route people came out and cheered and waved Union Jacks and clapped and offered us food and drink. Little did they know what we were in for during the next four years.

In his peculiar way of being at once typical and prophetic the Chief had presciently summed up the mood of these frenetic pre-war years in an end-of-term sermon in December 1907. He took as his subject 'Peace and Good Will'.

When is thy reign of peace
And purity and love;
When shall all discord cease,
As in the realms above?

He commented on the contrast between the Christmas message and the lavish expenditure on armaments. (There had recently been a press campaign to build eight dreadnoughts, 'We want eight, and we won't wait!') Francis imagined this expenditure being put to peaceful purposes and ameliorating the lot of the poor:

Shall not the labourer still be robbed of the fair wages of the sweat of his brow... and end a weary life of unbroken toil, through a despised old age, leading to the barely decent ceremony of a pauper's burial.

He expressed a belief:

... that all the convulsions of the present age, when the whole fabric of society was tottering, may seem that the evil spirit, which has so long possessed the nations is rending them

The Officers in 1912. Batterbee was a Master from 1906–46 and Housemaster of Old House from 1912–46. Williamson taught here from 1911–12. E.G. Peirce, moustached, gave seventy-one years' service to the School.

for one last hour before yielding up his citadel to the blest abode of the Prince of Peace and Goodwill.

He looked forward to a 'Parliament of Man' and a 'World Federation'. Having been 'prophetic' Francis then lapsed into the 'typical':

> *For a nation that may be called upon to defend its hearths and homes there is no better training than Sport, when a man pits his strength and imperils his life against powerful animals in their chosen fastnesses. Many of our generals have learnt the arts of strategy and tactics in the deer forest. The splendid disaster of Balaclava was only possible to troops led by officers trained in the hunting field.*

In conclusion he returned to his earlier theme and ended:

> *Have any of you who live in London ever wandered down some gloomy side alley, reeking with stale abominations and tenanted by helpless beings who literally think in farthings? Upon some eyes the socialist ideal looms like a ghastly spectre. To others, and they are not always the most foolish, it shows the radiance of an angel's wing and wears the serene countenance of Christ Himself.*

An unusual man. Not surprisingly, 'his' schoolboys responded to the call for sacrifice.

E.S. Cameron, SH 1905–12, Head of School, killed at Ypres, April 1915.

G.M. Paddison, DB 1906–12, killed at Hooge, July 1915. Cameron and Paddison must stand for the 197 Blundellians who died in the Great War.

Monsieur Georges Letoré 1909–14. The most decorated member of staff: Croix de Guerre, MC, Croix de Guerre de Belgique.

The cost of the war to Blundell's in particular and the Nation as a whole can be seen in the names graven on the walls of the School. Blundellians served and died in all the great battles in France, in the Cameroons, German South West Africa and German East Africa, at Gallipoli and in Mesopotamia, in Thessalonika and with the White Armies in Russia. They charged on horses, they commanded some of the first tanks and they flew with the various Flying Corps.

Before the founding of the RFC, comparatively few served with the Navy. And the School remembered all of them, especially the dead, at first with gallant cheerfulness, later with a sense of that grim determination to be summed up in the words *Invictis Pax,* but always with the meticulous care of a mother for her children. Sometimes the 'mother' was fooled by wartime propaganda. In 1914 and 1915 the *Blundellian* quoted many of the letters commanding officers wrote to next of kin and in all of them it was said that his death was 'instantaneous' and soldiers were either wounded or died instantaneously. The great toll was of the under-thirties, and probably something like a quarter of the Blundellians who left the School after 1900 died. There were 19 NCOs in the OTC in January 1912 and the names of five of them are on the Memorial: Martin, Harding, Stevens, Baillie and Ball. Harding, P 1909–13, died of wounds in June 1915. Stevens, OH 1907–13, was killed in May 1915. Baillie was killed in October 1915. Ball, P 1907–12, was killed in July 1916 on the Somme. Martin, P 1908–12, was wounded in 1914, gassed in 1915 and killed in October 1916. They had all volunteered in the first days of war, all Lieutenants, except Martin, who was a Captain, and none older than twenty-two. Five of them won the Military Cross: Lindesay, Comins, Gracey, Liesching and Wiltshire, and Gracey won a 'Bar' to his MC. Of the remaining nine, two served in the RAMC and the remainder in Thessalonika, Palestine and Mesopotamia, escaping the carnage of the Western Front. They had all volunteered before the end of 1914.

Out of the tragic years still come to us flashing yelps of pain. A.L.Francis paid a special tribute to Griffith, perhaps the first Blundellian to die in the war, and who had given all the time he could spare from a job in the City to working with the Blundell's Mission at Rotherhithe in the East End. Another occurred when E.S. Cameron, JH and SH 1905–12, was killed at Ypres in April 1915. He had been captain of cricket and hockey and two years in the XV. As the Blundellian wrote:

> *There has been no finer head of the School. His character was marked by an unswerving honesty of purpose that made him in his latter days here a true leader and king of men. He held his views with unflinching courage, but could command the respect and confidence of those who differed from him. He was a sportsman and played the game in everything... In his old School his fame is secure: a great cricketer, a sterling football player, truly tolerant and yet fired by the highest convictions, he ever laboured for the welfare of his House and School. He has died as nobly as he lived, honoured by every Blundellian of his time, and beloved by those who knew him best.*

And there were the four Paddison brothers, sons of 'Pot' Paddison, who taught here from 1906 to 1926 and whose sister married O.F. Granlund, Chaplain and Housemaster of Petergate. The first to die, in July 1915, was Lt George Paddison, DB 1906–12, who, while at Balliol, had climbed the Martyrs' Memorial. He was leading his company to recapture trenches temporarily lost to the Germans. By one of the chances of war his older brother, Lt R.H. Paddison of the Royal Engineers was in the same sector and found the body, only to be seriously wounded when trying to arrange for its burial. In 1916 a third brother, Henry Paddison, who had only left the School in 1915, won the MC for bringing back a wounded comrade in broad daylight. The wounded man was said to have been 150 yards out in no man's land. Henry was twice wounded during 1916, returned to the trenches in May and was killed in August 1917. The youngest brother, survived as a prisoner of war.

Many, both dying and surviving, were rewarded by medals and citations. I will only mention one more, the most regularly decorated of them all, Monsieur Letoré, who taught French for some years before 1914. As the French army mobilised before the British he 'vanished' during the summer holidays of 1914, to reappear as an interpreter attached to the 9th Lancers, who conducted one of the few cavalry charges of the war at Mons, where he had a horse shot under him. Later at Le Cateau he rescued a supply column and prevented its capture by the advancing Germans, for which he was awarded the Croix de Guerre. He was awarded the Croix again in 1917 for rescuing civilians from villages under German bombardment, and for a final time in October 1918. He was also awarded the MC. Behind every name on the War Memorial is a tale of pain suffused with pride.

The war was something of a watershed in the School's history. Many of the younger staff soon went to war. Of the 15 who were on the staff in July 1914 Letoré, Wheeler, Birchall, Hotblack and Rebsch went immediately and Batterbee left in July 1916 when the Army began to accept older volunteers. When the War Office wrote to the School asking if there were any staff available for conscription Francis replied, 'None, they have all volunteered already'. Those who stayed had more to do. Letoré's replacement was notoriously unable to keep order. As always in grim times recourse was had to women, four of whom joined the staff at various times: Mrs Wynne, Miss Hill, Miss Fletcher and Miss Underwood. Miss Underwood served until 1925 and it was said that her discipline was 'that of the quarterdeck' and that she was 'too invaluable to be dispensed with'.

The strain began to tell on those who remained. Francis, born in January 1848, was over sixty-six when war began, having already been Headmaster for over forty years. In 1914, his wife already injured by a stroke, had had a leg amputated and was wheelchair-bound. It was time to retire, but impossible to do so when problems were falling so thick and fast, so with the rest of his loyal old guard he struggled on. The first to fall was a man of great distinction, but over ten years younger, the brilliant maths teacher and Housemaster of Old House, J.M. Thornton, who had served the School for thirty-two years and produced many scholars. In a tribute A.V. Hill recorded that one of Thornton's most scathing criticisms was, 'That's the sort of argument they produce on a political platform.' 'Joey' Thornton quite rightly regarded loose thought and imprecision as moral evils. He was only fifty-six.

In the Summer Term of 1917 the Chief himself had a mild stroke and had to resign. For some time he had been failing. A few months after the Chief resigned the Clerk to the Governors had to write in the following terms to a generous Old Boy, Mr May of New York, who had set up a fund for the sons of OBs who had died in the war 'the late Headmaster, on account of increasing age and debility had been losing power.' His fellow Classicist, Henry Tatum, who had come to the School in 1884 retired simultaneously. A gentle lovable man with a first-rate mind, he also had produced a long list of scholars. By January 1919 only eight had served all through the war from pre-war days.

Obviously the Governors needed to make a quick appointment to replace the Chief for September 1917 and E.G. Peirce was their obvious man. He had come to Blundell's in 1892, had successfully developed the teaching of science almost from scratch, had run the OTC for many years, was Housemaster of North Close, was de facto Bursar and manager of the buildings and estates, later to be Bursar de jure, Governor and Borough Councillor. He was a man who loved the School with a fierce, possessive flame. But he was too fierce, too hasty, and his colleagues told the Governors they would prefer to work under Wynne, who had only recently taken Thornton's place. At first Wynne's appointment was only temporary, but the Common Room's instinct was shown to be right when under Wynne the School prospered and his appointment was made permanent.

The last eighteen months of the war were grim. The blackout against non-existent Zeppelin raids was introduced in 1916; the boys had to work on the land in 1917 as extra harvesters to produce as much food as possible in rationed times. Boys likely to join the Army had daily OTC drill parades, which gave rise to one of the odder Common Room Meeting decisions 'that boys should not bring bayonets into classes when wearing uniform' (June 1917). In 1918 there was a large deficit in the Sanatorium accounts because of the Influenza pandemic. A total of 180 boys out of 320 caught the bug.

E.D. Bellew, VC (N.C. 1894–06).

Keeping the home fires burning, The Theatre Royal, Petergate 1916.

The original Cross of Eyam.
Photographed by David Japes.

But before the end there were glimpses of the coming peace. In one respect the war had been good to Blundell's in that parents saw it as being in a 'safe' area, and in 1918 numbers topped 300 for the first time. In 1918, on Old Boys' Day, the Chaplain, C.G. Lowe, read the names of the OBs who had died in the war and thoughts turned to starting a fund for a War Memorial. But its grip was not easily broken and the *Blundellian* of November 1918 was very gloomy. One of Blundell's brightest and best, Denys Garstin, a Russian expert who had served on the Western Front and then been posted to the British Embassy in Petrograd was reported lost. Sent to Moscow, after the Revolution he had struggled through the winter largely on foot to Archangel, joined the British forces there, captured an armoured car single-handed, but was so badly wounded doing so that he later died. Only twenty-eight, he was already a well-known author. Fusty Wynne's eldest son was killed in Mesopotamia two days before the Armistice.

But the war did come to an end and in the rejoicings there were some amusing anecdotes, none more so than those recounted by A.V. Hill, the President of OB Day 1919. During the war he had been involved in investigating anti-aircraft technology and had taken part in the tests that discovered the existence of the Jet Stream, so that if you forced a Zeppelin up to 20,000ft it would end up in the south of France. He recalled a lady of Camborne who had written to the War Office to suggest that they 'froze' the clouds and then put on them guns and even lions and tigers to destroy the airships. How to freeze them she 'left to the experts'. There was even a man who wrote in suggesting that the moon should be blacked out by putting smoked black glass over a powerful searchlight and directing that dark beam at the moon.

Meanwhile subscriptions poured in to the Memorial Fund. A design and a site were chosen, the former a replica of the Cross of Eyam. On 2 November 1920, the Cross was dedicated in a ceremony in which there seems to have been no jingoism, only a sense of gratitude to the fallen and sober reflection. Poppy Day had not yet 'started' and wreaths of bay and carnations were laid.

Invicti Pax. *Bay and carnations.*

WYNNE AND WALLACE

A. L. Francis had been Headmaster so long that no Governor had any experience of choosing a Headmaster. When the Chief resigned in the summer of 1917 it was a time of great national crisis: Russia was disintegrating, U Boats had reduced the country to the edge of surrender and the blood and mud of Passchendaele had begun. Peirce was the longest-serving Housemaster, Commanding Officer of the OTC, Head of Science, dominant figure on the Hospital Committee and in charge of the maintenance of the school buildings. He was forty-nine years old and must have seemed to the average Governor ideal to replace Francis. By contrast Wynne had only arrived in 1916, yet the Common Room, when consulted by the Governors, voted overwhelmingly to recommend that Wynne be appointed to fill the headmastership.

Naturally there were numerous tributes to the great man, headmaster for an incredible forty-three years. Curiously, he submitted two poems to the same issue of the *Blundellian* that recorded his departure. One was called 'The Mountain Peaks' which some might call 'Wordsworth and water', but some of it is odd, for example verse 6:

> Mid flowers untended I my bed have made,
> Through rhododendrons traced my verdant lane:
> Alone, alone with Nature communed,
> Bidding the desert spices turn my brain.

'Fusty' Wynne, 1917–1930.

The second poem is a love poem which claims to have been, but is not, a translation of Lamartine. It was about Spring's lovely daughter Victoria, much admired by generations of NC boys, and who later married one of the surviving NCOs of 1912, Kiernander. No other retiring Headmaster has so marked his departure!

Fusty must have spent the summer holidays in hard preparation as in the Chief's last years the School had been drifting. On the first day of the Michaelmas Term of 1917 he made an announcement of such importance that it was repeated in full in

Mr and Mrs Francis. Perhaps the last photograph taken of the Chief. Mrs Francis had had both legs amputated.

the *Blundellian*. He welcomed new members of staff, who included his niece Miss Fletcher, and Mr Bygrave, Day Boy Housemaster and Head of Science. Then he reorganised the School into the Lower, Middle and Upper Schools. The Lower were to follow a set programme with no options. The Upper School was also divided into three: the Classical VIth, Mathematical VIth and the Science VIth, who would spend 60 per cent of their time on their specialism, 20 per cent on a subsidiary subject and 20 per cent on a common study of English and German literature. Mornings were divided into four periods of forty-five minutes and afternoons into two periods of similar length:

> *Throughout the School there will be four periods of Swedish Drill a week. This will be part of the School routine and will be taken very seriously. The war has taught us that physical fitness is very important. There are many men, who, from physical unfitness have been prevented from serving their country. In connection with this I want you to reduce to a minimum your unfortunate habit of wearing your hands in your trouser pockets. It is no use our trying to make you upright in the morning if you spoil our effort in the afternoon... There are penalties for disobedience, and I intend to see that those penalties are enforced.*

He continued with praise of Francis' achievements and ended:

> *Blundell's needs no praise from me, its reputation is worldwide. Its future is in your hands. To you who have joined us for the first time Blundell's will be as a second mother. See to it that you are worthy sons.*

However, this is not quite what happened. 'Fusty' Wynne may have wanted to say all that, but he got no chance. A new boy remembered in the 1977 *Blundellian* that Wynne was slow-handclapped and could not be heard and the whole school was dismissed with 600 lines each, to be completed 'by tomorrow'. At a later concert Fusty and Mrs Wynne sang a duet and were booed. Not a good start.

In the meantime the Wynnes had to find somewhere to live. When Francis moved to Horsdon he lived in SH and then built himself the present headmaster's house, which was his property and where he lived until he died in 1925, and his widow continued there until she died in 1938. Only then did the Governors buy it as the proper residence for the headmaster. The Governors bought 'South View', Blundell's Avenue for the Wynnes. As they acquired the property largely thanks to Thornton, who left the School his entire estate it became known as 'Thornton

The Junior House 1912 with Lowe as Housemaster, outside the present GH. Notice the Eton collars. The boys were eleven–thirteen years old.

The Junior House as a holding house in 1926. The boys are all thirteen–fourteen years old, the Housemaster is T. Pearman Stevens, 1920–26. No more Eton collars.

House'. The next step was the reorganisation of the relationship between the School and the boarding houses. Rooper, who had built Westlake, had retired in 1910, but kept ownership of the house and surrounding land, approached the Governors in 1920, suggesting that they rent the house from him and in 1921 it was agreed to do so for £250 p.a. In 1922 an element of crisis was injected into the situation because of a panic about the drains. They had been surveyed in the Christmas holidays of 1922–23 and it was reported that they were in such a serious state that Sir Ian Heathcoat Amory, the Chairman of the Governors, had ordered immediate work to be done so that the boys could return safely. Rooper hurriedly offered to sell for £4000, but the Governors refused until they knew the extent of the drainage bill. Eventually £3750 was the price fixed. Similar horrors were found in SH, always owned by the Governors and £1606.1s.1d. was needed to remedy that situation. In North Close the problem of 'drains' was not so serious and in 1924 the Governors bought it from the Springs for £4800. The Housemasters of these two houses, Peirce and Hotblack, were still very much their own bosses and paid the School a rent of about £300 a year for the right to make their profit out of running 'boarding houses'. Petergate was bought from Granlund in the 1930s and Old House, for which Cross had leased land from the School, fell back to the School once again.

As numbers steadily rose towards 350 a new house was essential. At a time when money was much needed for other things the School benefited from the generosity of a long-standing Governor, Girdlestone, who bequeathed over £10,000 to the School, which was to provide the finance for a new boarding house. There was the usual series of muddled plans as the staff, Headmaster and Governors grappled with

The Common Room before Fusty's new appointments, so it is probably about 1920. Wynne is fourth from the left. Splendid chaps.

The 1926 extension and the War Memorial.

the pleasant problem of the rising numbers caused by the combination of the School's pre-eminent reputation in the West Country and the post-war boom. A holding house for 12 boys was developed at Cowley Lodge; in 1924 plans were seriously discussed that the Junior House, the present GH, should become a fully blown boarding house, but this got cross-threaded with plans to put the Hospital there. So in 1924 Wynne persuaded the Governors to build a new house on the Francis Field, a piece of land recently donated to the School by Sir Ian Amory, move the Hospital to the Junior House and develop the Hospital as classrooms. The latter idea was obviously daft, as the Hospital was so far away, and dropped. Naturally the move to build a new house was strongly opposed by many of the staff, who wrote to the Governors saying the money should be spent on a new assembly hall and classrooms. The Chairman courteously replied stating their letter had been filed.

A start to the building of the new house was made and it was completed in 1926 and opened with some ceremony by the Bishop of Exeter, Lord William Cecil. It had cost £16,498, complicated by the contractors going bankrupt halfway through the project. Vernon Clough was the first Housemaster after Mr Bygrave had been offered the tenancy, but refused it, and in January 1926 the Governors decided to name it Francis House in memory of the Chief, who had just died. The Junior or Waiting House was extinguished.

Naturally this change in the relationship of Housemasters to School, led to the School Hospital, hitherto self-financing from subscriptions by the boarding Housemasters, being taken into the orbit of the School. In the later 1920s it was doubled in size by extension westwards.

More classrooms were provided when the Junior House was closed and the neighbouring property 'Penera', the present Bursary and offices, was bought. The former Junior House became a residence for bachelor staff and six classrooms. Some credit for the efficiency of this building programme must be given to Capt. Dixon who had been appointed Estates Supremo after the war.

On OB Day in 1930 Lord Seymour, SH 1896–99, proposing the toast 'Floreat Schola Blundellina', summarised the expansions that had taken place under Wynne. They were F.H., tennis hard courts, six Fives courts, the doubling of the Hospital's capacity, the building of the Chapel's western extension, the conversion of Milestones into classrooms, the new workshops in Penera, the enlargement of the Tuck Shop, the improvements and enlargement of School House, Westlake and North Close, a new cricket pavilion and the Masters' Club Room in the upper storey

The first Francis House photograph in 1926. Vernon Clough, the first Housemaster, died in 1930 and was succeeded by W. Lewin, and T.R.K. Jones in 1936. Nice foreground! Clough's son, Tom, was Housemaster of Petergate in the 1960s and later Governor. FH Album

of the Old Pavilion. And there was more: two cottages had been built for the groundsman and Sergeant Major by Tidcombe railway bridge, Gornhay and Mayfield had been acquired and squash courts had been built. The Headmaster's study had been relocated from SH to next door to its present position. No slow handclaps this time; the toast was received with applause and the singing of 'For he's a jolly good fellow'.

Wynne had also made some lasting appointments. Bygrave went on until the later stages of the next war. 'Jazz' Hall was appointed as the first Director of Music in 1922 and astonished the world until his retirement in 1961. T.R.K. 'Jonah' Jones, Cambridge rugger Blue and both Wales and England Trialist, came the same year and retired in 1959. Ronnie Seldon came in 1924 and stayed full time until 1964, and part-time for five years longer. Ronnie was an Oxford soccer Blue, but had a brilliance at cricket, in one Devon Dumpling game scoring a century and taking all ten wickets. He ran the first XI and later Westlake. Michael 'Toefug' Thoseby came in 1925 and left in 1945 and he was Seldon's fellow opening bat in those interwar years when the staff had a proper fixture against the First XI and almost always won. The 'baby' of the gang was A.R. Benedict 'Bendy' Thomas, man of wide sympathy and great integrity, who was English Chess Champion for many years, who came in 1926 and retired in 1967. Other Wynne appointments were W.W. 'Worm' French, 1926–45, arguably the best Geography Teacher of his time, and Housemaster of Petergate. His especial 'chum' was K.G. Edwards, all round schoolmaster and Housemaster of SH, 1927–45. R.A. 'Pot' Abigail, Chaplain, wartime commandant of the Home Guard, producer with Stan Davis of brilliant shooting teams, and Housemaster of Milestones, was appointed in 1926. Like Thoseby, French and Edwards he was to be driven away by later storms.

A.R.B. Thomas, 1926–67.

As they came, others departed. Francis Herring, Pot Paddison, G.N. 'Mother' Ley, O.F. Granlund, 1907–35, and the Chaplain from 1903–25, C.G. Lowe. Lowe is still remembered as the man who affected the role of the Monitors at Blundell's, whose name is perpetuated in the Lowe Medals, still awarded to Monitors on their appointment. He was another of that Franciscan band who had gained a First Class degree in Classics and his sermon 'The New Monitorial System', preached in Chapel on 12 June 1904, should be compulsory reading for all those about to assume powers and responsibilities. It was dedicated to 'The Monitors of Blundell's in all sympathy with their high calling and its noblest ideals, and in the earnest hope that they may find in duty, not privilege, their truest service now, and through after years their happiest memories'. He was succeeded as Chaplain by Granlund, keen cricketer and Housemaster of Petergate, who told a good story of the opening of FH. Sir Ian Amory, Chairman of the Governors, had asked Granlund to ask the Bishop to bless the House, but not to make an address as Lord Fortescue had that honour. It was Speech Day and things started in Old Big School. The Bishop, dressed in glorious scarlet, led the Governors and Wynne to the stage and sat in the Chair of Honour, reserved for the speakers. Sir Ian and Fusty roamed the stage uncertainly and made their speeches from odd corners. The Bishop then rose and dismissed the assembled parents and boys, who went to the FH dog run, but the Bishop insisted that Granlund wait with him until a suitable amount of expectancy had built up. 'Let us move on now slowly, carry my staff, we will make our own procession'. So Chaplain and Bishop processed, gorgeously and slowly, between the lines of waiting notables. The Bishop struck the door with his staff, blessed the House in the name of the Trinity and gave an apt address. Lord Fortescue was seen to replace the silver key and tear up his address. OFG is immortalised in stone near the south door of the Chapel.

O.F. Granlund, 1907–35. A gargoyle on the Chapel extension, Granlund was also Housemaster of Petergate as well as Chaplain.

Fusty ran a tight ship. Bendy Thomas, who taught in the room above the Head's study, only had his appointment confirmed after Wynne noted that boys did not shuffle their feet in his classes. Snappy notices survive along the lines that 'All staff teaching first lesson shall attend Chapel', 'Staff will be punctual at the beginning and end of all lessons', and 'I want to impress on Masters the importance of getting good and honest work from every boy.' His presence in Chapel was described as 'august and frigid', but arguably Blundell's most efficient Head, certainly the first to have a telephone in his study.

The Governors searched for a successor. In 1928 and 1929 they carried out private soundings and by the end of 1929 they had informally decided to appoint Alexander Wallace, aged thirty-nine and already the Head of a Scottish school, in spite of spending all his twenties in the Indian Civil Service. His experience was four years as an Assistant Master at Wellington College before his Scottish headship. Having made their decision, but to meet the demands of the Charity Commissioners, the Governors went through the charade of advertising and interviewing and then appointed the man their 1929 minutes reveal they had first thought of. Wallace was the third consecutive layman to be appointed, but like Wynne and unlike Francis, he took Orders subsequently. Wallace only stayed ten terms, before accepting a higher-paid post at Sherborne. Interestingly, the reason one of his

A.R. Wallace, Headmaster 1930–33.

referees gave for his quitting the ICS was the pay cuts introduced after the war. Not since Cholmleigh's supposed mastership in the years before 1604 has a Head left voluntarily after so short a span. Smith and Jones had had shorter reigns, but theirs had been ended by death.

The Governors had less time to get themselves organised as Wallace only gave them two terms' notice and left in April 1934, so they delegated their task to three wise men: The Master of Balliol, Thomas Knox Shaw, Fellow, later Master, of Sidney Sussex and A.V. Hill, Fellow of Trinity and Nobel Prize Winner. Rarely can a vacant Public School headmastership have had such a distinguished appointment panel. By processes known only to themselves they chose the Revd Neville Vincent Gorton, a Sedbergh master, with a poor degree and a reputation for a disorganisation that approached chaos. It is doubtful if any normal Committee of Governors would have even shortlisted him.

An aerial photograph of unknown date. It is obviously after 1926 as the Chapel extension is built. Yendle's is still a market garden behind NC. What appear to be Fives courts can be seen against the north wall of the old Gym. The Billyard Workshop has an extension so that may have been the enlarged Tuck Shop. The Glebelands estate is still fields along the railway and the Corps Ground, the old 'lower bather' is a wilderness.

GORTY

Gorty arrived for the Summer Term of 1934 and left to become Bishop of Coventry in December 1942. He was at the School for only 25 terms, and one of them was spent on sabbatical at Yale, lecturing on Theology, yet his shadow is so long that his memory has dominated both school and Old Boys for fifty years.

Immediately, the staid columns of the *Blundellian* begin to fizz and crackle with life. In December 1934 the Editorial began:

Few Christmas Terms have witnessed changes such as have taken place during the last term, and even the most stolid of us have been swept off our feet.

Mentioned in particular were the new Friday Club and the Horticultural Society, and that all forms had once again changed their names and the 'Direct Method' of teaching encouraged, and Big School the present Library redecorated. The next issue in April 1935 began:

Perhaps one of the most significant features of the past few months is the spirit of expansion which has swept through the School. At no other period during the last ten years has the old saying 'Joy of Living' been so well fulfilled as it has in the first part of 1935.

Pat McElwee, 1934–63. Producer of open-air plays at the Tower 1935–39. His 1940 production of Dido and Aeneas in Big School (the current Library) was long remembered. He succeeded 'Pump' Batterbee in Old House for fifteen years, 1946–61. Apparently his favourite dish was porridge. On his left, not in academicals, is Willi Soukop, the Viennese sculptor.

From 1937 School photo

Neville Gorton, 1934–43, Bishop of Coventry. 'In matters of school routine he could not be called efficient,' wrote a Blundell's Master, and his secretary set up a file for papers rescued from the waste paper basket. 'He was as near a saint as anyone I have ever run across' was Lord Amory's opinion.

From 1937 School Photo

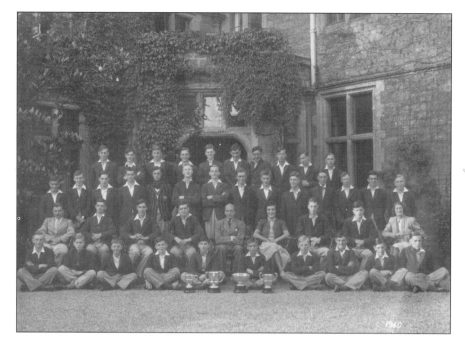

SH 1940. The Housemaster is K.G Edwards, a former Petergate boy, 1914–19, who joined the staff in 1927 and was Housemaster of SH from 1934 to 1945. He produced plays and was a close friend of the equally hairless W.W. French, next to whom he sat in the Choir. They were once described by 'Toefug' Thoseby as 'twin hairless cupolas of melody'. Fifth from left in the back row is Schidloff, later a noted violinist.

His most striking new appointment was David Ayerst, the *Manchester Guardian* journalist just expelled from Germany by the Nazis. He also appointed Pat McElwee and David Rickards. McElwee who left in 1963 was as disorganised and eccentric as Gorty himself, regularly getting lost on his rambling holidays in Europe. Before the war his great contribution was to school drama specialising in open-air plays in front of the Tower. In the summer of 1935 he produced a *Julius Caesar* with a cast of 124. (In the same term Jazz Hall carried a performance of Bach's B Minor Mass with 154 members of the Chorus and Orchestra.) In the remaining pre-war years McElwee put on open-air performances of *Twelfth Night, Murder in the Cathedral, Romeo and Juliet* and *The Taming of the Shrew*. In 1940 he and Jazz Hall put on Dido and Aeneas, but inside Big School. K.G. Edwards put on annual plays in December, and throughout the year Houses put on performances. Every winter season there were four or five subscription concerts, often bringing down such names as Moiseiwitsch and Solomon. Every year Hall put on a big choral event, interspersed with smaller concerts. About three times a term the Music Club met to entertain themselves with talks, recordings and performances. Until the Second World War plays and concerts spattered the firmament.

The 'Friday Club' was a joint creation of Gorton and Ayerst and it held its first meetings in the 1934 Autumn Term. All sixth-formers were members and, having heard a visiting speaker, they then went into a no-holds-barred discussion. Ten meetings took place in the first term on varied subjects, from 'India' to 'Hitler', from 'Unemployment' to 'The Jews in Post-war Europe'. In the following Easter Term political issues seem to have been left to the older Welt-Politik Group and the Friday Club had, among others, the BBC News Director, Eric Gill, W.H. Auden and Mr Burford a real-life miner. And of course in the Summer Term there were those performances of *Julius Caesar* and the B Minor Mass. The new Horticultural Society cleared land, planted fruit trees and learned how to propagate by grafting.

In the Autumn Term of 1935 there was more shaking up. Five Housemasters were persuaded to allow inter-house visiting and a year later the remaining two lowered their portcullises. Monday joined Wednesday and Saturday as a half-holiday so that there might be more time for extra-curricular activity. In 1936 French began his geographical expeditions and Blundellians might be found exploring the problems of Bristol or Tyneside. The first lesson of each day in the two lower years was set aside for supervised private reading. In 1936 games were made voluntary on Wednesdays to make more time for activities. The Science Society set about making a soil pH map of the area, visiting University College Exeter's science laboratories.

The Navvy Club set about the improvement and beautification of grounds and buildings. Drama, music, photography, wireless transmission and natural history flourished as never before. Hooray! One gets enthusiastic just researching Gorty's days! That cheerful duo French and Thoseby set up looms, and eight Petergate enthusiasts began making cushion covers, curtains, ties and an eleven-foot scarf.

To cope with the pace of change the *Blundellian* began coming out twice a term and to be written by boys for boys:

In the past reading the Blundellian *has too often meant searching for your own name in print. The idea is to make it look as little like an official publication and more like a magazine for the School to read and enjoy.*

Harvey Phillips developed sculpture in the workshops and in 1938 Lyons-Wilson, a much-respected artist, whose work has stood the test of time, lifted painting to new heights. But as the first issue of the new-look *Blundellian* pointed out, it was progress on a wide front:

The Workshop is the most interesting of all the School's varied activities. Its importance and its extent are all the more remarkable on account of its sudden development. Woodwork of course continues, but the most important part now is the new building [immediately behind the present bursary] *with the significant sign on the door 'Ceramics and Sculpture. Here the most important development has been the building of the kiln, where pots can be glazed and baked... Sculpture is also in full swing in stone and alabaster, and much fine work has been done. At the first Public Schools Art Exhibition held in London last September, great interest was aroused by the School's display, which included an excellent head in alabaster by Levi, a strongly masculine head by Frost and a horse's head by Kettle, – these last in Bath stone. The* Times *chose Frost's work for particular mention; the* Manchester Guardian *picked out the Blundell's exhibits for special praise and the* Listener *asked flatteringly, 'Why can't other schools do as well as Clifton and Blundell's?' Everywhere, in fact, the Workshop is running with great efficiency and further improvements and developments are always being seen or heard.*

W. Lyons-Wilson, 1938–68, a self-portrait. Inevitably nicknamed 'Lion's Willy', he was brought in by Gorton to improve art. A talented painter, he exhibited at the Royal Academy and his work continues to be appreciated.

The revolutionary Blundell's began to attract notice. Staff were invited to broadcast. Dakyns gave boxing commentaries, McElwee gave readings of Trollope; Ayerst and Gorton were frequently on the air. In 1937 the attention of the School was directed to the 'Condition of England'. The *Blundellian* of March 1937 stated:

It is time that we started to explore this hidden England. It is not enough to fraternise round a billiard table in the Mission. The visitor to the slums of Moorfields, [where the

The workshops in the present Bursary. This is post-war, but contains the young Bill Fisher and, at far right, the even younger Michael Mates, the Conservative MP.

The Blundell's Exhibits at the School Art Exhibition, South Kensington, 1936.

School had its mission], *who knows nothing of unemployment foolishly think that lazy people get a 'dole' for which he pays; who imagines that a bath is as natural a part of a house as a roof; who cannot imagine a school without a playing field or work without a holiday, such a visitor would return from Moorfields no better than if he had never left Blundell's. But his visit will have been worth while if he has discovered why people just like himself live in houses without bathrooms or send their sons to schools without playing fields and, which is equally important, how these things can and are being set right.*

The sixth-form was reorganised and three groups of eight boys were given a new programme. In some lessons and on activity half-holidays they would study and write about the problems. Out of school time they would investigate 'on the ground' in Bristol, where they would be supervised by Mervyn Stockwood, later one of the most inspiring Bishops of the century. Gorton's Group tackled the problems of Unemployment and Pensions; Ayerst's Group studied Housing; and Thoseby's Group investigated Schools and Public Health.

Gorton had plenty to say on Speech Day. The visitors had been round the various exhibitions and seen French's Survey Club work, which in 1939 was singled out for great praise in the *Times Educational Supplement* and French himself invited to address the Annual Conference of Geography Teachers; The Literary Society, The Sums Society under Bendy Thomas; the Horticultural Society, which was building a pigsty, later to be called the Pig Palace; The Radio Club showed its transmitter and the Photographic Society its snaps. Mr McElwee had just finished his open-air production of *Murder in the Cathedral*, General Fortune had praised the Corps to the skies and the first XV had beaten Sherborne, Clifton, Downside (twice), BRNC and Taunton. He ended his speech:

The schoolmaster in the old tradition doesn't believe he is doing his job unless, like the Ancient Mariner, he fixes 25 boys with a hypnotic eye while he whirls them through the sum of information he wishes to impart. I am wondering how much of the boys' energy is spent in resistance rather than in assimilation. I refuse, and I think the School is beginning to refuse to recognise the distinction between work in school and what is called work out... The modern world is all so much a muddle of inessential irrelevancies – telephones, cars, crowds. People haven't time to be themselves. All look alike and the motor-car face is worth observing as one of the most depressing of modern phenomena.

The guest speaker, Dr Lindsay, the Master of Balliol, supported him to the hilt:

The curse of all secondary education in the past has been that it was unreal. It is because I see the Headmaster here so successfully making these experiments, that I rejoice to come here.

Bowling	Overs.	Mdns.	Runs.	Wickets.	Average
B. A. Miller	158.1	42	409	56	7.30
D. Chapman	22	5	48	5	9.60
P. P. Bloy	129.1	21	436	43	10.14
A. A. K. Gifford	125.5	31	367	33	11.12
W. J. P. Olney	12.2	1	50	3	16.67
T. T. Cresswell	12	1	49	1	49.00

Also batted: G. J. C. Sumner 0, A. D. Symes 0, T. T. Cresswell 1, 3, B. S. Candy 2, 11, P. C. S. Chilton 10, 2*. R. C. M. Robinson played in one match but did not bat.

Also bowled: C. G. B. Gidley 10-0-23-0, A. D. Symes 5-0-17-0.

The 1938 Bowling Averages. The MCC were put out for 53, the Stragglers for 30, Balliol for 47, the Dumplings for 79 and the OBs for 101. Bloy played for Devon, Miller for the Young Amateurs v Young Professionals and Chapman for Young Kent Amateurs.

The 1940 Public Schools Sevens Winners. They beat UCS, St George's, Tonbridge, Stonyhurst, St Edward's Oxford and Dulwich. The team: Chapman, Penny, Hotblack, Thuillier, Mitchell, Baker and Lawson.

The Chapel before the alterations.

'Christ in blessing', a sculpture by Alain John, DB 1933–39. The most famous product of the Willi Soukop and Harry Phillips' Workshop.

Until the war the pace continued. The Monitorial system was recast with the emphasis ever more on service. House magazines were written. The 1937–38 rugger team was unbeaten against other schools and Ronnie Seldon always considered that the 1938 XI had the best bowling attack ever with Miller, Gifford and Bloy. There was a bewildering range of School societies and activities. The whole educational world knew that something wonderful was stirring in the West Country. Its modern visible trace is Alain John's statue of 'Christ in Blessing' on the Tower.

Given his faith and temperament it is not surprising that Gorty soon turned his attention to the Chapel. In the Chapel Minute Book the Chaplain, R.A. Abigail recorded events with elegant detachment:

During 1937 and 1938 the problem of improving the interior appearance of the Chapel was acute. The Headmaster was not alone in his opinion that the East End was too dark and too squat, and the glass unworthy: but it is easier to spot the trouble than to suggest a remedy. A multitude of counsellors propounded diverse remedies, and if all their advice had been taken the results would have been interesting.

There was naturally a strong body of opinion opposed to any change. They pointed out that panelling and other items had been given for a purpose, e.g. commemorating the departed. To this the iconoclasts retorted, with much justification, that 'the dead hand of the past should not be allowed to clog the channels of progress.'

In December 1937 E.G. Peirce, Housemaster of NC, Bursar and Clerk to the Governors, wrote a long and firm letter to Gorton protesting against any change on the ground that every inch of the Chapel was hallowed by the associations going back to 1882. The Governors tried to put on the breaks in January 1938 by allowing the Head to proceed only after consultation with staff and senior boys. They were too late as Gorton had already started by removing the pews nearest the altar, which as Abigail observed, resulted 'in an improvement in the spaciousness of the sanctuary with an acute shortage of seating accommodation.' In March the Headmaster came to the Governors with ideas and the Governors appointed a committee to meet the staff. Under the chairmanship of Derick Amory this meeting took place. It was laid down that nothing cranky should be allowed to disturb parents, boys or staff and that nothing should be done without a clear and known plan.

Abigail continued to record changes, but commented:

The conscientious historian must make certain comments:

1. *That nothing resembling a plan was ever prepared; and the rough sketches were subject to daily modification.*
2. *That it has ceased to be 'our' chapel and has become the Headmaster's chapel.*

The 'Gill' altar and the original cross.

Meanwhile, the new altar was being fashioned in the workshops, largely by the Art Master, Phillips, but with contributions from boys and descents by Gill, and an inlaid cross was being prepared for suspension above the altar, largely by Bill Fisher, but with help from boys. Abigail again:

> By the beginning of the war the new stone Communion table, designed by Eric Gill and executed by the boys, was in position. Above it hung a cross of inlaid wood also made by boys. The new sanctuary is not one about which it is possible to be indifferent: it has aroused, and will no doubt continue to arouse, the strongest expressions of approval and disapproval. About the same time new lighting was installed. This, although it gave the general impression of worshipping in an aquarium, produced the dim religious light which was necessary for the successful blacking out of the chapel during the hours of darkness.

More of this anon.

Gorton was an 'Appeaser' and like 80 per cent of the country thought Chamberlain had done a good job at Munich and said so in the *Blundellian* of November 1938. It fell to another Blundellian, Vernon Bartlett, 1906–09, journalist and broadcaster, to challenge the mood of Munich in a by-election at Bridgwater, then a rock-solid Tory seat. Standing as an Independent on an anti-Chamberlain ticket Bartlett dislodged the Tory, who was a relative of the Chairman of the Governors.

Bartlett, not Gorton was right; it was time to stand up to Hitler even at the risk of war. War when it did break out merely increased the pace of life at Blundell's and added an extra dimension to change as teachers came and went. The Headmaster used his connections to get some great men. Northcote Parkinson left in 1939 and was replaced as Head of History by Manning Clark, doyen of Australian historians, who sadly had to return to Australia after Dunkirk with his wife, who taught Modern Languages at the School. Stephen Spender taught here for a term and Professor Hooke, a theologian of world repute came in 1942 for a year. He dissolved into tears of merriment when asked by some academic groundling, who, poring over foot-notes, asked who this chap 'Ibid' was. Thereupon was founded an ephemeral society 'The Ibids'. A distinguished Teutonic refugee, Dr Honigmann from Heidelberg,

The altar, a longer view.

taught biology until he was interned. He organised an ingenious experiment to see if chicken could learn, which involved pasting corn to paper in triangles and circles, to see how well they could distinguish different shapes. Another distinguished academic, Dr Aufricht, as a Czech, lasted until 1945. More interesting to the average older adolescent was Miss Dawson, who definitely had 'it', slim, elegant, beautiful and known as 'the Pocket Venus'. Etheridge from FH stated that there was a queue at a knothole in the Bath fencing to watch her swimming and that the front desks of her class were always crowded, and her effect on the Common Room was likened to that of Zuleika Dobson's on Oxford.

An evacuated Dover College came for a space before disappearing towards Exeter.

An immediate problem was the loss of servants. Before 1939 there had been one servant to every five boys and boys had their beds made and shoes polished by servants as well as their studies cleaned. So a School Duties Scheme was drawn up with boys allotted to all sorts of jobs, from painting to grass cutting. In March 1940 fagging was abolished for the duration and all had to get stuck in. The Housemasters rapidly agreed that separate house dining-rooms were an impossibility and the Gym (the former Language Block) was adapted and called the 'Central Feeding Facility'. Much work was organised by the Horticultural Society in growing as much food as possible, geese were kept and the Pig Palace was always tenanted on a series of short lets. Every harvest, gangs of boys sallied forth to help local farmers, and that help and their attitude to work was much appreciated. By 1942 there was no petrol for mowing and the groundsman had to resort to the horse-drawn mower, last pulled ten years earlier by the much loved Bendigo.

The Corps doubled its number of parades from September 1939, but there was a different tempo after Dunkirk. R.S. Soames, then in the Upper VIth and in his last term, wrote:

> *My diary records that on a morning in May a Petergate boy got up early to work and switched on the seven o'clock news to hear that the Germans had invaded Holland. He*

Petergate 1940. The diarist, R.S. Soames is wearing glasses in the front row. The Housemaster is W.M. Thoseby, 1925–45. His articles in the Blundellian *were often even more beautifully written than the author's. I.G. Davies was Gorton's war winning weapon in the Battle of Crediton (Blundell's Home Guard v Regulars), when, disguised as a girl, he was sent in to chat up the enemy and discover their positions: middle row, second from the right.*

The Church and Blundell's Militant. The Blundell's Home Guard led by Chaplain Abigail. 'Come the four corners of the world in arms and we shall shock them!'

burst into 'A' dormitory to tell them the news. In the next few days we listened avidly to the wireless and were disgusted at its non-committal and frankly misleading statements. Finally, one day before Chapel the Headmaster warned us that only a miracle could save the BEF. On the six o'clock news after house matches, we learnt that Italy was fighting us, and in a discussion in No 2 Study we decided that we could give the ice-cream merchants hell... France fell and we discussed the news during a 2nd XI match; in the evening we went to a service of intercession in Chapel. And looking back, it was then that there came a transformation. We dug air-raid trenches at frantic speed in school time. Gas masks were taken to dormitories. The LDV was formed of boys over seventeen and, very self consciously wearing our tin hats, we rode to guard a post. We spent one afternoon a week at Chevithorne range. Every evening we put benches on Big Field to obstruct enemy landings. The LDV was called out one night and told that the invaders had come: we went to bed at one o'clock with our rifles beside us. The Headmaster refuted a rumour that we were to be evacuated to Canada. On the last night of term we were roughly awoken by a whistle, a crash, repeated three times. The Housemaster's cigarette glowed in the dormitory and we assured him we were none the worse.

The LDV soon became the Home Guard and the Blundell's unit was seventy strong, led with ferocious patriotism by the Chaplain. Each house took in it turn to fire watch from the Tower. Nightly in that dangerous summer, platoons guarded the factory or other 'vital' points. There was an emphasis on fitness and daily parades for Swedish Drill were introduced; total war came when boxing was made compulsory for all fourteen and fifteen-year-olds in 1941. Meanwhile, in fortnightly Field Days with other units of the Home Guard, Blundellians did their best to become a fighting force. Gorty himself was a Private in the Home Guard and was so inordinately pleased when he got a stripe that he gave the School a half-holiday. Visions come to us of that unmilitary figure marching back to School, the only one to have his bayonet 'fixed', but still scabbarded; the dashing Lt French defending Heathcoat's and striding through the factory brandishing a loaded revolver, terrifying the workers; of patrols scouring the golf course or Newte's Hill looking for the invader. One patrol arrested Sir John Amory and held him until someone could vouch for him. There

BLUNDELL'S SCHOOL
MUSIC CLUB
(1927—1943)

The 100th CONCERT
In BIG SCHOOL,
6.30 p.m., March 27th, 1943.

President:
Mr. J. W. E. Hall.
Secretary: Treasurer:
J. A. Reynolds.   J. E. S. Russell.
Committee:
P. N. Clancy, Mr. A. R. B. Thomas, Mr. A. Barton, Mrs. D. Hall.

Open Concert given to the School, Old Members and Visitors by all Members of the Club
and arranged by the Committee.

BLUNDELL'S SCHOOL
CONCERTS
1943—1944
IN BIG SCHOOL

LÉON GOOSSENS

Tuesday, October 12th, 1943,
at 5 p.m.

BLUNDELL'S SCHOOL
CONCERTS
1941 - 1942

MOISEIWITSCH

Saturday, September 27th, 1941, at 5 p.m.
IN BIG SCHOOL

'Jazz' Hall concert programmes during the war.

were even 'blitzkrieg' patrols, trained to dash out to Puddington or Uplowman in Housemasters' cars to deal with any parachuting Hun. A trench system was excavated to enable the Blundell's Home Guard to defend the 'Home Base' to the death. Eventually, on 3 December 1944 the Home Guard was stood down. All the local units joined together on Big Field for the final parade:

We represented a fairly good cross section of life. Next to us stood the men from the factory, and next to them the sturdy farmers from Witheridge, who had come in by bus, sturdy Chestertonian men, redolent of beef and ale, the spirit of England incarnate. Many of the uniformed men around us we knew well by sight, and it seemed absurd that they or we should be clad in uniform and equipped with lethal rifles. Looking around the field it was hard to realise that we were the army that stood between Germany and world domination. Nevertheless at this last parade we felt a justifiable sense of pride and awe. Well it's all over now; but another ghost has come to join Jack Russell, Peter Blundell and the rest – a ghost dressed in tin hat, camouflage net, battledress and gas mask, with a Sten in one hand and a sticky bomb in the other; and as you approach, he will peer from his hidey-hole and croak, "pass friend and all's well." And so it is, thanks to him!

The days of war, when the *Blundellian* reported the term's casualties on its front page, 13 in 1940, 19 in 1941, 35 in 1942, 17 in 1943 and 36 in 1944, did not dim the appetite of Gorton's Blundell's. McElwee had gone to the war, but Wilfred Hall continued to attract superb artists to his subscription concerts: Solomon, Peggy Ashcroft and Natasha Litvin, the Philharmonic harp trio, the London Pianoforte Quartet, Isolde Menges, Cyril Smith, and Moiseiwitsch. He continued his annual Choral Concerts, in 1941 the Messiah, which was particularly praised, in 1942 works by Parry and Purcell and in 1944 Mozart's Requiem. A key performer was Exelby, the Porter, who had a marvellous tenor voice. And it was business as usual for the Music Club. K.G. Edwards, in spite of being Housemaster of SH and an Officer in the Corps, seems to have produced a play almost termly. And then he would ask sixth-formers to join him of an evening in SH where the guests might be Stephen Spender and C. Day Lewis! Occasionally it all got too much, especially on one occasion when a concert had been arranged for the evening after the Russell. Aldridge of OH 1936–41, described the artist as 'an appalling soprano who made the most excruciating noise for two hours'. On the following Monday a special assembly was called and Gorty told us that we had behaved admirably in difficult circumstances and so he was going to grant an extra half-holiday.

Aldridge's account of these days tells of those days from within. Parkinson, though brilliant, sneered and was lazy. His friend 'Basher' of NC was given 'twelve' for being found in possession of alcohol, cigarettes and a firearm simultaneously. Then there was 'Basher sailing in to Toefug Thoseby's Latin class and asking brightly, 'Where's that boozy old bastard, Toefug?' and Thoseby saying from an invisible position behind the blackboard 'Hear I am, boy!' Abigail, whose habits were 'eatin', beatin' and sleepin', was fat, and was called 'Pot'. Gorty was apt to invite chaps into Blundell House and forget where he had put his lighted cigarette, light up more and circle, talking, round the room with three or four of them on the go. Eventually, he would absent-mindedly put one of them into his pocket, which, of course, caught fire. As Aldridge said, 'He was a lovely man: kind, imaginative, full of ideas and sometimes more than a little mad.'

In December 1942 he left to become Bishop of Coventry, and the Governors appointed the youngest Headmaster since Francis, with a First in Mods and a First in Greats, experience at Rugby and recommended by William Temple: R.L. Roberts.

R.L. ROBERTS

R oberts had a First in Mods and Greats and had been a star turn teaching Classics at Rugby from 1934–40. After a brief spell in the R.A. and Coastal Defence he had become Chief Instructor in the War Office School of Education. He was only thirty-one years old when he arrived in May 1943 to take up the reins from 'Pump Batterbee', who had been in charge for the Spring Term.

Most of the Governors were probably relieved to see the back of Gorton. He had been far too daring for all but the likes of A.V. Hill, and they approved Roberts' whirlwind drive to return Blundell's to the ranks of the normal, organised Public School, and even his best friend would never have accused Gorton of the vice of 'organisation'. Roberts began by making termly in-depth reports to the Governors. By the end of 1943 he had reorganised and improved the salary scales and increased the pay of the Housemasters and defined conditions of service. He had introduced clear regulations for new pupil entrants based on known Common Entrance standards. He had insisted that a clear written book of School Rules be produced. He reported that not enough prep was being set, that he was planning to tighten up staff classroom performance as pupils were being treated more like undergraduates than

R.L. Roberts in the School photo of 1947 with , to his right, J.E. Lloyd Lewis, 'Jonah' Jones, A.R.B. Thomas, and to his left, Jazz Hall and Ronnie Seldon.

the sixth-formers with an average age of just over sixteen that they were. He had introduced monthly meetings with the Housemasters. He had curbed the incidence of, and established routines to control the use of, corporal punishment. He reported that the Oxbridge candidates were few and of low quality and declared his intention of recruiting staff with high qualifications.

In 1944 he announced that all pupils who stayed on would work for the Oxford and Cambridge Higher School Certificate (a more prestigious board than the one Gorton had used) and that the new two-year course would start being taught in September 1944. The two fifth-form years would do the O and C School Certificate and science teaching would be beefed up to ten periods a week. The two fourth-forms would be amalgamated to make one year group, which was now possible, as entry standards had improved. Each academic department would draw up a revised and accurate syllabus of teaching. In the aftermath of the Butler Education Act he persuaded the Governors to agree to the surrender of the Grant Aid status, which A.L. Francis had obtained in 1903. Oxbridge Awards, which in the 1930s had been thin – though in Gorton's last two years there had been 11 – now increased to eight in 1943–44, ten in 1944–45, four in 1945–46, and nine in 1946–47. So far so good; in many ways the Roberts' douche had been a necessary corrective to some of the dispersion of effort in the Gorton years, so that Roberts could end his report to the Governors for the Spring Term of 1947 with the following words:

> It is now four years since I assumed my appointment, and I am confident that a general progress report upon the School should indicate development which can only be described as remarkable in the organisation of school work, in academic successes, in the quality of the staff and their teaching, and in the discipline, manners and tone of the School. The credit for this is largely due to the really excellent work, which is now being done by an extremely able and loyal staff of Masters and to the very fine spirit of energetic co-operation displayed by the great majority of the boys. I have of late received constant and regular evidence of the unqualified support for the present policy and administration of the School from senior boys, Masters, parents and also, I am very glad to add, the Old Blundellians.

The Old Blundellians had been particularly pleased at a recent event. At the first OB Day after the War, on 29 June 1946, the School had retaken possession of Old Blundell's, thanks to a grant from the Goldsmiths' Livery Company, whose Warden was a prominent OB, Professor Hutton. The day had begun in the School Chapel, the Head, now a deacon, preaching eloquently on the text 'the Lord is my light and Salvation'. Making allusion to the importance of SOUND learning, he moved on to comment on the new Memorial to the 163 dead of the Second World War and how the Chapel was the link between the living and the dead. He quoted from a former Rugby Headmaster, Frederick Temple. The company moved on to Old

Handing over Old Blundell's at its repurchase in 1946. Sir John Amory (left), the Duke of Somerset, SH 1924–30, and the Headmaster, R.L. Roberts, 1943–47.

Blundell's, where Roberts, this young Welshman, now thirty-four, again took pride of place. He referred to the presence of Governors, Officials of the Goldsmiths Company, Old Boys and present pupils and continued:

On this unique occasion, the memories, associations and the romance of centuries are crystallised in one historic moment of time – I cannot but think that we are also encompassed about with a great cloud of witnesses who are indeed with us in spirit in this place today: Peter Blundell himself, the long line of Governors, Headmasters, Ushers and boys of more than 300 years, the Bishops, Generals, statesmen, scholars, men of every profession and calling, who have gone through these gates to serve God and King, country and people, in every corner of England and the Empire.

He continued in a similar vein for some time before calling upon the Chairman of the OB Club, the Duke of Somerset, who told how the matter had occurred: first a rumour in 1939 that the building was on the market, then fund-raising by writing to 12 of those City companies who had benefited from Blundell's will, and how the Goldsmiths had been so generous. Sir John Amory and Professor Hutton then spoke in practical vein.

Then the Luncheon and further speeches. The President of the Day compared Roberts to A.L. Francis. In reply Roberts made his third great oration of the day, and it was a brilliant paean in praise of the School, singling out Messrs Thomas, Seldon and Hall for particular praise. As he expounded in a further speech a month later on Speech Day, it had been a great year. Francis Clayton had produced *She Stoops to Conquer*, the first of his scintillating productions, Jazz Hall had performed Bach's Christmas Oratorio, Vaughan Williams' Christmas Carols Fantasia and Britten's Ceremony of Carols, and the Ashburton Shield had been won for the first time ever

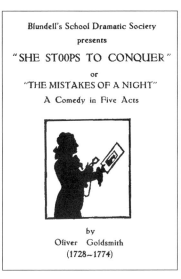

The Stoops to Conquer, *Clayton's first play, 1946. The production was successful in every way except financially – there was a deficit of £8.*

The 'Ashburton' won. *This was Abigail's last term. Stan Davis had a long and distinguished career. He came in 1938 but left for the war in 1939. After a Japanese PoW camp he returned in 1946 and retired in 1967. He, and Jazz Hall, had the distinction of being awarded MBEs while working at Blundell's.*
Standing, left to right: *Major Abigail, P. Tibbitt, W. Wood, A. Byrne, B. Burns, J. Williams, RSM Davis.*
Seated: *J. Fraser, J. Chick, G. Smith, M. Sole, C. Heath, A. MacIntyre.*

by the Shooting Team. Moreover the Chapel Trustees had just agreed to the removal of the cranky furniture in the east end of the Chapel. He emphasised yet again his belief in the twin principles of sound learning and good discipline. Maybe he had weathered the storm that any dynamic reformer finds when he takes over from a much-loved figure. And whatever Gorty's faults or disorganisations he had been loveable, and, of course older and wiser.

A storm had brewed up as early as October 1944. The staff called themselves together for a private meeting as the bullying of the Headmaster had become unbearable. Enraged, Roberts threatened some of them, such as K.G. Edwards, with dismissal. The staff then wrote a joint letter to the Governors, who had a special

The XI of 1945. The captain, R.J. Morris scored over 500 runs and took 43 wickets at an average of 7. He won a Cambridge Blue. E.R. Crowe is seated front left.

meeting on 7 November to discuss the matter and to meet H.H. Batterbee, the Second Master. They unanimously passed four Resolutions, the main three being:

The Governors express their complete confidence in the Headmaster and refuse to accept his resignation.

The Governors strongly deprecate the terms of the joint letter, dated 20 October 1944 received from the Assistant Masters

The Governors have authorised the Headmaster to make certain changes in the staff.

Professor Hooke had already been sent on his way; W.W. French, the geographer superb, left in March 1945 to become an Inspector; K.G. Edwards, producer of plays, left at the same time to join the Old Vic; Miss Dawson, the Pocket Venus, left, as did Willie Soukop, the great sculptor. A.R.B. Thomas offered his resignation, but Roberts managed to persuade him to stay on. 'Toefug' Thoseby left at the end of the summer to become Headmaster of St Edmund's Canterbury, in company with four others. Chaplain Abigail was driven out at the end of the Summer Term in 1946, immediately after his great success at Bisley. It was not all net loss; in their stead came Ted Chanter, Neddie Clayton, Donald Beatty, W.P. Brook-Smith, Lloyd-Lewis and Burton. 'Jonah' Jones and Pat McElwee, and Rickards returned from the wars. It was still a very able Common Room, but it was the manner of the change that had been so hurtful.

Roberts was deeply admired as a teacher by many of his pupils, but rarely can a Head not only have so lacked the ability to inspire affection but also to have inspired such dislike among his subordinates. He was a driver not a leader, as the Monitors' Record Book shows (a Book written up termly by the Head of School and passed from one Head of School to another). It records Roberts' desire to strengthen discipline, have more roll calls and to set the Monitors almost inhuman standards of 'Duty'. (One of his calls to action had the amusing result that Ted Crowe was caught

Ted Chanter, 1945–76. Head of Physics, Head of Science, Housemaster of Milestones 1946–58 and of SH 1958–71 and Second Master. Formidable, in any language.

School photo 1949.

smoking in a Halberton tea shop and given 'six'.) In 1944 one of the shrewdest of Head Boys, Bullard, wrote that Roberts was determined to attack the old spirit, but that 'Gortonians' would be more loyal to their principles and to the School than to the Head. Another, explaining some incident of rowdy behaviour, noted 'The Headmaster was away and that automatically means a general uplift of spirit.' When trying to insist on extra roll calls the Head exploded when one Monitor observed that it would infringe freedom. In 1946 there was a general consensus that as little would be told him as possible 'for the Headmaster's reactions are sometimes drastic.' The Head is shown as definitely imbued with an evangelical dread of sin, always on the alert for signs of homosexual behaviour, which in an all-male, largely boarding

A.R.B. Thomas, the FH Monitors (Richards, Taylor, Lyon-Maris J, Rattray and Lyon-Maris D) of 1947, House Tutor Mr MacIlwaine, and Matron.

The 'restored' Chapel. The 'Gill' altar was rescued and taken to a home for 'fallen women' in Coventry.

school, an environment where sentimental and harmless relationships abound, was chasing mirages, but also on occasion resulted in expelling vulnerable souls.

But he might have survived if he had been an older, wiser man and have grown into a great Headmaster, worthy of that comparison with the Chief. In 1945 he had been only thirty-four, when he appointed Pat McIlwaine to the staff. At that time he was only too conscious that he was fighting evil. He became friendly with Mrs McIlwaine, who managed to convince him that Abigail celebrated Black Masses in the Chapel, and that she was sadly mistreated. This was at the time when Roberts removed the cross and burnt it and restored the chancel, removing the altar, and carried out a service of exorcism. He took Mrs McIlwaine into Blundell House and in the subsequent divorce case, during which Mrs McIlwaine retracted all her accusations against her husband, the Headmaster appeared with Mrs McIlwaine and the Chaplain with Mr McIlwaine. The end came from an oblique direction. Roberts was due to be ordained priest in a few months, but there were protests from those who were appalled at his violent behaviour. The Archbishop of Canterbury came down to investigate, was also appalled, and postponed the ordination. This was an issue that conservative, upright Governors could understand. On 9 April 1947 they called another Special Meeting and passed a confused motion to the effect that, if Roberts promised nevermore to visit Mrs McIlwaine, he could stay on, but, if not, would he please leave at the end of the Summer Term. No official record exists as to Roberts' reply, but in their May meeting the Governors heard a statement from the Headmaster, who tendered his resignation. They accepted it with effect from December 1947. He was only thirty-six.

The War Memorial 1939–45.

15

MODERN TIMES

In their different ways the old Headmasters had had a great impact and those who had stayed long enough and were loved or hated had nicknames: 'The Chief', 'Fusty', 'Gorty' and 'Bloody Bob'. The old-style Head had taught the sixth form and, if he had the personality to do so, had dominated the life of a School which then had very few specialist teachers. Provided he had a mathematical brain and knew a bit of science he could have some insight into what was going on in every classroom. There may have been a plethora of different exams, but the scope of the work was comprehensible by one brain. But soon after the war had ended O-levels and A-levels replaced School Certificates. Until the mid-1960s the average Blundellian passed five O-levels and two A-levels; then the competitive explosion began. The burden on Headmasters has grown exponentially. Whereas Roberts was responsible

J.S. Carter, Headmaster 1948–59. His nickname was 'Clueless', but he wasn't. It derived from his habit of muttering White Rabbit-isms under his breath. Here he is striding out to celebrate the 350th Anniversary in 1954 with the almost seventy-year-old A.V. Hill and the almost ninety-year-old 'Fusty' Wynne.

Blundellian

for a boys' school of 350, the present Head is the centre of a constellation of three schools, ranging from crawlers in the crèche to eighteen-year-olds, who are legally, but incredibly, adults, offering 16 subjects at GCSE and probably as many at A-level and 4 A/S subjects. Central supervision and Robertsian domination is now quite impossible; the Blundell's of 2003 is a different animal from the School of 1945. In 1945, indeed as late as the 1960s, Monitors beat malefactors, and Headmasters and Housemasters did so until the 1980s. Now we have the Social Services and Childline. Even mothers have changed and become even more 'caring'.

When Carter came in January 1948 he had the fundamental asset that he was not R.L. Roberts. Like 'Fusty'Wynne he lived in the shadow of towering predecessors; like 'Fusty' he did good things without panache and was underestimated. There were serious problems to be faced. These were grim years when the level of food rations was actually lower than at any stage during the war, without the sense of exciting emergency to help the drab food go down. The transformation of the old Gymnasium into the 'Feeding Centre' had only emphasised the need for a new gym, and the fact that the Feeding Centre itself was not a lovely place meants that sooner or later a new dining hall would be needed. Numbers steadily increased from a low point of 346 in 1949 to 400 ten years later when Carter left. Removing the day boys from their rooms in the area of the present Registrars' Offices in 1936 across the road to Milestones (presently GH) had created some classroom space, but there was already urgent need for more and better teaching facilities, which the extra numbers exacerbated. Old Blundell's needed urgent work to repair the end nearest the Lowman, which had been sadly damaged by a fire in December 1941. All this was in a time when the economy was so stretched by post-war demands that building permission had to be sought from the Government, because building supplies were so scarce. Inevitably and sadly the Governors could not see their way both to finance the repairs necessary at Old Blundell's and to contemplate the necessary expansions at Horsdon, so in the early 1950s an arrangement was made with the National Trust and Old Blundell's was handed over to them.

In 1948 the Governors commissioned a report from Oswald Milne, a specialist in educational architecture. He listed the following as 'essential in order to keep the School up to modern standards': three or four new classrooms as the Library, Tuck Shop and the Masters' Smoking Room were being used for teaching. There should

The Gym is built, with the Archbishop of Canterbury, Geoffrey Fisher, in attendance.

THIS STONE WAS LAID BY
ON DERICK HEATHCOAT-A
THIRD JULY 1954

also be either a new dining-room or a new gymnasium. The third 'essential' was for more music practice rooms. Less urgent needs were listed as:

> ... a large assembly hall (Old Big School, the present Library, was much too small), exten-
> sions to the workshops and art rooms, then housed higgledy-piggledy in the area of the
> present Bursary, additional Fives courts and more laboratories.

In 1950 the Governors launched an appeal for £45,000 and out of this came the Gym, and the four classrooms of the History Block, both in operation by 1956, and an upgrading of the Feeding Centre. Interestingly, Milne suggested that the new classrooms should be built eastwards from the chemistry labs and connected to them with an arch through which traffic to SH would go. In 1956 work was begun on the physics labs, largely funded by a grant from the Industrial Fund and some firms, including Heathcoats.

To staff the new Gym, Carter appointed Stan Munday, 1954–78. He ran all the PT lessons, learnt to run Judo after the School doctors had declared boxing danger-ous, ran fencing and swimming and was to the fore in athletics. They need a whole department now to do what Stan did!

Milne also suggested that 'should further buildings become practical, such as a large hall, staff quarters, etc., they should be sited between Petergate and North Close'. Thinking about this had begun in the last years of Carter and an appeal for £100,000 was launched in 1961 for a dining hall, Big School with Music School, updating the Library (the present Staff Common Room) and enlarging the Chapel. In the less optimistic climate of the 1960s, the scheme got pruned to the Dining Hall, Big School and Music School. An attempt to tack a new hospital to the back of the kitchens, thereby releasing the Old Hospital for service as a new boarding house came to nothing. The Queen Mother opened these new buildings with panache in 1967. One day posterity may regard them as one of the best sets of

The Queen Mother opening the new buildings in 1967. Beside her is John Stanton, Headmaster 1959–71, and next to him the Chairman of Governors, Sir John Amory. The Consultant Architect was Raglan Squire, SH 1926–30, who was the son of the author, Sir John Squire, SH 1901–03.

Colin Beale, SH, 1925–30, Bursar 1953–77.

buildings to come out of the 1960s. The consultant architect was the OB, Raglan Squire.

Much of this remarkable achievement was due to those patriotic stalwarts who founded the Peter Blundell Society in 1951. It had been conceived by Knox-Shaw, its first Chairman was E.G. Peirce and strong supporters were Graham Yeatman, NC 1922–26, and Sir Dan Mason, OH 1925–28. Originally, it was open to all friends of the School and the minimum subscription was a guinea a year. Most members, taking advantage of the tax laws, covenanted their subscription, which, at the then rates of tax, meant that the guinea became £2. The whole purpose of the Society was to provide funds for 'the maintenance and extension of the school buildings' and the Society soon began to produce a reliable covenanted income, which could be used to service the large loans necessary to finance the Gym, History Block, Dining Hall and new Big School. The PBS also provided the four staff houses in Tidcombe Lane, 'Beaks' Row', which until so recently were such an invaluable adjunct to the School. Between 1954 and 1979 the PBS raised over £225,000.

Behind all this fund-raising lurked the eminence of Blundell's finances, Colin Beale. It is difficult adequately to praise Beale's tenure of the Bursary. A former pupil of SH from 1925–30 he was Bursar from 1953–77. His staff worshipped him, because he led from the front and cared for them. In a tribute to him by one who

Sir John Amory, Governor 1931–72, Chairman 1939–72.

Blundellian 1972

Derick, later Lord Amory, Governor 1926–39 and 1945–81, Chairman 1931–39 and 1972–81. With his brother, he was donator of the workshops and many other gifts. Here he is gamely leading the 1974 St Peter's Day procession with Clive Gimson, the last Headmaster to wear a mortarboard with conviction, and Chris Cuff, SH, Head of School.

Blundellian 1974.

Sir Ian Amory, Governor since 1973, amidst the 2001 Governors in their summer pomp. Sir Ian is next to the 'Church'. Sir Ian's mother, Lady Margaret Amory, was also a Governor.

Blundellian 2001

Sir John H. Heathcoat Amory, Governor 1861–1904 and Chairman 1888–1904.

Sir Ian Murray Heathcoat Amory, Governor 1898–1931, Chairman 1905–31. He gave Gornhay to the School, though at first it was called Macdonald's, the name of the Gornhay farmer of the time.

knew what he was talking about it was said, 'Colin made it his business to look after others, and never to do anything he would not do himself.' The author can remember John Pilkington and Colin rodding OH drains late on a rainy Saturday winter's night and repairing to the Club Room, reeking, in weatherproofs, looking for whisky. His staff, consisting of Bill Maple 1949–84, Doreen Gidley and Bette Dolling stayed for years, as did successive Porters, George Blair, John Pilkington and Brian Hacon.

Special mention too should be made of the great generosity of Sir John and Derick Amory. Both brothers had become Governors before the war, Derick in 1923, Sir John in 1931. Derick served as Chairman until the outbreak of war when Sir John took over and he served until his death in 1972. Then Derick, by now Lord Amory, having been Chancellor of the Exchequer and Governor-General of Canada, took up the reins again until his death in 1981. Those who attended any meeting which he chaired, left having witnessed art of the highest kind. That such a man with such gifts was prepared to serve as one of our Governors for fifty-eight years says a very great deal about him and not a little about the School. Lord Amory's father and grandfather had both been Chairmen before him in almost unbroken line since 1890. The family's generosity to Blundell's has known few bounds. They were always to the fore in any of the Subscriptions and Appeals in the last 125 years and special record must be made of their quiet generosity in providing Fives and Squash courts. In 1962 they gave Gornhay Farm to the School and that gift was valued at the then large sum of £50,000 for Stamp Duty. As splendid was the gift of the present work-shops in 1974. The family's connection with Blundell's continues through the presence of Sir Ian, their nephew, on the Governing Body.

The post-war School of 400 pupils had many successes, the most notable perhaps being connected with shooting. Between 1946 and the 1960 Blundell's was one of the most famous of shooting schools. Abigail saw the VIII win its first 'Ashburton' before his unfortunate departure in 1946, when W.P. Brooke-Smith, 1945–65, took over, but the key to the teams' successes was the presence of Stan Davis. Davis came to Blundell's in 1939, but was immediately called up. His coaching led to the winning of the Ashburton Shield and the Kinder Cup in 1946. Regularly the VIII

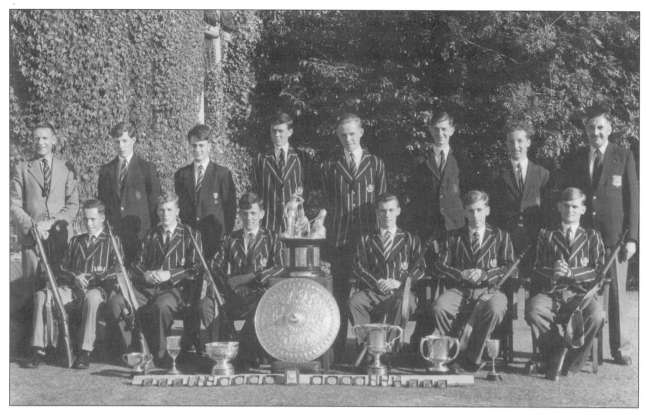

The successful 1956 shooting team. W.P. Brooke Smith, 1945–65, took over from Abigail. He said of Stan Davis, 'A great coach and a very fine man'.

The Chevithorne Range. The OB match of 1954. From left to right: C.W. White, P 1913–17, father and grandfather to many other Whites, J.A. Batten, SH 1953–57, B.H.B. Wrey, W 1953–58, and A.V. Hill, CH, OBE, FRS., DB 1900–05 and Governor 1919–44.

came high in the Earl Roberts' Trophy for the best school team in the Empire and almost invariably won the English Schools' section. The Bisley Grand Aggregate was won in 1952 and 1956 and the Ashburton again in 1956. Perhaps 1956 was Stan Davis' annus mirabilis as the team won the Ashburton, the Marling and the Grand Aggregate. The *Blundellian*:

> *Unfortunately examinations clashed with Bisley this year and two people, Maunder and Craig were compelled to remain behind. This left one place in the VIII to be filled. Keen competition arose for it and only on the eve of the Ashburton was it finally decided. Monday 23 July was spent practising and P.M. Jones (W) scored 34 out of 35 at 500 yards to win the Countess of Iveagh Cup. On Tuesday at 9.00 the first detail was on the firing point for the Snap and Rapid competition. Everyone shot up to expectation and we scored 474 out of 600, 5 points behind Whitgift. We knew then that we had a team that 'really had something' and we were determined to put everything into the Marling, which followed at 10.30. Our efforts proved successful and we produced our first record score of 362 out of 400, 14 points better than Cheltenham. With the encouragement of these fine scores we were determined to do our best on Ashburton Day, Wednesday. It was the splendid coaching and captaincy of J.M. Palmer, who himself scored a 'possible' at 200, which guided the VIII through the sweltering heat and tricky wind to win the most coveted of Public School Shooting Trophies, the Ashburton Shield. This produced our second record score, winning the Aggregate Trophy with 1467 out of 1700.*

This team included some notable shots. Both Bentata, FH 1951–56, and Wrey, W 1953–58, won Blues for shooting, and Wrey went on to shoot for England.

Of course even with such gifted coaches as 'Pot' Abigail, Brooke-Smith and Stan Davis, who was awarded the MBE in 1951, such successes did not come out of nowhere. In the aftermath of the Boer War shooting had taken off and before 1910 matches were shot against other schools and teams were sent to Bisley. Before the First World War the School was winning the Devon Shield, a competition for Devon schools and won it every year from 1906–14. Thanks to the nearness of the Chevithorne range the School continued to shoot and, in the 1920s had a very full fixture card. When he came in 1930 Abigail ran shooting with fanatical zeal and the VIII continued to win the Devon Shield. He was so keen that, when war put an end to Bisley, he started up a JTC Spring Championship in which 50 schools participated. After the glory days of the 1950s and the retirement of Stan in 1967, increased pressures on the Summer Term and the closure of the Chevithorne Range have led to the dwindling of shooting.

Davis was not the only Blundellian to win official recognition in this period; Jazz Hall was awarded the MBE in 1959 for services to music, and what 'services' they were too. He was not actually a musician, but one whose first commitment was teaching Classics to the Middle School. When he took over the direction of what school music there was from Francis Herring in 1921, Hall rapidly built up the Choir and the Orchestra so that they were capable of performing part of the St Matthew Passion in 1924 and Part 1 of the Messiah in 1926. The Bach B minor Mass in 1931 was his first full work, which he repeated in 1935, 1948 and 1961. A big choral work became almost an annual event and he performed the German Requiem, Mozart's Requiem, Dido and Aeneas, the Messiah, Bach's Christmas Oratorio, Fauré's Requiem, Vaughan Williams' Carols Fantasia, Britten's Ceremony of Carols and many Bach Cantatas and shorter works. In his last two years, 1960 and 1961, the Choir performed a fifteenth-century Mass in Bideford Church; the Missa Brevis by Palestrina; they had broadcast English, French and German carols on the BBC West of England Service; Part III of the Messiah and the Overture for St Cecilia's Day, and Bach's B Minor Mass, with repeat performances of the latter in Exeter Cathedral. This emphasis on choral work was an inevitable consequence of there being virtually no music practice rooms, although Miss Danvers Martin did wonders with the string players.

But that was not all. Hall had also started a very active Music Club, a Motet

'Jazz' Hall and the School broadcasting. Please help the author date this photo.

Choir and Subscription Concerts. The Music Club was founded in 1927, just after his marriage, when he moved to Hillands, where the club met two or three times a term. Programmes were drawn up by club members, boys or staff, who performed the music they had chosen. The last of Jazz's club meetings, the 210th, took place in the Summer Term of 1961. The Motet Choir was of such quality that it was called on to broadcast almost annually after 1945, and its zenith must have been going to Brussels in 1953 at the invitation of UNESCO to represent the musicianship of English Schools at the International Music Conference. In 1956 the Motet Choir flew to Darmstadt to demonstrate the English style of choral singing to Germany. The Subscription Concerts allowed Hall to use his wide contacts in the musical world to lure down a galaxy of great musicians: Solomon, Moseivich, Dame Myra Hess and Leon Goosens. In his penultimate year the Subscription Concerts were performed by musicians who had been taught by him: the violinist Peter Schildof with the Amadeus String Quartet, John Burden with the London Horn Trio, the pianist David Parkhouse and Peter Hurford, organist at St Albans Cathedral. And all achieved before the School had a proper Music School.

'Jazz' Hall and the Motet Choir, 1956.

Blundellian 1956.

The key to J.W.E. Hall's success was a streak of ruthlessness. He started an article on the subject of 'Music in Schools' in 1950 with the words:

A well-known Headmaster when asked whether there was any music in his school is said to have replied: 'No, the Music Master does not know how to fight.'

Readers who have experienced from the inside the self-confident pressure of the sports' fraternity will know what that mythical Head meant. Jazz knew how to fight his corner. Wallace told a story of how, from his study window he once saw Jazz Hall approaching up the drive, and so terrified was he of Jazz's bustling earnestness that he crouched down on the floor behind his desk until the daemon had passed on.

In these years of high musicianship, drama was not neglected. On the rather limited stage of Old Big School Francis Clayton put on many excellent productions. He started in 1947 with Shaw's *You Never Can Tell* and the Easter Term usually ended with a sparkler. Clayton never got stuck in a rut and he attempted Goldsmith, Sheridan, Shakespeare, Terence Rattigan, Dorothy Sayers and Ibsen, as well as running a Play Reading Society that met weekly, usually on a Monday in the Clayton home near Jazz Hall's in Hillands. In 1958 he succeeded Ted Chanter as Housemaster of Milestones and invigorated the house drama there. After 1960 others have carried on the tradition of the annual School Play, but none has done it for so many years and also kept such exemplary records. *Si monumentum requeris*, keep the files! All the stage sets were largely produced by 'Bill' Fisher, who must have given up a great deal of time beyond the call of duty.

Another area of excellence in the Carter years was science. A Natural History Society had existed in A.L. Francis' time and made scholarly collections of flora, fauna, lepidoptera, minerals and fossils, even forming a 'School Museum', whose contents, sadly, have been scattered. In 1947 the Science Society was reformed to meet on six to eight Sunday evenings in a winter 'season' to hear talks on scientific matters, either by members of the Society or by distinguished visitors. The Society was run by a particularly brilliant trio of science teachers, E.W. Chanter, 1945–76, W.H. 'Bunny' Dowdeswell, 1946–51, and Dr Ashby, 1945–58. Dowdeswell and Ashby started the Science Society's magazine, which carried on and developed the scholarly traditions of W.W. French's Survey Club of the 1930s. In May 1953 the *Blundellian* recorded:

The success of the current edition of the Science Magazine *may be judged from its reception in British Universities… While another University Lecturer concludes his letter: 'I should be pleased if you could include us in your distribution list. Your magazine is a shining example of what can be done in schools.' We have recently had enquiries for back-numbers of the magazine from research students at Glasgow University and the University of California.*

When Dowdeswell left for Winchester, Dr Ashby continued the magazine alone, until he too left in 1958. Not surprisingly Blundellians gained a remarkable number of Oxbridge Awards for Science in these post-war years. Geoffrey lucas, 1947–65, did just as well with the Classicists.

As would be expected in a vibrant School of 400 pupils, sport flourished. The rugby fixture list is almost entirely made up of games against 'bigger' schools such as Sherborne, Downside, Clifton and Cheltenham. Grahame Parker, an England cap, coached the XV, with assistance from T.R.K. 'Jonah' Jones who helped with the forwards.

As a result of the effectiveness with which Grahame Parker ran the rugby, many representative honours were won. Rugger Blues were won by G.L. Bullard, SH, at Oxford in 1950 and 1951, that year as captain, when he had N.A.H. Creese, W, in the side. P.W. Watson, SH, played in 1954 and 1955 and R.A.W. Sharp was in the XV for three years 1959–1961. The solitary Cambridge Blue was R.C.C. Thomas in 1949, but after Grahame Parker left to become Secretary of Gloucester Cricket Club, P.R. Price and T.M.R. Lintott won Cambridge Blues and C.P. Kent won a Blue at Oxford, before playing for England. Sharp also played many times for England between 1960 and 1967 and Thomas won 29 caps for Wales between 1949 and 1959.

Two brilliant post-war scientists who added flair to the Science Society's magazine:

Dr Ashby, 1945–56, now living in Winchester.

W.H. 'Bunny' Dowdeswell and family; the youngest is Colin who taught music at Blundell's, 1976–82, exactly the same length as his father's stint as a science teacher, 1945–51.

Graham Parker and Westlake 1963/4. Graham Parker, 1946–68, played rugger and cricket for Cambridge and rugger for England. OBs from his 'reign' over the XV included R.C.C. Thomas who captained Wales and R.A.W. Sharp, who captained England. But he was more than a rugger and cricket coach. He commanded the CCF and was awarded the OBE for his outstanding work. He was also Head of Geography.

Both captained their country. A memorable Commemoration Match to celebrate the Centenary of 'Football' at Blundell's was held in September 1968 when an Old Blundellian XV, which included many good club players, played a very distinguished XV collected by R.A.W. Sharp. It was an excellent game of rugby, but they had missed the centenary of the game at Blundell's by at least seven years as a manuscript copy of a *Blundellian* dated 1861 witnesses that 'Football' was played then. 1969 was a particularly good year, certainly Ted Crowe's best when ten games were won and only one lost on a tour after term had ended.

There were also some useful cricket XIs. R.J. Morris, W 1940–45, and F.J. Davis went on to play for Oxford and Cambridge and the latter played for Glamorgan, where his brother R.C. Davis, FH 1959–64, was a key player. The most successful teams, also largely coached by Grahame Parker, were those of 1956, 1960 and 1963 when eight matches were won in each year. An important event of these years was the expansion of OB cricket by Ted Crowe, who began Cricket Weeks in 1951, and has been organising them and a Midlands tour ever since. There was a brief burst of excellent tennis, always the Cinderella of Blundell's games in the mid-1950s, thanks to the coaching of Hugh Silk who was on the staff from 1952–58.

A 'relic' from that era is the presence in the present Common Room of Richard Giles, M 1950–55, whose housemaster was Ted Chanter, who imposed his personality on the House. His daily arrival after lunch to issue sides from a broom cupboard at the end of the passage was accompanied by the whispered frisson, 'He's coming' as he made his way up the dog run. His simple refusal to accept anything less than one's best in everything from work to the Russell led to a swift improvement in the numbers and reputation of the House. Anecdotes about him are legion, but it is striking how one so cordially detested by his charges became an object of veneration and even affection to many of his former pupils in later years. One of the best stories concerned a straw-haired new boy from Westlake who joined Ted's Junior Colts. When he received the ball he jinked his way to score under the posts. This happened

The XV of 1969. Played 11, won 10, lost 1. The team contained C.P. Kent, who captained Oxford and played for England and T.M.R. Lintott who won a Cambridge Blue. But there is so much hair that I cannot name them. An example of the importance of 'naming' all photographs as soon as they are taken!

Blundellian.

A period piece: The Common Room in 1960 with their dutiful and supportive wives. In white on the right is Viv Chanter.

The Revolution, September 1975: Clive Gimson, Headmaster 1971–81, and Arabella Ashworth the first girl!
Blundellian

A rose among thorns, Milestones 1976. Ashworth would later marry R.I.G. Whitehead (both highlighted). Next to Whitehead is David Park who taught from 1957–93. For many years he ran cross country and athletics and he developed Adventure Training in the CCF. An immensely loyal and hard-working colleague. In two years' time Milestones would have almost 100 boys.

a second time. After he had scored a third time EWC was heard to say 'Auxh, auxh! You'll never get away with this in big rugger you know.' It was Richard Sharp.

The 'You've Never Had It So Good' years eventually came to an end and the School entered a long tunnel of difficult years of change, the 1960s and 70s. These were the years of the great questionings: compulsory games, compulsory chapel, the Russell, corporal punishment, school uniform, compulsory CCF, single-sex education, and above all 'hair': everything was up for discussion and change. At Blundell's the debates were as fierce as anywhere else as the School was led by two headmasters, J.M. Stanton and A.C.S. Gimson, whose niceness and Christian characters made them less apt to deal with revolutionary situations. Part of the knack of being a great Headmaster is not to live in interesting times!

The sixties were a time of steadily declining numbers, from just over 400 in 1960 to 374 in 1970. This was disappointing considering the vast improvement in facilities that the new build of the 1954–67 period had produced. Stanton made a big effort to leave a full school to his successor and 402 were collected in 1971. The kernel of the School was its 340–350 boy boarders. These numbers fell to under 320 by 1980, a problem, as Bursars love boarders! The School's numbers slowly increased during the 1980s, but this was largely as a result of an explosion of day boys as Milestones mushroomed from 45 in 1970 to 98 in 1980. This was due to parents voting with their children's feet against the destruction of the Tiverton Grammar Schools and the coming of Comprehensive education. In 1974, largely under persuasion from the Common Room and parents who wanted to send daughters where they had already sent sons, Clive Gimson and the Governors took the decision to admit girls, but only in the sixth-form.

In retrospect, the admission of girls seems grudging and unplanned. Arabella Ashworth joined her brother at Blundell's in 1975, and for a year was the only girl in the School. Five others joined her in 1976, who were based in the top floor of Blundell House. For these two years they were nominally in Milestones under Robin Wellesley, who was coping manfully with the growth in day boy numbers as well and now had the responsibility for six girls and 76 boys. In 1977 the girls moved into Gorton House which Thornton, the confirmed bachelor, had bequeathed to the School in 1916, and Barry and Anne Wood became House Parents, relinquishing their home in Beaks' Row for Terry Barwell to come to revitalise the rugger. The girls stayed in Thornton's house until 1982, but, as their numbers grew, they found niches in staff houses and even in NC. The day boys, 45 in 1970, 60 in 1973, 70+ in 1975 and 98 in 1980, were coped with in old Milestones and then a sub-house was created in portakabins with David Park in charge. In Clive Gimson's last Summer Term, 1980, a 'house' event of great excitement occurred: North Close burnt down. Luckily, no one was hurt, but a lot of exam revision notes went up in flames, although one canny German pupil, Christian Engelhart, tipped a fireman to

The North Close Inferno, 8 June 1980. Dr Blake, 1973–87. was Housemaster and he and Geoff Clark his House Tutor did a great job picking up the pieces.

Colin Blake

John Patrick and the XI of 1973.
Seated: *Walker, Wright, Marks, Lloyds, Murrin.* Standing: *Forsythe, Vallance, Pridham, Coles, Cockram, Seymour.*

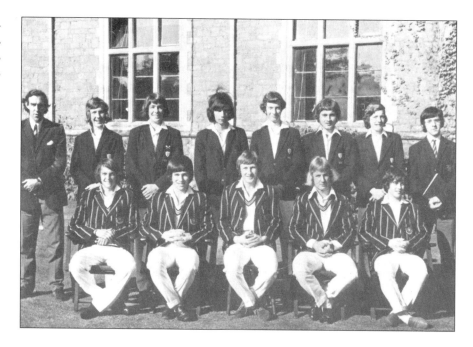

The 1970s was the age of the 'silly' House photo. This is the 'silliest' I could find: SH in 1980. The Housemaster in bandsman's hat is R.B. Richards, 1965–90. Alan Furse, 1971–2001, is the House Tutor. He was Head of Chemistry, Head of Science, Director of Studies, Housemaster of Petergate and a musical sailor.

Petergate being more sensible. The Housemaster is Derrick Denner, 1967–1996 who was also Head of English and driver of all matters cultural. There were in 1979 still six full boys' boarding houses.

go in and get his A-level revision notes out. Meanwhile, on the games fields the traditions of Grahame Parker and Ted Crowe were being ably continued by others. At the beginning of the 1970s John Patrick, 1965–75, produced some excellent cricketers and teams. He had a vigorous no-nonsense approach and minimal toleration of the asinine. His competence and fierce love of the game inspired Blundell's cricket, which had been in the doldrums in the later 1960s. In J.W. Lloyds and V.J. Marks, both exact contemporaries in FH from 1968–73, he had two stars, but they were merely the spearhead of a good all-round team. His early and sudden death was a great loss, as was the death a few years later of Chris Reichwald, Master from 1954–80. In many ways Reichwald was the personification of Blundell's sport, with his utterly inexhaustible appetite for sporting minutiae. His war record had been most distinguished, but had left him with a stiff limp, which did not stop him playing high-class Fives, squash and cricket. He was responsible for improving Fives at Blundell's and coached James McClachlan and Richard White to be Schools' Doubles Champions in 1959 and in two spells coaching the XI began the end-of-term Cricket Festival with Oundle, his old school, Uppingham and Ampleforth.

It was fitting that the headmastership of a man with such a Christian vision as Clive Gimson should be sealed with the consecration of the Lady Chapel.

THE TWO JONATHANS

The burning of North Close and the death of Chris Reichwald marked the end of an era. There were now no staff who had served in the war and only a handful who had done National Service.

Colin Blake, whose housemastering motto might have been *Ars est celare Artem*, supervised the rapid rebuilding of the house with improved accommodation, and North Close continued in its old ways for a few more years under Trevor Powells and Clive Hamilton. When Robin Wellesley moved to Westlake to take over from Nick Swarbrick, who was to concentrate on his duties as Second Master, it was obvious that something had to be done with the swollen numbers and in 1981 Gimson's successor, the young, dynamic and flamboyant John Rees, decided to create two day boy houses. Charles Noon would take half the day boys and the Milestones name to create a new house in part of the former Hospital and Peter Dickinson would recreate Thornton House in Thornton's old house with the other half. Barry and Sarah Wood collected up the girls and escorted them to the old Milestones, which

1983, the new Milestones on the site of the 'Hospital' built in the 1890s. Back row: *Barwell, Browning, Brook-Webb, Powney, Lobb, Hodson, Northwood, Gabriel, Giles, Paul, Patrick, Jones, Caskie, Empson.* Middle row: *Cavey, Varney, Japes, Granger, Tidball, Maunder, Barrow, Shipman, Mackie, Marshall, Hake, Conway, Valentine, Petticrew, Whitworth.* Seated: *Pinches, Barwell, Guest, Valentine, Tidball, Lockyer, Dr Brabban, C. Noon, D.J. Park, Whitehead, Chadwick, Halfacree, Caskie, Jones.* Ground: *White, Tidball, Martin, Batth, Kerr, Pinches, Roughton, Curtis, Brenchley, Webber, Glendinning, Barwell, Long.*

1983, the new TH. Peter Dickenson, 1964–97, was Housemaster of TH three times, the first when it was a holding house for thirteen-year-olds, the second when it was a sixth-form retreat, and the third as a full day house based in Joey Thornton's bequest. PDD was Head of Maths and a loyal contributor to Choir and Chapel. The two House Tutors are Rob Courtney, 1981–88, Head of Modern Languages and Derick Coulthard.

1983, the new GH, 44 sixth-form girls. Barry Wood, 1975–2002, taught chemistry and for many years was OC CCF. Tim Dyke became Head of English, editor of the Blundellian, *producer of plays. On the right-hand end of the front row wearing the 'illegal' stockings is Juliet Tricks, 1982–84, the first Head Girl, and one of at least three in this photo to marry other Blundellians.*

Old House 1983. P.J. Salter, Housemaster, with Mrs Salter to his right and Mrs Barwell, Matron, to his left. On the ends of that row are Paul Rivett, now Director of Studies, and Alaistair Deighton-Gibson with Chris Barton. Mike Coe, who married the first female Head of School, is behind Jerry Salter's left shoulder.

Westlake 1984. A useful photograph as it shows the slow decline of full-time 'boarding', only 39 boys. Robin Wellesley (1967–93) had been Commander of the CCF, Housemaster of Milestones and finally Westlake. To his right is R.F. Julier, 1968–91, Head of Art. To his left Mrs Wellesley, E.D. Fursdon, 1979–84, now Chairman of Governors, and T.J. Powles, 1981–96, later Housemaster of NC and Milestones. Until NC and TH became girls' houses, the girls were 'attached' to the boys' houses for music, drama and photos.

The unbeaten XI of 1981. E.D. Fursdon coach and Ernie Steele umpire. Standing: Beard, Dee-Shapland, Faye, McKinnel, Trafford, Taverner, Craze. Seated: Selley, Langdon, Hugh Morris, Watts, Eustace. Morris (Glamorgan and England) scored 953 runs, average 184.6, Selley and Langdon both scored over 500 runs and averaged over 40.

became the new and expanding Gorton House. There they truly became part of the school and 'history' was made when Juliet Tricks became the first girl 'Head of School' in 1984.

The other boarding houses continued in the even tenor of their ways. In Old House fifteen years of Ted Crowe merged imperceptibly into fifteen years of Jerry Salter. In Petergate Tom Clough had become Derek Denner and then Alan Furse. In Westlake Nick Swarbrick succeeded Grahame Parker and was himself followed by Robin Wellesley. In SH, Lloyd Lewis was followed by Ted Chanter, who was succeeded by Brian Richards and Peter Lanfear. After the long reign of Bendy Thomas, 1940–55, changes were more frequent in FH. First Hugh Silk then Chris Reichwald, 1958–73, who was followed by Chris Tomlinson and Paddy Armstrong. It seemed timeless and the boys' boarding houses were still recognisably those of Cross, Rooper, Norman and Spring. By the time they were appointed, the Housemasters, however radical their temperaments may have been, were steeped in the ethos of the place.

In retrospect the early Rees years were halcyon. Cricket results improved again when David Fursdon, 1979–84, took over. The core of his teams was Hugh Morris, W 1976–82, whose eight centuries for the XI is a record – so far. In his short time Fursdon produced two of the three unbeaten Cricket XIs in the School's history, 1981 and 1982, to accompany that of 1889. When he left he was 'irreplaceable' until Nick Folland arrived in 1990.

Terry Barwell's start with the XV had been inauspicious, but the new ideas and freshly original approach slowly but surely brought dividends, and progress was continued under Norman Ridgway. By the 1980s the XV's results were better than ever before: nine wins in 1982, 13 in 1983 and 11 in 1984, nine in 1986, and 11 in 1988 and 1989 and 13 in both 1990 and 1991. Arguably the best decade in the School's long rugby history was when the XV won 104 games and lost 40. The icing on the Barwell cake was the winning of the Rosslyn Park Sevens in 1982 in a period when Blundell's reached the quarter-finals in four years out of eight. In 1983 the Seven reached the finals again, losing by the narrowest of margins, 16–18.

Unbeaten cricket teams and good rugger was matched by a new zip. The Music department, first led by Paul Matthews, 1969–84, and Colin Dowdeswell, then by Andrew Barlow and Reg Thompson, began to hum. Paul Matthews set the department very high standards and instituted a House Music Competition that led

Winners of the 1981 Rosslyn Park Sevens. Team: P.G. Whitlock, R. Maltby, S.A. Watts, J. Massie, W.T. Carden. Kneeling: I.M. Brierley, R.J. Taverner, G. Watts. Also pictured are Cardinal Hume and T.I. Barwell.

to ferocious antagonistic artistry and who will forget his valedictory concert in the summer of 1984. In the late 1970s Colin Dowdeswell, 1976–82, collected together a small orchestra of enthusiastic young musicians, who took the name of 'The Camerata' and brightened up the musical year with a series of excellent concerts. Among a number of notable musical pupils, Graham Caskie shone at the piano, a product of his own ability and the teaching of Paul Matthews and Reg Thompson. Reg, a former distinguished Professor of Music, came to Blundell's as Paul left and possessed unusual skills as a performer, teacher and musicologist. His work with the more able pianists and in conducting chamber orchestras of the such pupils produced performances of the very highest standard. His gravitas as a conductor and his total absorption in the music will long be remembered. After his death in the summer of 2000, the depth of loyalty he had inspired in his former pupils was revealed when Caskie came to help fill the gap that Reg had left.

Part of the Reesian Blundell's was a deliberate policy of opening up to the outside world. He encouraged activity and in some terms a week's evenings might be taken up with Arts Week, Politics Week and Poetry Week and one wag managed to get 'Work Week' into the calendar. But these events did expose Blundellians to outer realities and a whole number of artists, poets and politicians descended on the school in the 1980s, including the infant Tony Blair. The event that hit local headlines was the visit of a deputation of miners, then picketing the Exmouth Docks during the Miners' Strike. John Rees strongly defended their right to address the sixth-form.

In the mid-1980s the Sports Hall was built and opened by Vic Marks in 1984. It enabled the School to explore a whole new range of sports including basketball, badminton and indoor hockey and football. To balance this extra sporting asset Christopher Ondaatje, P 1947–51, provided the funds for the single most generous gift since the foundation, 'Ondaatje Hall', which was built in the gap between the Music School and NC and opened in 1987. It contains a magnificent theatre, an Art School and well-proportioned surrounds, as well as two other classrooms. The new Art School allowed all of the Amory Workshop to be used for design technology. This was not the end of Ondaatje's munificence as he built and endowed the Blundell's Room at Taunton Cricket Ground, over which his friend Ted Crowe presides.

Another spectacular event of John Rees' time was the repossession of the Gorton altar. Since the Gortonian diaspora the altar had reposed in the chapel of a Home

Opening the New Sports Hall, October 1984.

Blundellian, December 1984

for Fallen Women at St Faith's, Coventry. Requests at the time of the celebration of the Chapel centenary in 1983 for its return had been refused, but the Trustees of St Faith's, realising that an altar with associations with Eric Gill was valuable, decided to sell it. The auctioneers, Phillips, informed the School of the sale and a group of OBs and well-wishers clubbed together to raise sufficient funds (over £30,000), and Gorton's son attended the auction and successfully acquired the altar, beating off the under-bidder, a Californian funeral parlour. After seeing the altar at St Faith's, the author described it as a 'jewel' and it is a matter of rejoicing that the 'jewel' is now in its rightful setting.

The purchase of the altar occurred in John Rees' last term. In his time the facilities of the boarding houses had been modernised and at last proper provision had been made for day boys. Sixth-form girls had been integrated into the School. Above all, things had happened and he had embedded into the School a sense of energy and a new confidence. But there were problems, which afflicted not only Blundell's but also all boarding schools for thirteens to eighteens. In 1987 numbers had peaked at over 490 pupils, of whom 100 were day boys, 40 were girls and 350 were boy boarders. In other words, the school was as it had been in Fusty Wynne's day, except for 50 extra day boys and the girls. By 1995 numbers were about 360; the day boy numbers had stayed the same and girl numbers had increased to 50. Boy boarding numbers had fallen by 30 per cent, something that had not happened since the difficult 1890s. First of all boarding Prep Schools, such as Ravenswood, had started dying like flies and secondly by 1990 every other Independent School in the area was taking pupils in at eleven.

Luckily, Jonathan Leigh and the Governors were alert to the problem and grasped the solution dynamically. By coherent stages the School changed to being genuinely co-educational and to taking boys and girls at eleven. As part of the progression the ancient division between 'day' and 'boarding' has gone and there are now boys' and girls' houses where are found full boarders, 'flexi-boarders' and day pupils. (Flexi-boarders can sleep over as boarders or go home each night.) To cater for the girls NC became a Girls' House, with David and Susan Hamer in charge, and a few years later Sue Rumble reopened Thornton House as a Girls' House. In 1997 SH changed to being the base for the eleven–thirteen-year-olds under John and Dee Brigden. It was all remarkably smoothly done. Numbers are now well over 500.

And that is not all. When the other main feeder school, St Aubyn's decided to close, the Governors took over the name and St Aubyn's was moved to the Hospital and the necessary new buildings were erected on the Hospital Field that the Governors had bought from Batterbee at the beginning of the century.

NC 1995. Having survived two world wars and a fire, Spring's North Close became a Girl's House when girls were admitted at thirteen. David and Sue Hamer were Houseparents until 2001. By now the girls are present in force in all age groups.

The new St Aubyn's Hall.

Andrew Barlow and musicians some-where abroad.

During these changes, governments were imposing the new GCSEs and the new options systems, the new A-levels, then the new A/S-levels and the even newer A2s. With all these changes to the House structures going on, the Director of Studies, Alan Furse, 1970-2001, never lifted his eyes off the ball and guided the School through with aplomb.

In a different style Jonathan Leigh has continued the dynamic of John Rees. Ondaatje Hall has allowed an explosion of high-quality drama. When he came in 1981 Tim Dyke could only use Big School for drama and as Big School had to be used for so many other events he was only able to produce one major production a year: *Oh What a Lovely War*, *Twelfth Night* (who remembers James Patrick in a gauze tent?), *A Man for all Seasons*, *Romeo and Juliet* and a version of the Medieval Mysteries. In those pre-Ondaatje Hall days the Houses put on excellent productions of their own, but with home-made sets and home-made electrics, which, in retrospect make one's hair curl. These House plays would now be banned by the Health-and-Safety spoilsports.

So Ondaatje Hall was doubly welcome. More plays of a higher standard could now be put on, so that keen actors and stage managers, who continue to throw their energies into House plays, can now be let loose on the real thing. Moreover, Tim Dyke and the other thespians can now entertain with a whole range of School productions. The dramatic year starts off with a musical produced in the first ten days of the Autumn Term. Then follows the main School play in November and the School House play in the Spring Term. That is not all, for the GCSE and A-level drama classes produce at least two other plays during the year. Bill Fisher has been succeeded by a full-time theatre manager and technician. Happily Jerry Pilbeam's workshops are a matter of yards away.

Andrew Barlow's appearance belies the fires of energy that fuel the engine. Since 1993 the academic year has started off with a September musical. Concerts sprinkle all three terms. There is a large choral work after Christmas and a full orchestral concert. That dreaded monster, the Brass or Big Band, caresses the ear. Since 1991 the musicians have taken to going on trips. In 1991 the Choir went to Berlin and since then they have been to Chinon, often to the Czech Republic and to Hungary. Not to be outdone the Big Band have started exporting their decibels, first in 1997 to Jersey, subsequently to Brittany.

In the last decade the sportsmen have also been active. Nick Folland's career with Somerset and then Devon has matched Ronnie Seldon's, although one fears the former will never, against any normal cricket side, take ten wickets in an innings. He really took over the coaching of the XI in 1994, the year Gompertz hit four centuries and ended the season with an average of 125. (Thanks to John Smith and his groundsmen the wicket is superb.) Folland and Peter Gordon organise a year-long

Jemba Bull in flow. This must stand for the seasons of 2000 and 2001, during which the XV have played 29, won 23, lost 5 and drew 1. Norman Ridgway, who came in 1987, continuing the traditions of Ted Crowe and Terry Barwell.

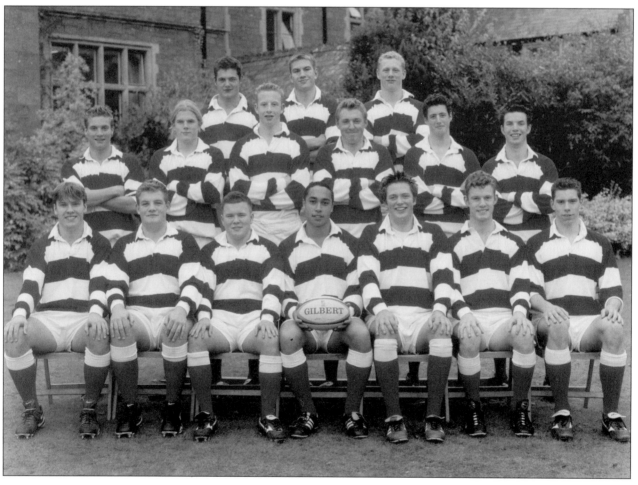

The XV of 2000.

coaching programme, which in recent years has borne fruit. The XIs in 1999, 2000 and 2001 had one exceptional cricketer, Tom Wright, but were canny all-round teams, who won 45 games, lost 16 and drew 2. Old-timers will immediately spot that the paucity of the draws is unrealistic and realise that the School circuits are playing the dreaded limited-over game. But that is the way of the world these days. It is a much more professional approach and we amateurs can only sit on the boundary edge, muse and admire.

Recent rugby has been equally successful. In 1999 and 2000 the XV won 21 games and only lost 5, scoring 632 points to their opponents' 265. The star of the sides was Jemba Bull who went on to represent England Schoolboys. Ryan Hopkins of the 1998 team also played for the England Under 18 squad.

Part of the explanation for these excellent results may have been the building up of *esprit d'equippe* during pre-season tours. In the summers of 1999 and 2000 over 20 Blundellians toured South Africa and on both occasions played seven matches in three weeks. Such an expedition could not be held without enormous support from parents who helped raised the funds necessary, and from the staff who accompanied the tour. In October 2000 the Girls' Hockey team went to Barbados and the Boys' Cricket team followed them in the following March. Girls' Hockey teams have also been to Ireland in the last few years and the Boys' Soccer teams to Spain, allegedly to play football.

As can be seen from all this, Blundell's girls have been no whit behind. Indeed, the latest Rugger Blue has been won by a girl, Kate Chidgey 1996–2001, and the last Blundellian Rugby International was Nicola Coffin. The building of the all-weather pitch and the arrival of Nicky Klinkenberg in 1997, Debbie Hoskins and Sue Norman to reinforce the old guard of Jeremy Shrimpton, Andrew Barlow and Charles Noon, have changed girls' hockey out of all recognition. Charles Noon ran girls' hockey with two grass pitches, and matches were begun as soon as there were enough girls to raise a team. The first match was won under Juliet Foster's captaincy in 1980, but standards could hardly rise until the facilities were there. Now that they

Rugby tour to Australia and New Zealand. The author has lost track of the great number of tours entered into by the Girls' Hockey and Boys' Rugger and Cricket teams. Norman Ridgway and Mrs Ridgway are seated between A.J. Deighton Gibson and John Brigden.

Nicola Coffin, GH 1990–92, who has played international rugby, here collecting a cup as captain of Richmond.

The Girls: The School's latest Oxford Blues were Carolyn Robson, GH 1984–86, Cricket...

are there, hockey has taken off with a vengeance. In the 2000 season ten different teams were produced and 150 girls out of 184 had the opportunity to play team hockey. No less than 17 Blundellians represented Devon at various age groups, with Caroline Lomas and Polly Salter heading the list with the Devon Under 19s. The Under 16s were Devon Indoor and Outdoor Champions and the Under 15s Devon Indoor Champions. Old 'Slash and Run' coaches like Noon and Barlow have been relegated to the 3rd and 4th XIs on farthest Amory.

Tennis also flourishes. In 2000 the Boys' First VI, run by Rod Tranchant, won six out of eight, and the Under 16s five out of six matches. The girls put out nine teams ranging from the Under 12s to the First VI, captained by Kate Chidgey, and they won most of their games. Girls also play netball, squash, and take part in athletics and swimming, as well as playing unofficial cricket, soccer and rugby.

The ubiquitous Norman Ridgway plays the leading role in organising athletics and cross country. In the 1970s athletics and the Duckworth relays filled a gap in the Spring Term and old-hands can well remember Duckworths being run in snow flurries. *Mais nous avons changé tout cela.* Athletes work at their thing as thoroughly as the cricketers. Indeed, in the current academic year (2001/2), Oliver Robertshaw has represented Oxford Freshers against Cambridge, and in 2000 Rhys Griffiths, Rachel Cotton, Gavin Vincent and Alex Jeffrey all won their events in the Devon Championships.

Sport, drama and music are all more photogenic than 'work'. But under Alan Furse's methodical leadership as Director of Studies the successive challenges of the

... and Kate Chidgey, GH 1996 –2001, Oxford Rugger Blue.

The Girls' XI of 2001. Standing on the right is not one of the girls but the coach, Mrs Klinkenburg, Housemistress of NC.

And to redress the balance, male aestheticism: Ben Rice, TH 1986–91, Shell Young Poet of the Year, 1991. Ben's father Douglas Rice, 1969–98, taught English at Blundell's.

R.N. Swarbrick, 1964–97, English Master, Westlake, and Ted Chanter's successor as Second Master, now the Staff Governor. Good at everything except goalkeeping.

Blundellian 1996–97

academic changes introduced in the last ten years have been more than met. In 1999, 2000 and 2001, well over 50 per cent of A-level grades were at A or B, and in each of those years A, B and C grades amounted to over 75 per cent. This represents a vast improvement in the last ten years. The picture is similar at GCSE. In Alan's time A★s have risen from five per cent to 17 per cent of the grades gained at GCSE and recently in some subjects over 70 per cent of the candidates have gained A or A★ grades. It is fitting that this story should end in the classroom, where the successors of Samuel Butler and his Ushers attack the main business of education in a way worthy of any period in the School's long history.

As Peter Blundell's 'Grammar School' approaches its 400th birthday it is a vibrant and busy place, but no list of things being done can adequately give the impression that it is also a happy place to be a pupil and a good place to be a teacher. If these pages have given the impression of favouring staff associated with memorable highlights, at the expense of sterling performance of the routine of teaching Blundellians at GCSE, A/S and A-level, that is the fault of the very nature of a commemorative book As for the pupils, the vast majority of Blundellians over the last few years, even more so over the last 400, cannot be mentioned by name, but they are as valuable members of our community as the he or the she blest with the most sparkling of talents.

This author has not the slightest desire to live for ever, except… except that he should like to know how Blundell's will be faring at the 500th!

The staff in 2001. I will only mention those who left that summer after many years' service. A.J. Furse, 1971–2001, Director of Studies, sits appropriately at the Head's right hand. The Chaplain, David Hamer, 1973–2001, was Blundell's longest-serving Chaplain. He and Susan Hamer, just visible in the back row were the first 'Houseparents' of North Close as a Girls' House. P.J. Salter, 1969–2001, Head of Geography and Housemaster of Old House, did not make the photo call. He was probably tidying his classroom.

THE MISSION

The first suggestion for a School Mission came in a 'Cambridge Letter' printed in the *Blundellian* in December 1884, written by 'G.M.', almost certainly George Martin, 1875–83. He wrote:

I must now give you a little information about St John's College mission to South London. The reason I mention it is this: some of the larger Schools have undertaken a similar work, why should not Blundell's do the same? Such a mission would be in accordance with the wish of Peter Blundell.

George Martin deserves to be remembered. He died in 1947 and the following is his obituary:

I know of no man so entirely unworldly, so wholly self-sacrificing, at the same time so fully wrapped up in religion as he was in his long life of eighty-two years.

While still comparatively young he resigned his comfortable living of St Michael, Caerhayes, offering all that he was and all that he had to the Bishop of London, to become a leader in Church work among men; and when his proposal was refused he gave himself up to living in the slums of southeast London, occupying one miserable top attic in the scarcely habitable purlieus of Southwark.

Without creature comforts or anything of beauty, he devoted all his time to his holy religion and to helping his neighbours, both spiritually and bodily. He regularly rose at six in the morning to engage in hours of prayer and always kept three hours of silence on Fridays.

The saints of old must have been very difficult people to live with. Martin was pre-eminently saintly, but his accentuated unworldliness, together with the neglect of his person and of his clothes, unfitted him for ordinary society. However, his charity knew no bounds. His substitute for an annual holiday was to accompany East Enders when they went to toil in the hop fields of Kent, though he chose to walk thither, for Christ always travelled on foot. He would share the labours of the porters in the Borough market and of villa servants; and when friends supplied his needs by presents of food, he would give them away to the poor.

He read no newspapers and he was a trouble to the police, who had to arrest him because his strong convictions about sacrilege led him to set fire to a wooden stand erected outside a church, where seats were set in preparation for a royal event. However, 'Father' Martin gained the profound respect of the slum-dwellers. The old age of this Cambridge graduate and son of a Canon was spent in a London work-house, where he occupied a place in a very large common ward with a crowd of unfortunates of all sorts. The indefinite announcement that he 'had died recently' is a true reflex of the obscurity of this holy man of God. When the memory of his saintliness and good deeds has perished, there will remain the massive granite cross, which he erected on Dodman Point as a sacred reminder to seamen who pass along the south coast of Cornwall.

In 1889 the idea of a 'Mission' achieved a focus on the new parish of Emmanuel, carved out of the larger parish of St Thomas, Exeter, and a Committee was formed, led by T.U. Cross and G.H. Norman of Petergate, with boy representatives from each House. In November 1889 Cross led a party of Blundellians to visit Emmanuel and to meet the Curate in Charge, the Revd C.H. Williams. They saw his corrugated-iron church and realised the inadequacy of the facilities. They noted the 'squalor, poverty, misery, overcrowding and evident lack of the most ordinary needs of sanitation.' Early activities were termly House collections. A Ladies' Association was formed to organise gifts of clothing. The first term's collections raised £22.13s.8d., as well as much clothing and books. In Spring Term 1890 the sum rose to £31 and a term later to over £50.

The Mission prospered for a time. At the annual meeting in 1898 it was reported that there were three Mission Rooms in the Parish, one called the Blundell's Mission Room, and that there were now many games clubs and other societies. The new stone church on the site of the old iron shed was nearing completion, and the School was providing stalls for Clergy and Choir, Pulpit and Lectern. The Mission was already paying £50 a year towards the Assistant Curate's stipend, as well as renting a cricket pitch for the Parish. The church was opened for worship in 1899 and proudly in the Chancel are the crossed keys of St Peter and the School Crest.

Then in 1908 there was a special meeting of the Mission Committee to take stock. Since the 1880s Emmanuel Parish had gone up in the world and the Church itself would now pay the Assistant Curate. With the consent of Revd C.H. Williams the Committee decided to direct its energies towards a London parish and Rotherhithe was chosen. At early meetings E.G. Peirce reported on his visit to the area and the problem of the boys who left school at thirteen. The School opened a 'House' in January 1910, 670, Rotherhithe St., and Scout Troops were formed named 'School House, Petergate and North Close' by the Missioner, C. de M. Rudolf. Two further clubs were started by Rudolf, one for boys with collars and one for more ragged types and a call went out for an OB who could teach boxing on Tuesdays. In a termly newsletter Rudolf reported Scout Camps and visits from OBs, who included A.V. Hill and C.E.M Joad. A useful thing was the provision of reasonable clothes so that boys could get better jobs. A reflection of the grinding poverty of the area was its insatiable appetite for cast-off clothing.

After the First World War the Mission was usually in financial trouble. The termly collection from boys generally raised £40, but costs had escalated. Nevertheless, the connection continued and in 1924 a camp for 19 boys was held at the School in June. Each Mission boy was paired off with a Blundellian 'mate'. It seems to have been a success, though the Mission boys could not be persuaded to go to Chapel twice on Sunday. The camp was repeated in subsequent years from 1925–32, but the financial problems would not go away, nor would the problem of visiting the Mission; Charlton and Rotherhithe were too far away. In March 1933 the decision was taken to transfer the School's attentions to Moorfields Parish, Bristol.

The Bristol Mission began with a flourish in 1934, when the Lord Mayor and the Bishop of Bristol performed an official opening ceremony of St Saviour's Mission in St Matthew Moorfields Parish. The first Missioner was the Revd E.M. Hall. A fortnight's camp for Mission boys was held in August on Mayfield, which was repeated in 1935. Gorton encouraged boys to make weekend visits to the Mission to help with clubs and sports and the Mission served as base for other Blundellians who studied Bristol's economic life. In 1936 Mervyn Stockwood replaced Hall as Missioner and a call went out for £300 to improve the Mission's facilities. In 1937 three parties of sixth-formers descended on the Mission led by Gorton, Thoseby and Ayherst to do in-depth studies of the area and the lives of the poor. In 1937 and 1938 the School workshops hummed with activity to produce an altar and a crucifix for the refurbishment of the Mission Chapel. The boys and staff responsible attended the reconsecration of the Chapel on 3 July 1938.

After 1945 parties of Blundellians continued to visit Moorfields, but the Boys' camps did not restart. Fund-raising for the Mission increasingly devolved onto the Summer Term fête. Then in 1959 the proceeds of the fête were passed to St Andrew's Church, Tiverton, and in the February 1960 *Blundellian* it was announced that 'the name of the School Mission has now been changed to the Blundell's Association for Christian Service.' Latterly this has been known as Blundell's Action.

The granite cross on the Dodman, erected by Martin.

The Blundell's lectern at Emmanuel Church, Exeter.